The Pursuit of
PRIME

The Pursuit of PRIME

MAXIMIZE YOUR COMPANY'S SUCCESS WITH THE ADIZES PROGRAM

Ichak Adizes, Ph.D.

KNOWLEDGE EXCHANGE

Santa Monica

Knowledge Exchange, LLC
1299 Ocean Avenue
Santa Monica, California 90401
In association with Wordworks, Inc.
Boston, Massachusetts

Jacket design by Russell Gordon
Text design by Lee Fukui

1 2 3 4 5 6 7 8 9-VA-99 98 97 96
First printing November 1996
ISBN: 1-888232-22-6

Knowledge Exchange books are available at special discounts for bulk purchases by corporations, institutions, and other organizations. For more information, please con-tact Knowledge Exchange, LLC, at: (310) 394-5995 (voice) or kex@kex.com (e-mail).

To my wife, Nurit,
and our children:
Atalya, Topaz, Shoham,
Nimmy, Cnaan,
and Sapphire

Contents

The Pursuit of Prime

All living creatures progress through stages of growth and decline in an arching curve that begins with birth and ends with death. Organizations, however, do not have to decline and age; it is not preordained that they have to do so. Businesses can remain at or near the high point of their vitality for a very long time, perhaps indefinitely. Organizations can even return to those peaks from stages of decline.

This book explains how for-profit and not-for-profit organizations reach the prime of life from either direction—by advancing from youth or returning from old age—and maintain their position there. It contains the principles not for achieving eternal youth but for pursuing and maintaining perpetual vitality.

To say that businesses peak and decline is like saying that life is unfair. Both statements are true, but they are incomplete truths. Life is indeed unfair; businesses do indeed decline. But that doesn't mean that life has to be unfair to you or that your business has to get swept into the dustbin of history. In this book, I urge you to take fate into your own hands and manage your organization's lifecycle. My goal is to demonstrate in hard, practical detail how you can take your business to the stage I call Prime and keep it there.

I have devoted my career to the development of a profession that coaches organizations to achieve and maintain their Prime. I call that profession organizational therapy. If you are a Californian, you won't laugh if I call it organizational healing. After all, the purpose of therapy is healing. As organizations change and transform themselves, moving from one stage of the lifecycle to the next, they develop problems. Some of their problems are not transitional in nature, and they stymie the organizations, requiring professional assistance—organizational healing—to overcome the barriers that block their advance to Prime. I have established the Adizes Institute and designed a graduate program licensed to grant master's degrees and doctorates in organizational therapy.

Do not be confused. I do not work as a consultant. Consultants advise you what to do. What you need if your organization is having problems you cannot handle alone is an organizational therapist to coach you and help you learn from your own experiences. This book presents my own experiences coaching companies to Prime.

I have treated hundreds of companies, from those in their developing and growth stages to those in the aging stages, in a dozen countries. I have personally trained hundreds of people around the world in the principles presented in this book, and I have monitored their success to verify that the application of these principles generates reproducible results.

This book describes the results of a tested program that has helped companies grow and/or rejuvenate. One company increased its revenues from $12 million to $800 million in only ten years, with no dilution of ownership. Another took only seven years to rocket from $400 million to $4 billion, showing no signs of debilitating strain. What's more, that company is poised and energized to reach the $10 billion mark within five years.

Prime organizations passionately nurture both their expansive, creative energy and their need for structure and discipline. That is the dynamic of truly successful organizations.

But the process of bringing and maintaining an organization in that enviable state of Prime poses many challenges.

In the process of writing this book, I have further honed the principles that govern overcoming lifecycle challenges, and I have clarified my perspective on the problems that even my own company confronts. As a result, I believe, more than ever, that whether you are leading a corporation or a division within a corporation or you are aiming to start your own business, you will find this book helpful.

Showing you how your organization can preserve, multiply, or jump-start that dynamic—how it can reach Prime and stay there—is this book's mission.

Organizational Vitality and the Nature of Problems

*S*o you've got problems. Well, thank God! Problems come with change, change is a necessary characteristic of growth, and no company ever achieved peak performance—Prime—without changing. The struggle for success, for Prime, is a struggle with problems. Rejoice. Without problems you'd be dead.

But there are problems, and then there are problems. One familiar distinction is that some problems threaten while others beckon. To some managers the limited sales life of products poses a terrible, continuous danger; to others it means never-ending opportunities to come up with other winners.

Some problems you need to have: Normal problems come with change. Some problems you don't want to have: They are abnormal; they stymie change and interfere with growth. The distinction between normal and abnormal problems is critical.

Consider the example of a well-known software company. Sales zipped from nothing to $40 million in just three years. Since its earliest days, the CEO and the company have been sidestepping such near disasters as inadequate cash flow and failing quality control. The faster the company grows, the more extensive and complex are the difficulties that confront it. Has the CEO despaired? He has been concerned, yes, but he doesn't despair. He knows that problems are attributes of growth through change. He knows that as long as the organization is growing, he will continue to face an endless succession of problems.

Even in Prime—the stage that intrepid CEOs struggle to reach, sustain, or regain—a company has to contend with the problem of how to remain there. In other words, there is no end to it; the solution to one generation of problems leads inexorably to the challenges of the next generation of problems. Should it reach a condition with no problems, the company will have stopped changing. And that means that the company has reached the end of its life.

Like every good parent, that CEO knows that some problems are just not worth getting all bent out of shape over. They're the normal (that is, perfectly appropriate and even predictable) maladies, stresses, strains, and pitfalls that are consistent with successful corporate growth and development. He avoids those stresses by taking the available preventive vaccines: He continues to create new revenue streams by hiring a good development manager who can engineer new product lines. He treats challenges promptly and skillfully, lest they fester or spin out of control.

If the normal problems of organizations are those that occur at specific phases of predictable change, then abnormal problems are those that should not occur within particular stages in an organization's life: like mumps, say, in middle age or prostate trouble in adolescence. For an infant organization, cash-flow problems—if they are anticipated, confronted, and handled—are normal. Cash-flow problems are abnormal in an organization that, in spite of its experience and maturity, is unprepared to handle such crises. When CEOs don't or can't deal effectively with the normal problems that confront their growing businesses, their problems will persist as chronic, recurring abnormalities.

In a company beset with too many problems, normal or abnormal, it is common for one or more executives to suggest that it is time to slow down. If the other executives agree, the company slows down. And you might ask, Why not? It is like cooking on a stove, isn't it? If the fire is too hot, the cook should lower the heat.

But that metaphor is misleading. What the executives are really saying is: Let's slow down change because we cannot handle our problems. But when are there no problems? Only the dead have no problems. Life is change, and no change is death. Slowing the rate of change, therefore, means slowing down life. It is a protracted suicide. The dinosaurs were not equipped to handle the accelerating change. Where are they now, these giants that dominated earth?

If you adapt to changes only as fast as they happen, you will be doing just enough to survive. To thrive, you must precede the curve, anticipate, and act faster than the speed of change.

Do you know the story about the two tourists on safari on the plains of Africa? They see a lion approaching rapidly. One of them starts to put on his running shoes. His companion asks, "Why are you putting on your running shoes? You can't possibly outrun a lion." The first traveler replies, "I'm not trying to outrun the lion; I'm trying to outrun *you*."

Japanese automakers developed concurrent engineering to meet the shifting tastes of motorists in new markets. By learning to perform simultaneously several activities that had, in the past, been sequential, Japanese engineers were able to change their models in half the time traditional manufacturers required. The ability to get new products to market before other auto manufacturers gave the Japanese a tremendous advantage.

If you let change-induced problems slow down your growth, change will pass you by. This, in essence, is the question this book answers: How can companies use change intelligently to arrive at, or return to, Prime and stay there?

Years ago, during outings with my small sons, I arrived at my understanding of the need to anticipate ever-accelerating change and speed up solutions to its challenges. The boys used to drag me to a local arcade where they loved to challenge me to play their favorite video game: auto racing. What surprised me was that my sons, who were certainly much too young to have driven a car even once, always beat me. They had played the game so often that they knew the road ahead and could drive proactively. They could predict each turn and anticipate when other cars would try to pass. To me each turn offered another opportunity to mishandle the situation. I crashed. I tumbled. I stalled.

When I drive in foreign countries, the locals hoot and toot. They quickly lose patience and get annoyed that I slow down traffic. They are not better drivers. Knowing the road ahead, they do not need to slow down. This book can help you know the road ahead of your organization, anticipate future problems today, and gain an advantage in accelerating advances.

DO YOU HAVE THE RIGHT PROBLEMS?

Managers must make sure that their organizations focus on gaining optimal control and/or flexibility for their company's stage of development. Companies in Prime have both flexibility and control in balance.

Growing companies with no cost accounting systems, for example, will soon pay the price. With no control over costs, there is no way to keep up with where or why a company is spending money. Managers of companies with insufficient controls may find that their companies are losing money even though sales are rising. As I write this, a specific company comes to mind: Oddly enough that company was in the field of financial reporting and analysis.

In a push to increase revenues, that company awarded discounts on volume sales, paid generous commissions to its sales force, offered highly favorable rates to distributors, and mounted an aggressive advertising campaign. To finance its expansion, the company borrowed money at heavy interest rates. When we conducted a thorough analysis of the cost of sales, the results revealed—to everyone's surprise—that by the time the company had paid the bank, salespeople, distributors, advertising media, and so forth, its variable costs exceeded the prices it charged: The more the company sold, the more money it lost.

Ego, combined with entrepreneurial zeal, can create a dizziness that makes people lose sight of reality. By failing to track a normal problem that every growing company experiences, rising costs of sales, the financial services company created an abnormal problem: a cash crisis.

When an abnormal problem begins to develop, no red flag pops up on the CEO's desk. An abnormal problem insidiously creeps up, and when it is almost too late (sometimes when it is too late), it generates a crisis. Abnormal problems aren't abnormal right from their origin. They are the extensions of normal problems that people ignored, treated too late, or handled incorrectly. When they loom over the organization, management gets overwhelmed.

Abnormal problems seem to have more lives than a cat. When you think that you have taken care of them, they reappear as if you had done nothing, or they appear in a new, more virulent form. Abnormal problems have a nasty tendency to turn chronic, threatening the life of the organization.

Leaders who cannot handle their normal problems should call for professional help before they have abnormal problems on their hands. If, for example, you have a cold and can cure yourself, good for you. If, however, that cold persists, you must get medical help before it develops into a serious illness. If you came down with pneumonia, you wouldn't try to nurse it yourself.

I emphasize the need for professional help because I find too many managers who believe that because they know how to read and write—or, worse, because they have an MBA—they can treat any organizational problem. The more arrogant the manager, the higher the chance that he or she will miss or ignore the warning signs of a chronic organizational disease.

I have been following the history of Apple Computer for years. The newspaper reports painted—for me—an increasingly troubled picture. I noted the first indication of a problem when I read that Steve Wozniak, Apple's cofounder, was starting to show more interest in rock 'n' roll than in computers. At that time in the company's lifecycle, that was not an abnormal problem: By and large, successful founders of companies get so excited by their success in one field that they have to try their hands in another.

The signs of abnormality appeared following Wozniak's departure. Entrepreneurial and creative as Jobs was, without Wozniak to provide balance, Jobs became an unguided missile.

The journalists were no help. They lauded his genius, and he behaved as if he believed his own press releases. Managerially, Jobs was speeding over a cliff. Growth was too rapid and uncontrolled. So the board recruited a professional manager, John Sculley, to impose some controls.

I saw my red signal flash once. Would they, I wondered, work together? If they had, the problem would have been solved. Sculley and Jobs could have formed a complementary team to provide flexibility and control. However, Sculley eased Jobs out, and my red lights started to flash furiously. I knew Apple was suffering from a seriously abnormal problem: premature aging.

Sculley had jettisoned the entrepreneurial spirit Apple needed to stay alive in the fast-changing computer industry. Not yet having institutionalized the entrepreneurial spirit embodied and personalized in Steve Jobs, the company now had an abnormal problem. It was far too early, and perhaps not at all necessary, to get rid of the founder. The question I asked myself was, What will Sculley do now?

The newspapers reported that he was attempting to change the culture by cutting out some of the freewheeling behavior. More controls, I said to myself. Next, Sculley united manufacturing with research and development—a clear indication that there would be much more control and distinctly less R&D. I knew that Sculley was handling it badly. The red lights were flashing, and the sirens were wailing.

Sculley's brother, a senior executive with H. J. Heinz Company, had attended one of my lectures. I asked him to take his brother a marked copy of my book *Corporate Lifecycles*. I directed him to the pages that described Apple's position on the lifecycle. "Tell him," I said, "to read those pages if nothing else." Even without the brother's letter telling me that Apple's Sculley had no interest in what a consultant might have to say, I might have predicted that my message would fall on deaf ears.

Something has been left out of this discussion, as you will have noticed. I have made assumptions, perhaps unfairly. When I talk of problems being appropriate (normal) or inappropriate (abnormal), I've begged a question: appropriate or inappropriate to what?

Well, what is left out, or assumed, is the notion of corporate lifecycles. What follows is a brief overview of that theory, as it forms the basic intellectual armature of this book.

Most of us, given the choice, would want to be at the peak of our vitality, the high point, the apex, enjoying the best years of our lives—that is, at Prime. When it is in its Prime, the ideal stage of its lifecycle, an organization combines the creative daring of youth with the control it gains through a series of pleasant and unpleasant experiences.

In Prime, the company enjoys the vital balance of flexibility and control. The organization wants more than it has and calls the shots. Though it seems to overreach, it repeatedly grabs what it reaches for. It is a dynamo, humming with realistic optimism.

Like athletic prime, organizational Prime is a period during which perfect self-control unites with flexibility. Before Prime an organization is flexible but not under control. An organization in Prime is both in control and flexible. In the aging stages it has controls, but it has lost its flexibility. When a business is in Prime, its balance is evident in effective, efficient management. In Prime the organization is in the best of health: The ailments of Infancy and childhood are far in its past, and the potential maladies of old age have not yet become matters of concern.

But to get to Prime, of course, you first have to pass through the developing years. You may also have to experience some part of the declining years. You must pass Prime to realize where it is and to know how to stay there. Prime is not a destination: It is a condition. It is not a dot on a curve but a range on a curve. To stay within that range, you have to struggle to maintain the condition. Before you can manage to challenge and defy fate, you must learn what undefied fate has in store for you. In short, you must understand the lifecycle of the organization.

Reaching, maintaining, or retrieving the condition of Prime is the goal to which every organizational leader, whether young founder or seasoned CEO, should devote his or her planning, dreaming, and most efficient doing. Only in Prime can companies dominate their markets; only in Prime can they retain that leadership.

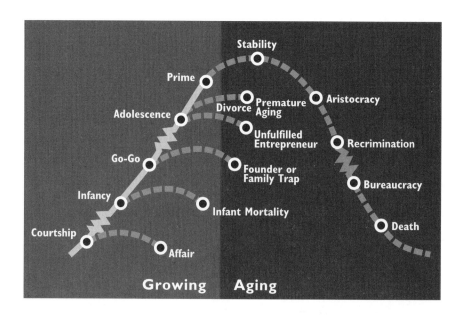

CORPORATE LIFECYCLE Companies, like people, follow definitie growth stages as charted above. It is in the stage of Prime that both humans and companies are at the pinnacle of health and prosperity.

THE TEN STAGES
OF CORPORATE LIFECYCLES

In my experience, organizations evolve, and dissolve, in a series of ten stages. They are:

- Courtship
- Infancy
- Go-Go
- Adolescence
- Prime

- Stability
- Aristocracy
- Recrimination
- Bureaucracy
- Death

THE DEVELOPING STAGES

STAGE 1

Courtship

This is the stage of dreaming and making a commitment to a dream. The would-be founder focuses on ideas and future possibilities, making and talking about ambitious plans either to change the market or to create a market niche. Courtship ends and Infancy begins when the founder assumes risk.

STAGE 2

Infancy

During this stage, the founder's attention shifts from ideas and possibilities to results. In the business world those results take the form of sales. Sales drive this action-oriented, opportunity-driven stage. For a nonbusiness organization, results take whatever form is critical for the survival of the organization. For a fledgling political party, that form would be in positive media write-ups that generate the votes or donations that keep the organization afloat. During Infancy, nobody pays much attention to paperwork, controls, systems, or procedures. The founder works 16-hour days, six to seven days every week, trying to do everything. Because a small problem can escalate and turn into a major crisis overnight, the founder makes all decisions—big or small. Infancy ends and Go-Go starts when the organization's cash flow stabilizes and is predictable and positive.

STAGE

Go-Go

This is a rapid-growth stage. Sales are still king or queen. The founders, seeing their companies flourish, believe they can do no wrong; their arrogance leaves their businesses vulnerable to flagrant mistakes. They see everything as an opportunity, and too many opportunities can present big problems. The leaders organize their companies around people rather than functions; capable employees can-and do-wear many hats, but, to the consternation of key employees, the founders nevertheless make every decision. What was normal in Infancy is becoming abnormal in Go-Go. Go-Go ends and Adolescence begins when the Go-Go gets into serious trouble.

COMING-OF-AGE STAGES

STAGE

Adolescence

During this stage, the company experiences the problems of uncontrolled growth and takes new form. The founder hires a chief operating officer but finds it difficult to hand over the reins. An attitude of us (the oldtimers) versus them (the COO and his supporters) hampers operations. Company goals languish while the battle rages. There are so many internal conflicts that people have little time left to serve the clients. The company suffers a temporary loss of vision. If the company sails successfully through Adolescence and develops controls without losing flexibility, it enters Prime.

STAGE

Prime

This is the stage of life when everything comes together. Introducing and enforcing discipline without losing vision, the company in Prime establishes an even balance between control and flexibility. The organization, disciplined yet innovative, consistently meets its customers' changing needs. New infant organizations sprout up, and they are decentralized to provide new lifecycle opportunities: The organization is vital and vibrant. If the organization does not work on staying in Prime, it will age.

THE AGING STAGES

STAGE

Stability

The organization is still strong, but without the eagerness of its earlier stages; it is starting to show the first signs of aging. Instead of getting what it wants, it wants what it gets. Members of the organization welcome new ideas but lack the degree of excitement that characterized new ideas during the growing stages. The financial people begin to impose controls for short-term results. The emphasis on marketing and research and development wanes. Employees admire past achievements but find it difficult to muster energy for the future. If this stage does not get treated, the company will age further.

STAGE

Aristocracy

Not making waves becomes a way of life. Outward signs of respectability (dress, office decoration, and titles) take on enormous importance. The organization acquires companies rather than incubates start-up businesses. Its culture emphasizes how things are done over what's being done and why people are doing it. The company appears to be stalling, and the organization's leaders rely on the past to carry them into the future. Inaction in a changing environment has a price. The time of Recrimination will arrive.

STAGE

Recrimination

In this stage of decay, the company conducts witch-hunts to find out who did something wrong rather than trying to discover what went wrong and how to fix it. Cost reductions take precedence over efforts to increase revenues. The reason for this behavior seems to be that it is easier to see how cutting costs improves the bottom line. It is far from certain, however, whether stronger efforts—even with an unchanged cost structure—will increase revenues and affect the bottom line. The company, therefore, does what is certain and expedient for the short run, rather than what is uncertain, in spite of being significant, for the long run. Some companies cut costs to the point that they suffer from corporate anorexia: They have no strength to do anything. They die. Backstabbing and corporate infighting rule at this stage. Executives fight to protect their turf, isolating themselves from their fellow executives and demonizing their customers. Petty jealousies reign supreme.

STAGE

Bureaucracy

If the organization did not die during the previous stage, it becomes bureaucratized; it is politically protected or it survives in a regulated environment. The critical factor for its survival is not how it satisfies its customers but how it satisfies those who grant its resources and control the predictability of its behavior. The organization's procedure manuals thicken, paperwork abounds, and rules and policies choke innovation and creativity. When employees question procedures or processes, management's answer is, "It's the policy." Clients, forsaken and forgotten, find they need to devise elaborate strategies to get anybody's attention. There are systems for everything. Employees play by the book.

STAGE

Death

This final stage may linger for years while the company slowly dies, or it may arrive suddenly with one massive blow. The organization crumbles when it cannot generate the cash it needs to cover its payables, when the outflow finally exhausts any inflow.

For each defining stage there is a set of actions: Those are the steps required to bring growing companies to Prime or aging companies back to Prime. Again and again, real companies have challenged perceived fate, and their success validates the principles presented in this book.

WHICH STAGES ARE NORMAL?

Since no organization is born in Prime, the problems of development that organizations confront during the stages preceding Prime are normal. Since a leader can retard organizational aging, all aging problems and aging itself are abnormal. If the Taj Mahal is maintained properly, it can endure forever.

How? All systems act the same way. What happens to an old car? It falls apart. An old house? It falls apart. An old person? The same.

When a system ages, it disintegrates, but growing systems disintegrate, too. The common denominator in both cases is change. Change disintegrates, accelerating aging or causing premature death. But here is the antidote to aging and the secret to perpetual vitality: If we can retard disintegration, in spite of change and with change, we can extend our lives.

Disintegration can cause premature aging and the decline of young systems. Within the normal growth stages, there are abnormal turns an organization can take. The abnormal stage in Courtship is an affair. An affair is characterized by excitement and passion, but it lacks true commitment. At the first sign of risk, commitment evaporates. There will be no marriage and no birth of an organization.

I call an abnormal Infancy infant mortality. Either the founder loses commitment, or the risks are such that the organization loses liquidity-cash—irretrievably.

The abnormal stage in Go-Go I call the founder's trap. The founding father, mother, or family cannot move on to allow others who are more qualified to manage. The guerrillas from the mountains who won the revolution try to lead the industry and the economy when all they know is how to ambush a convoy.

In Adolescence, it is abnormal to get rid of entrepreneurs before the entrepreneurial spirit is institutionalized. The forces for control try to rid the organization of what seems to be the source of unpredictability. But such ill-conceived attempts to slam on the brakes often cause the steering to lock and the organization to stall. The organization may seem to be better controlled and more profitable, but the improvement is only short-lived. Depending on the speed of change in the company's industry, the company will cease to be creative. Its products will become obsolete, and the company will wither away.

Do You Need Help?

The problems of organizations are so familiar to me that, by examining companies for key symptoms, I can tell them where they stand in the lifecycle and how they can progress. Once companies know where they are in relation to Prime, they can learn what they need to do to get there—either for the first time or as a return trip.

The aim of this book is to show you the road ahead. The future should not take you by surprise, making you feel that God, the fates, the industry, the government, or pure bad luck is the cause of your troubles. It is not your predicament alone. Raising an organization involves normal and abnormal problems, much like the normal or abnormal problems of raising a child.

When you have your first child, every problem is a crisis. By the time you get to your fourth or fifth, your children are pretty much raising themselves: You have learned the difference between normal and abnormal problems, and you can, more or less, predict behavior and conserve your energy. You can discriminate between the normal and thus trivial, and the abnormal and thus significant.

I have based this book on my experience with hundreds of companies, in more than 15 countries, over a period that spans more than 30 years.

In the chapters that follow, you will learn how to diagnose where organizations are in their lifecycles. You will become familiar not only with your company's position in its own lifecycle but also with the content, as it were, of that position. You will know what your company ought to be doing at that stage and how and who ought to be doing it.

CHAPTER 2

Getting Started

Remember, this is a book about how you can control the lifecycle of your company or organization. While the future may appear to the untutored to be governed by fate, we will see that if you follow tested principles, the future can be predictable and manageable. You can bring your organization triumphantly to Prime, nurture it, and stay there. If it moves beyond Prime, you can learn how to return to that desirable condition. Be warned, though: The proposition that men and women might conquer fate is radical. It defies the most ancient beliefs of the human race. Nevertheless, institutions, like businesses, can defy fate—at least for a very long time.

People who lead companies and other organizations, however, can foil fate in two ways. They can fail to take advantage of the growing years, when fate leads their businesses toward Prime, and they can fail to resist decline, when the lure of fate pushes and pulls businesses from Prime to weaken and die. The defiance of fate is a matter of knowing how to ride its upward thrust as well as how to resist its downward push.

First we have to mark our current position on that curve. This chapter explains how to use certain signs and indicative symptoms to identify stages of organizational development or decay.

AGE, SIZE, AND SELF-CONTROL

Before we consider the diagnostics, I should make clear that neither chronological age nor size determines the stage an organization occupies on the corporate lifecycle. That observation may be counterintuitive. Many people assume that a large organization is, by definition, bureaucratic and therefore on the downward slope of the aging process. People automatically assume that larger companies respond more slowly to challenges—both external and internal—than do smaller companies. But do they?

When I first examined it, Philip Morris had sales approaching $9 billion. It was young despite its size. Proof? Today annual sales are $40 billion, and despite the FDA's challenge to the tobacco industry, I don't see Philip Morris slowing down. On the other hand, I have seen companies with $2 million in sales that are aging and slow to respond to market forces.

Another misconception is that there is an inevitable causality between time and age. Recently, I met with a prospective client who had assumed that since her company is 17 years old, it must be in the adolescent stage of the lifecycle. I explained that it was no more a foregone conclusion than it would be to assume that all teenagers were adolescent. Some teenagers act with the maturity of adults, and some adults behave as irresponsibly as a young teen. I have seen 70-year-old Indian yogis with the heart rate and blood pressure of 17-year-olds. I have also seen young men in their twenties who, because they smoke, eat, and drink too much, exhibit the vital signs of someone approaching middle age. I have seen companies that are 108 years young: flexible, adaptive, changing, and growing; and companies that are five years old: aging, ossified, stale, predictable, and out of touch.

Where a company is positioned in its lifecycle depends on two conditions that could be correlated with chronological age and size but are not caused by them: flexibility and self-control.

Let us examine the relationship between corporate flexibility and self-control. When a company is young, its self-control, like a baby's, is limited, but its flexibility is high. A baby gradually gains control over its bodily functions, its mind, and its emotions. Eventually the baby becomes an adult, taking full responsibility for its actions. In that process, however, the baby—little by little—loses flexibility. A company that has achieved self-control while maintaining flexibility is, we say, in Prime. Until that point, the company has been flexible but uncontrollable. After Prime it is controllable, but it has grown rigid.

Some companies never reach Prime. They die young or age prematurely. What brings about the healthy advance to Prime? What causes premature aging and death or aging and death after a company has reached Prime? Here, in a nutshell, is the answer that I discovered after thirty years of work. Once I realized it, it seemed obvious.

Change is the cause of all problems because change causes disintegration. Think about your own life. Your body is, say, 40 years old, your thought processes show the wisdom and experience one might expect from a 70-year-old, but, at the same time, your spouse criticizes your emotional behavior, saying that you act like a teenager. Spiritually, perhaps, you have not yet been born. If those sentences describe you, you are falling apart, or one aspect of yourself is holding you back. Therapy might, as they say, help you "get it together."

In a young company, marketing and sales strategies usually change rapidly while accounting stays locked in the Stone Age, and concern for human resources has yet to emerge. Such disintegration manifests itself as what we casually call problems or crises.

If disintegration is the cause of all problems, the antidote is obvious: integration. We are healthy when we are a unified whole, whether psychologically or physically. Psychologists talk about "oneness or illness," and in most languages, the word that means to heal derives from the word to make whole.

If you want to diagnose and solve a problem, you should ask yourself, What is falling apart? Will my actions bring the pieces together, or will they lead to even more disintegration?

Consider the situation that confronted Lee Iaccoca when he came to take over troubled Chrysler Corporation. In general terms, the company was badly integrated with the marketplace. Its product line did not respond to the needs of the customers. Iaccoca's solution: He asked the unions for concessions, and he, in turn, offered to work for an annual salary of $1. He created goodwill and cooperation and was able to get the company to make necessary changes. Was his a good solution? On the surface, yes, it was. He saved the company, and he recreated himself as an icon of leadership.

Let us look a bit deeper now. When the company turned the corner, Iaccoca rewarded himself with tremendous bonuses and stock options worth millions of dollars. The union workers, who had conceded so much to save the company, got to keep their jobs. What happened to mutual trust? I suggest Iaccoca caused considerable long-term disintegration.

Take for another example a company that is overstaffed. To cut costs and improve profitability, management decides to reengineer. Good or bad? The what and why of the reengineering choice may be legitimate, but how the company executes the reengineering may leave long-lasting scars on the organizational psyche. People remember wrongs. The stories of people who had to leave after years of loyal service pass from generation to generation. People do not forget betrayal. When the company asks for their forbearance, they will pay in kind.

As you diagnose problems and the disintegration that causes them, you must differentiate between external and internal integration. External integration connotes the energy a company expends to identify its clients and their needs, and to satisfy those needs with products and services. Internal integration is what it takes to coordinate efforts within the company so that there will be products and services to sell.

When an organization devotes more effort to internal than to external integration, sales and profits begin to deteriorate, customer service slackens, and repeat orders decline. That stems from rules of physics: According to the laws of conservation, energy can be neither created nor destroyed, although its form can be changed. Because people have fixed energy at any point in time, the energy they expend on internal integration is not available for external integration. The longer internal integration exceeds external integration, the more difficult, expensive, and painful it is to regain and return to organizational equilibrium.

Complicating the diagnosis, however, is the nature of disintegration, whether external or internal. When a company is growing, it does what it needs to do to bring in sales: It is externally integrated. At the same time, however, that growing company might well be disintegrating internally due to inadequate inventory controls, faulty production plans, nonexistent cost accounting, or compensation practices that fail to elicit optimal performance or create feelings of injustice and jealousy.

Companies grow and/or decline depending on the nature of their external and internal integration and disintegration:

- A growing organization in the Courtship, Infancy, Go-Go, or Adolescence stage is integrating externally while it might be disintegrating internally.

- A developing organization is integrating both internally and externally.

- A Prime organization is both externally and internally integrated, the optimal condition.

- An aging organization in the Stability or Aristocracy stage is externally disintegrating while remaining internally integrated.

- A decaying organization in its final stage of Recrimination or Bureaucracy is externally and internally disintegrating.

- When it is no longer disintegrating, it is irreversibly disintegrated.

- The organization is dead.

Integration is a prerequisite of creativity. A company that is disintegrating—either internally or externally—is unlikely to find the energy and resources to focus on creating new ventures, new systems, or new anything. The organization directs all of its efforts at survival, fighting the many fires that erupt almost spontaneously. The organization's employees simply try to keep their turf from burning up. Such an environment is not at all receptive to constructive change; it is changing destructively.

Entrepreneurship fades with a decrease in risk-taking, and risk-taking is inextricably tied to commitment. When an organization is disintegrating, commitment is missing. In such circumstances, even the organization's brilliant founder has lost interest.

Integration is brought about by mutual trust and respect. In operational terms, respect enables learning from differences. Immanuel Kant describes that as the legitimization of the sovereignty of the other. When we recognize that each of us has the right to think differently, there is a chance we might learn something. Functioning diversity of thoughts enabled by mutual respect enriches the organization. How about trust? Operationally, trust stems from the perception that, at least in the long run, people share a common interest. When we perceive a lack of common interest, we become suspicious of those with whom we are involved.

To diagnose whether your organization's problems are normal or abnormal, ask yourself whether mutual trust and respect exist. You should interpret the word organization to extend beyond your payroll. Your organization includes everyone you need to accomplish your task: your suppliers, distributors, temporary help, and sources of capital. If mutual trust and respect among all parties remain strong, the problem is predictable and transitional, and you should be able to handle it.

If the problem has been plaguing your organization for some time, resisting successive attempts to solve it, and—more important—if mutual trust and respect have all but disappeared, the intensity and persistence of that problem classify it as abnormal. It is time to call for professional intervention. Your company needs an outside party to coach it toward solutions that will enhance growth and development.

One result or manifestation of a company in Prime is its full integration. On one hand, it is well integrated with its external environment—customers, vendors, investors, and the like. And, on the other, it is well integrated internally: All business processes work together smoothly. A company at the height of its Prime is heading—so long as it maintains its controlled flexibility—for a long life. That is a reflection of human life. Statistics show that married people live longer than single people, probably because they are often better integrated internally, as individuals and with their communities. Love does conquer all because love is a force for integration. Hate causes those possessed by it to age rapidly.

All companies develop unevenly, and uneven development is to be expected because systems develop their subsystems in sequence. A system does not develop all its subsystems in unison. Therefore, the sequence of development and its attendant problems are predictable and repetitive for any organization of any size, profit or nonprofit, in any technology. Some problems are not normal. The abnormal lifecycle stages and the abnormal problems within each lifecycle stage are manifestations of unexpected disintegration.

As you read through this book, you will be tempted to identify your company's stage in the lifecycle. Be careful not to oversimplify. Like the continuum of human life, organizational behavior varies constantly. When we are threatened, feeling vulnerable or scared, we may revert and behave like children. When we feel accomplished, confident, and successful, we show indications that we are progressing to the next stage closer to Prime. And occasionally, when we feel run down, we act old.

How old are you? You are as old or as young as you act most of the time, under most circumstances. The same is true for organizations. You will find that your organization exhibits traits from many locations on the lifecycle.

Another complication is that different parts of the organization can be, and usually are, at different stages of the lifecycle. Marketing should always exhibit signs of perpetual youth: continuously sensitive to changes, aggressive, and creative. On the other hand, it is normal and to be expected that accounting—organized, deliberately inflexible, totally predictable—ages rapidly. Different branches, some old and some new and vibrant, will also behave distinctively.

Where is your organization on the lifecycle? There is no simple formula. Your analysis should focus on individual units: department, branch, corporate headquarters, or the company as a whole. Determine the characteristics of each of those units.

Another warning: The purpose of my work is not to diagnose companies. My aim is to give tools to the organization's members so that they can diagnose themselves. When all the players agree on what is happening to the company and why it is happening, you will begin to reap rewards. People will start acting in unison. I suggest, therefore, that you not read this book alone or come to conclusions alone. Have your team discuss the book together and agree on the diagnosis as well as a plan of action.

Changes made to your position on the lifecycle must be incremental. A company does not jump from Infancy to Prime or from Bureaucracy to Prime. It needs to move through the lifecycle one stage at a time. The transition from stage to stage can be rapid, but there can be no leapfrogging.

An endless stream of problems attracts the attention of those who lead an organization through its transformation to Prime. Leaders must understand which problems are critical to the success of the company and which are not, which problems they can delegate to lieutenants and which they cannot. This book will help you set priorities and focus on what is crucial for the success of your organizational transformation.

DENIAL: THE ENEMY OF DIAGNOSIS

All improvement starts with the admission that help is necessary. Denial is exhausting: It consumes a company's resources, diverting everyone from constructive business. It inhibits healthy development. Denial (lack of awareness, reality-blinking) is dangerous because it indicates a detachment and disintegration from the purpose of one's existence. Loss of awareness breeds trouble. The precondition of valid diagnosis is conscious awareness. Companies that suffer from denial and mutual deception will derive faulty diagnoses.

How does a company heighten awareness? Its people must become conscious of their surroundings, dealing honestly with one another. Openness among members of an organization is paramount. Barring organization-wide openness, you should get professional help for creating an openness that will allow the organization to proceed to Prime. The higher a company's self-awareness, the more receptive it will be to change.

Elements of Organizational Diagnosis and Therapy: Touchstones of Managerial Responsibility

To solve problems and move the company to Prime, I invoke the contributions of six classic managerial responsibilities: style, structure, strategy, staffing, rewards, and planning and goals. Their relative contributions are variable and different at every stage of the lifecycle. The actual practice of each of those variables changes (or ought to change) over time and according to the stage of development the company is in.

To lead your company to Prime, you must first get it to the healthy part of its current stage in the lifecycle and prepare it to advance. Company leaders must be like parents who know how to treat their child one way when it is a baby and to modify their parental approach as the child grows to adulthood and beyond.

STYLE

How leaders make decisions and carry them out is crucial to morale, which, in turn, shapes an organization's performance. Founders necessarily manage their newborn companies in a kind of heroic or authoritarian way. Without a strong-willed leader, an infant company may die. A decaying company, slipping into bureaucratic paralysis, also needs a strong-willed leader—one capable of changing direction and effectively rousing everyone to follow. This need, once again, parallels life: A teenager joyfully exercises with little cajoling or coaching, but a person in middle age often needs a personal trainer's encouragement and instruction.

At other stages, over-centralized decision-making quashes creativity, bringing about a fatal paralysis. China's leaders rigidly insist that the country's clocks all run on Beijing time, even though that means that high noon comes to Mongolia in the middle of the night.

STRUCTURE

Each stage implies an optimal structure. In the freewheeling days of Infancy, when the entrepreneur and a few colleagues do everything, the best organizational structure is no structure at all: Just praise the Lord and pass the ammunition. Structure would suffocate the organization, cutting its flexibility and bringing about premature old age. In the hard-won harmony of Prime, a healthy company thrives in an atmosphere defined by well-crafted rules and responsibilities. Later, as a company begins to decentralize (giving life to babies, as it were), it requires a diverse management team: Some managers need to be able to handle headquarters, whereas others need to run satellite units that evolve at different rates and stages.

STRATEGY

If the strategic concerns of parents of a child in the "terrible twos" differ from those of a "twenty-something's" parents—and they do—then the same must be true of companies. A young company must plan for rapid sales growth, for example. But having achieved booming sales, it must direct its attention to building structure, controlling costs, and insuring profits. Otherwise, the deluge of orders will overwhelm its cost structure and operating systems, and the company will crumble as sales increase and profits fall dangerously. In short, it is time to confront adolescence. A Prime company, on the other hand, needs to avoid aging by producing new infants with the energy to regenerate the parent company.

STAFFING

In the early stages of a business, its founder should hire at least one alter ego who admires his or her creativity and—at the same time—functions as a hard-nosed realist, keeping the whirlwind boss from self-destructing. An aging company, on the other hand, may lose vitality if its many realists overshadow its few risk-takers. The key hires are the top managers. They, and the strengths they bring to the table, have to change continually to meet evolving leadership needs.

At various points, risk-takers must inspire the company; nuts-and-bolts producers must steady it; administrators and accountants must systematize it. In Prime, when all three groups converge to work in unison, the company needs a fourth kind of manager: an integrator with an ability to harness diverse talents and direct them to the company's goals.

REWARDS

Different kinds of rewards attract different kinds of people and encourage different kinds of behavior. Each stage in the corporate lifecycle implies its own best style of compensation.

An infant design company might attract gifted young artisans for little money simply because they value the sheer exhilaration of creating exciting new products. That same company might find it necessary to pay big commissions to sell those exciting new products: The company, strapped for capital, needs to carry higher variable costs to lower fixed costs. The hard-charging salespeople who have to move the products value quick payoff above all else. By contrast, an adolescent company has more need of long-term loyalty than hard-charging (and highly mobile) performers can give.

An adolescent company might do well to encourage and motivate loyal employees with generous profit-sharing or deferred-compensation plans designed for long-term payoff. That is something a start-up could not and, I strongly suggest, should not offer. I have seen many situations where the founders gave up too much too early. When rough times arrived (and they always do), those employees had no motivation to stick around: They had no voice in their highly centralized companies, and the centralist founders of those companies had lost interest when they gave up controlling ownership. The result was doom.

When a company is operating at Prime, its competitors vie for the services of its key employees. At one time (and, to some extent, today), companies in IBM's industry—even companies in vastly different businesses—competed to have IBM managers join their ranks. IBM lost many of its top performers when they responded to the lure of new and promising opportunities.

When the potential for losing key employees is a factor, and it usually is for companies in Prime, companies retain their best people by offering them what amounts to irresistible challenges: starting new divisions, launching new product lines, engaging other companies in joint ventures, and giving them equity. The more millionaires a company has created by its results in the marketplace, the better it is for all the other shareholders, too. All those devices help organizations retain their top performers who, simultaneously, open new vistas to maintain Prime. In Prime companies, top performers need more than the challenge of new and exciting ventures; Prime organizations can afford to share equity. But for a company in its Infancy to share equity would be premature—like giving away the store.

By the same token, a Go-Go organization that offers profit-sharing to its key people is engaging in an exercise in futility: A Go-Go organization does not know its cost structure and is in no position to assess individuals' impact on its costs. For key people in a Go-Go company, profit-sharing is a windfall. Some richly deserve it, and some do not.

Each company must, therefore, craft a reward system suitable for its stage in the lifecycle. Again, business mirrors life: A lollipop that motivates and rewards a toddler would be an insult to a teenager.

PLANNING AND GOALS

At every stage of the corporate lifecycle an organization needs to reassess its immediate and future needs. From Infancy through Adolescence, the immediate goal progresses from survival to sales volume to net profit. A company entering Prime should be grooming future businesses and leaders; an aging company achieves rebirth by plunging into expansion and innovation.

As it matures toward Prime, a business should pursue oscillating priorities: first going after sales, then building cost controls, then improving market reach. That repeating cycle—expansion, consolidation, expansion—is the dynamic that turns opportunities into profits. The discipline of focusing on exactly the right set of priorities for each stage is clearly the key to propelling a company toward Prime.

To help a company determine its position in the corporate lifecycle, I examine it for factors that influence long- and short-term organizational effectiveness and efficiency.

- An organization that is highly creative but has not yet taken any risk is still planning or dreaming in the Courtship stage.

- If its orientation is short term and survival-based (do it first, we'll talk about it later), it is in the Infancy stage.

- A company, all function, little form, mostly results oriented, with overconfident management increasingly involved in deals and projects the company is ill prepared to handle, is in the Go-Go stage.

- When form and function are in conflict and there is a struggle between those who want short- and long-term effectiveness and those who want more efficiency, when management has internal conflicts about what to do next, the company is in Adolescence.

- In Prime there is order and aggressive, well-evaluated planning. When form starts to overshadow function, when people in administrative positions have more power than those in productive positions, when authority and power migrate to staff, and when authority and responsibility start to get bifurcated, the company is departing Prime.

- In Aristocracy, form dominates. Whom you know and how you behave are more important than what you actually do or the results you actually produce.

- Recrimination is characterized by witch-hunts. Instead of uniting to solve their problems, people are attacking one another. The company experiences loss of liquidity and the resources necessary for survival.

- In Bureaucracy form is all that is left, and the goals are not to serve those who need the services but to secure the funds that are driven by political considerations.

In the following chapters, we will delve into each of those stages on the lifecycle. I introduce each chapter with an illustrative parable and close each one with lists of the normal and abnormal problems that challenge and trouble organizations during that particular stage of the lifecycle. In the book's final chapter, I discuss common management myths in light of my lifecycle theory and findings.

From Courtship to Cradle

— *From Courtship into the Future: A Parable* —

Richard Harrow loves to start companies—so much so, in fact, that he has done it twice. In 1969, he spotted an unserved niche in, of all things, the market for campground accommodations. While on vacation, he had tired of hauling his family and their 16-foot Winnebago into crowded, run-of-the-mill, dingy, state and private camping sites. A lot of people would pay thousands of dollars, he figured, for the right to visit safe, clean, attractive, well-maintained camping "preserves" with swimming pools, woodsy trailer pads, and other attractions. The idea sent him dreaming and to pencil and paper for a few calculations.

His dream took shape in sketches around the dinner table. Before long, Harrow made a pact with his wife: She would pay the mortgage and sundry bills with paychecks from her nursing job at the local hospital. He would drain $41,000 from their savings account as a start on building the first members-only campground, in a vernal glade in the Cascade Mountains, an easy drive from Seattle. They would call the company Outdoors Club.

The family's savings rushed through Harrow's hands, faster than he thought, what with buying materials, paying seasonal help, printing promotional materials, and developing the systems to enroll, track, and serve members. He begged a $10,000 loan from his brother. When he lacked cash, he made up for it by pouring his personal energy into every project—even cajoling his kids to help him cut down trees, clear trails, frame the campground club house—anything to get the new preserve open.

Harrow proved he had a winning idea the first summer he was in operation, filling his first campground to an average 80 percent of capacity. And by 1981, he had built Outdoors Club into a $40 million company, with 22 preserves in five states, visited by 29,500 members. But as one success led to another, Harrow's energy for the business grew.

Harrow went back to do more of what he loved to do. He launched a new company, Seattle Airlines, reveling again in rolling up his shirtsleeves to build a business, rather than sitting on his rear to run it. Though initially an airline with only two airplanes serving three cities in Washington and Oregon, Harrow was bent on showing people that he could build a business that served passengers better than all the other airlines. Unlike the financing of his first start-up, Harrow could bankroll this one himself. Even so, he took financing from outsiders because there were so many opportunities.

When Seattle took possession of its first plane, a used Fairchild F-27 from Alaskan Airways, Harrow helped scrape the body to get it ready for painting with Seattle's logo. On the day of the company's first scheduled flight, he greeted passengers at the gate. And then, after walking a red carpet from the terminal to the plane at Seattle–Tacoma International Airport, he boarded the flight to enjoy Seattle's maiden voyage, serving every passenger a glass of champagne.

Harrow was in his glory. This was what he lived for—to run

against the conventional wisdom, to make a business burst to life against the odds of survival. Although his first flight had only six paying passengers (in a plane built for 40), the anxiety of an uncertain future didn't faze him. For the moment, champagne in hand, he celebrated his company's birth.

COURTSHIP

Courtship, the first stage of a business, feels like new romance. Passion is its sine qua non. Without passion, a would-be entrepreneur never gets beyond the anxiety and confusion of those early days of uncertainty. A person who is overwhelmed by hard truths and cold reality will never create anything. Realists adapt to their environment, but the people who dare to be founders of businesses try to change their environment. Founders, therefore, are not quite realistic, not even reasonable. No surprise there: Business advances—civilization's advances—are the fruition of the dreams of unrealistic people.

STYLE

The Courtship stage is inherently limited. Founders dream of bringing their ideas to fruition. Then, abruptly, they stop their dreaming and declare, "Enough. We know now what we have to do. Let's go do it." They grab their fledgling idea by the scruff of the neck and drag it to the next stage of the corporate lifecycle, Infancy. Entrepreneurs who can do that are leaders.

Leadership theorists describe only one type of leader. I, however, say that we are all leaders—depending on the circumstances. The style that, in one situation, makes a leader of a person eliminates that person as a leader when conditions change. In Infancy we need doers, realists, overachievers, risk-takers, people who drive to the heart of a problem. They say, "Show me the tracks. Okay, now that we know where the tracks are, get out of my way. Let's get going." They are not prophets, and they are no longer simply dreamers. Their compulsion is to achieve results and get done with it. I call people who have this quality producers.

A successful Courtship demands dreamers, prophets. But just as doers (that is, producers) alone do not conceive, prophets alone do not give birth. The successful Infancy needs a prophet-doer: a person who dreams and wakes up to take action. An arsonist-firefighter all in one, he throws the firebomb and then rushes in to extinguish the flames. To insure a healthy birth, the organization needs the leadership of either one person with both those qualities or of a doer-dreamer partnership. Consider the combinations of Moses and Aaron, and subsequently, Moses and Joshua, or Karl Marx and Friedrich Engels. Incidentally, it is interesting to note that the dreamers usually get all the credit and blame while the complementary member of the team remains in the shadows. That, I believe, is a reflection of our Western cultural bias that favors individualism.

Here is the place for me to point out that there are founders who introduce abnormal problems to Courtship. I think of them as the flirts. Among all the would-be entrepreneurs out there romancing reality, this type deserves special notice. One type of a flirt is the inventor, an especially appealing breed—first sight, anyway. Every so often I meet inventors so excited by their latest ideas that their contagious enthusiasm makes me happy. It is like seeing young people in love. I want to help them get started. The problem is that the people who come up with great ideas are not always the people who can carry them out.

Not long ago, for example, I met an inventor who wanted my advice on how to retain control of his ideas. He had invented many devices. For a variety of reasons, he lost control of every one of his inventions. When he came to me, he had another brilliant idea—an answer to the potential disaster of fires in high-rise buildings—and he was determined that time to control his fate. People caught in a high-rise fire can't jump or take the elevator, and, because the stairs are choked with toxic smoke, they may never reach a helicopter on the roof. That inventor had devised the first (and thus far only) solution: a safe, flexible chute that connects all floors along the outside of the building and leads to safety below. The chute is made of material that allows people to step inside and easily control the speed of their descent with their elbows and knees. He had demonstrated his marvelous idea on at least one television show. With a potential market of hundreds and hundreds of high-rise buildings around the world, it looked like a classic winner, the seed of a major corporation.

It failed.

Why?

A truly creative inventor doesn't have one invention. He or she seems to have a new invention every morning. If it is not a new invention, there may be new marketing ideas that inevitably destroy the chances that earlier ideas have for a fair chance. Little if anything ever really happens. Like people who are in love with love, some inventors are addicted only to spawning ideas. Sales, financial negotiations, product reliability: All that bores them. They derive 80 percent of their gratification from the first 20 percent of the innovation experience. They usually avoid the remaining 80 percent—the painful nitty-gritty of working out operational details.

That's what happened with the inventor of the chute. No sooner had we agreed on a marketing strategy for his chute than the inventor had another idea—and another, and another, and another. He ran in so many directions that he accomplished practically nothing on the first idea.

Eventually, he offered me 30 percent of all his inventions in exchange for holding his hand and protecting him from the wolves in the forest. Instead, I urged him to focus on one of his many ideas: car-window holograms that would replace temporary license plates. "Make your first million out of it," I said. "Maybe then we'll talk about something else."

Such inventors are the business romantics, the entrepreneurs who can't help playing the field. They are like people who are so appealing, smart, funny, or powerful that they attract willing partners of the opposite sex time after time but just can't commit to a long-term relationship. Before they realize it, those people have reached their late forties, and their opportunities for marriage are slipping away.

Other flirts are the forever creative entrepreneurs who do not submit their ideas to the reality test. They have no doubts, or they do not allow for the consideration of doubts. They believe that if they are excited about an idea, the whole world must also be excited. So, rushing forward, they use their enthusiasm to convince people with no business acumen to invest. Only after they have the capital, do they contemplate doubt. By that time, though, the money is gone.

An entrepreneur with whom I worked lived through two Courtships: one failed, and one progressed successfully to the next stage. In his first Courtship, the entrepreneur committed the classic error of spreading himself too thin: He had too many ideas, and he loved them all. He did not focus. When he abandoned all but one of his beloved ideas, he was then ready to make the transition from Courtship to parenthood; he was ready, in other words, to nurture an infant business. That accomplished, he positioned his business to pursue Prime.

When I examine organizations in Courtship, I want to identify what it is the founder is really committed to. If the entrepreneur is committed to the continuous excitement of creating, I know that I am dealing with a Don Juan of business: a person who will never make the commitment to marry any one idea. The Don Juans cherish the chase. They derive no pleasure in making a success that grows and endures.

In such abnormal situations, I pass on the opportunity to coach their creations to Prime. Although I find those entrepreneurs extremely exciting and charming, they are nevertheless seductive robbers of time. Either nothing really happens, or worse, people lose a lot of money. It is not that they deliberately con investors. They truly believe in their creation and its merits. What generates the disaster is their lack of commitment to endure the pain and problems of raising a company. Their romantic notion that building a company must always be exciting, in the end, always inhibits their commitment.

Entrepreneurs—those who in their passion have won investors, leased office or manufacturing space, hired employees, resigned from paying jobs, and gone into debt—cannot return to their former lives. Their former lives no longer exist. Entrepreneurs who have made the ultimate commitment in business life are the founders of new enterprises.

When their enterprises emerge as infant corporations, romantic, passionate dreamers may not have what it takes to lead them: The moment founders undertake risk, their organization's culture undergoes a dramatic transformation. Infancy is the time to *do,* not to dream and talk but to do. The founders can no longer pass the time visualizing. Nobody has time for meetings. There is much work to do, and everyone should pitch in. Founders award only doers. The people who climb the ladder of success in emerging companies are those who go into sales and production. In those heady days, the founders have no patience for anyone who muses and says, "You know, I've been thinking . . ." They can't use thoughts. Not now. They need results. They need product. They need sales. Now.

Don't misunderstand me. I am not saying that ideas are not welcome. Certainly they are. But in young, growing organizations, deeds are gold. Growing companies have insatiable appetites for cash, sales, and results. Thus, while it is important to be a dreamer, it is equally important to have the doers on board. In Infancy the doers take their turn, and the dreamers take a rest. An organization needs both doers and dreamers to make a healthy transition to Prime.

The Courtship-to-cradle transition to Infancy can be painful, especially for romantics who shy away from the reality of doing. It is difficult for individuals to alter their styles, and when several people are involved, the process can be dangerously painful, politically charged, and even lethal.

Consider what happens to the prerevolutionary idealists once the insurgents take power. Following a revolution, who are the first people thrown in jail or trundled off to the guillotine? They are the people who are still dreaming. Why? Because the new society has no need for dreamers. It needs doers, and it needs them desperately. So, too, founders of new businesses have to protect their newborn companies.

They are understandably autocratic, hardheaded, protective, central-ist, and opinionated.

Their new businesses are, quite often, one-person operations. Their founders serve as sales force, customer representatives, inspec-tors, service engineers, and production managers. They are their companies. They are authoritarian, self-centered, opinionated, and hard-nosed. They work long hours, make every decision, do every-thing from the small detail to the major policy. They do not delegate.

Is such behavior good or bad? Most consultants condemn it. I do not. I welcome and accept it. I applaud it. My experience has shown that their behavior is a necessary condition of success. The founders, protective of their offspring, are both passionate and committed. They fear someone might threaten, abduct, or hijack their infant.

Despite all the current talk about centralization versus decentral-ization and delegation, founders must control everything during the growing stages: Obligation precedes delegation. Their commitment to the dream and their ego gratification sustain the company's early life. Before they can delegate tasks, they need systems that inform oth-ers about what, how, when, and where tasks should be done. At that early stage, however, founders themselves are still learning about the job, experimenting with how to do it, and making improvements on the fly. So even if they want to delegate, they cannot possibly know what or how to do the tasks that need doing. How can they delegate those tasks? And of course, they shouldn't. Hands-on management is both normal and desirable. Delegation with no systems for control ends up being abdication. Not long ago, I saw a cartoon that showed two homeless people sitting on a bench. One guy said to the other, " . . . and then the consultant advised me to delegate."

How can they delegate? First, they need a structure.

STRUCTURE

During the early stage of Courtship there is no talk of structure, and that is just as it should be. It is too early. Talk of structure would be ice water on the enthusiasm of the founding parents who still have no clear vision of the future. Partisans' guerrilla forces do not have clear structures with ranks and division of responsibilities. During this stage, commitment to do whatever needs doing takes the place of structure.

During Courtship, founders house their enterprises almost entirely inside their heads, and they fuel them with their passion. As to physical surroundings, consider the mythology of the computer industry, which holds that great electronic tycoons typically begin their careers tinkering in their garages. One day lightning strikes, turning IOUs into potential IPOs. Other founders have launched companies from humble attics and basements, equipped with nothing more than a Rolodex, fax, and fanatic faith in a fantastic idea.

Structure provides a form that decreases flexibility. An organization in Courtship needs maximum flexibility. Its idea is tested only in people's heads, and no one can guess exactly what needs doing, much less who will do it or how to do it.

Young MBAs often fail in start-up organizations because their training has prepared them for more structured environments. I remember when my company was still young, I interviewed an MBA to join me. His first question was about the career ladder at my company. At the time, I had about $5,000 in the bank, and the company was going to be just the two of us, at least for a while. "Look around," I said. "There's just you and me. We are the company. There is nobody else. But I will tell you about your career ladder. You are standing on top of it, and the other end is buried in the ground. If you want to climb it, just pump it up."

STRATEGY

The optimal strategy for founders during Courtship calls for vision tempered by reality. Founders need to think big while asking themselves, "Am I committed to the idea of providing a value-adding product or service to the market? What is that value? How valuable is it really? Am I interested mostly in raking in profits? Am I willing to take risks and spend my own money? Do I want to devote years of my life to raising a healthy business? What exactly is my company going to do? Why? How? When? My idea is great, but what exactly will I do? Do I know who my customers are?"

Here is a very important tip for those who want to start a company. Remember: You are not the customers. Who are they? Are you starting this for yourself? If so, how many are there like you? Where will money be coming from? Do the capabilities of your team match your ideas and needs? Are their styles correct? Are they workaholics? Are they willing to sacrifice sleep and family until the company is up and running?

The strategy for a healthy Courtship incorporates two aspects:

- Commitment as expressed in sacrifices commensurate with future risks and realities

- Realistic evaluation of the business idea.

Those two factors must be in balance: The more committed you are to your idea, the less realistic you will be. The more realistic you are, the less committed to your idea you will be.

I deliberately use the word idea because the word opportunity forces unrealistic analysis. Opporthreat, a word I coined by translating a Chinese word that means both opportunity and threat, is much closer to what I mean. Many ideas are opportunities that, when mishandled, turn into threats. Many threats, if they are handled right, can be opportunities for learning and strengthening the organization.

Founders—even in the most preliminary stages of their dreaming—make business plans that are often quite detailed. But it is important not to lose sight of the crux of Courtship: The founder needs to focus not on what and how something will be done but on why it needs to be done at all. Because Courtship occurs so early in the lifecycle, details are negligible, and it is premature to evaluate the concreteness of the founder's proposition. What really counts is motivation. Has the founder subjected his idea to a reality test? That is where the business plan comes in. The plan is not the purpose; it is the test of the purpose, of the passion.

Passion manifests a deeper factor, commitment, which is critical for success. When I applied for my doctorate, an adviser told me that writing a dissertation is extraordinarily grueling, and unless I picked a topic I truly loved, I would fail.

Likewise, passionate commitment will be critical for sustaining the newborn organization as it confronts the hard realities of life. Look at would-be company founders. They are constantly selling their great ideas. Whom are they trying to convince? Themselves. Why, then, the big sell? It is all part of the process of building commitment: the higher the potential risk, the more intense the requirement for commitment.

A productive and healthy Courtship shows commitment commensurate with the risk. Are you committed? Instead of measuring commitment in absolute terms, measure it in relative terms: What percentage of your resources will you commit to your endeavor? By resources I do not mean only money. Time and energy are equally important. What are you willing to sacrifice? How about your marriage? Say your idea will require you to be away from home at least three days a week, maybe more. Are you willing to sacrifice your part in your children's youth? One day, you may find they are fully grown, and you do not remember their ever being small. As the founder of Banco de Commercio in Mexico once told me, "Starting a business is like going to sleep young and waking up old."

Business founders face overwhelming odds. Realists often assume that entrepreneurs are in it for the money. But if they were only after money, they would probably be happier working for someone else. At the beginning of a new venture, there is very little money, if any, for the founder. True, there is the potential to make money, but wealth is far from guaranteed. Money, I maintain, is simply not enough to compensate for the sacrifices. Do revolutionaries sacrifice their lives because they anticipate a huge gross national product after the revolution succeeds? Of course not. They do it for truth, justice, and freedom. So it is for the founder of any business or organization.

Motivation is everything, and, in business as in any other undertaking, it must be the right motivation. Profit is not enough. Because new businesses rarely make money, profit-driven founders will not easily find the enthusiasm to sustain them until profits appear. Profitability is the scorecard, but it is not a significant factor until later, after the company has progressed to another stage. Ask successful entrepreneurs what makes them pour their energies into their businesses, and they will tell you about other concerns besides money. "It was something I had to do," they'll say. "Challenge is addictive. I love it. Making it on your own is the greatest high. I want to make a difference, and I know that I can. I just can't help it; I have to do it. The call is too strong for me to resist." That call has the strength of the call of motherhood, which many find irresistible.

Passion for making a difference is the rising tide that lifts the spirits of entrepreneurs, giving them the strength to follow their dreams of a new reality. In the early stage of Courtship, founders subsist on the transcendent thrill of planning to bring something unique to market—a fresh answer to a perceived need. They fuel that thrill with the certainty that the world will embrace their creation. The best founder is not a profit seeker but a market prophet, a person who defies skeptics and "safety-firsters." The best founder is one whose prophecy is self-fulfilling.

Obsessed? Let's hope so. After all, obsession never hurt Ford, Edison, or Gates. To launch a successful start-up, obsession is a necessary and desirable pathology.

Still, obsession alone is not enough to nourish a healthy Courtship. Entrepreneurs are romantic obsessives who are romancing in an all too real world, and they soon feel its exigencies. Almost every entrepreneur needs money or credit. A new company needs a business plan, an assessment or calculation of the necessary resources—people, materials, space—to get the enterprise going. Having consorted with reality, the fledgling founder inevitably bumps up against the hard fact that all those resources do cost money. Among the first realities entrepreneurs romance is the reality of credit. Creditors admire entrepreneurial passion—even insist on it—but they also expect budding entrepreneurs to risk their own money.

But let's not get ahead of ourselves. We're still in the Courtship stage of the corporate lifecycle: The romance slowly but surely meets reality. Commitment to an idea has conjured up a new market niche, a new product brand, a new service. Relentlessly, that vision drives the entrepreneur beyond ambiguity, fear, and doubt.

Passion without commitment is just noise without the benefit of music, and some creative, excited people are passionate about their ideas only until they confront difficulties: Their romanticism evaporates when the specter of reality looms over them. Those would-be founders substitute their passion for their ideas with a new, fierce passion against those they imagine failed them. To progress successfully, entrepreneurs find that there is no substitute for quiet commitment and a willingness to pay the price—in time, energy, and resources. During Courtship, there is nothing tangible: no company, no credit, no investment. There is, in a manner of speaking, no marriage, not even an engagement. What, then, keeps founders going? It is, as they might tell you, the dream of making a difference.

Commitment to ideas has cost many founders their marriages. Once they give life to their organization, it will require unconditional dedication. Like a new mother giving up on a husband who doesn't understand the demands of motherhood, certain entrepreneurs give up on their spouses when the needs of the newborn organization conflict with those of family life. And, like a wise new mother who recruits her husband to wash and care for the newborn baby, smart entrepreneurs involve their families in their creations.

The realities of the next phase, Infancy, call for us to assure that the conditions for a healthy birth exist. The questions are: Is there sufficient commitment? Is the spouse supportive and understanding?

The founders of start-up companies are, in effect, the parents of newborn children. The company is like a squalling baby whose every need demands immediate and total attention. Customers, banks, investors, and employees clamor for founders' attention. And founders feel the need to respond personally to all of them: In the beginning each question seems as critically important as every other. Founders need to share the care of the newborn company with their partners. Just as parents cannot easily raise children alone, founders need the involvement and commitment of the people close to them. If they do not involve their spouses, they may find themselves leading a company and facing life alone.

STAFFING

Whom should founders recruit during the early stage of Courtship? Founders need to work with dream-sharers—not just employees—who are willing to do any job that needs doing. Even the toughest revolutionaries need hand-holders and co-conspirators. They need one or two close friends or disciples, but I do not recommend involving lovers. Working with one's lover may seem like a great idea: During the Courtship stage, dreaming is quite enjoyable and contagious. The problems arise when the organization enters its Infancy. Lovers' quarrels get confused by and with fights for control of the organization, and founders need to control their infants. Those arguments can and do destroy emerging enterprises, and they can end love affairs, too. When it comes time to make critical, strategic decisions, lovers have a penchant to introduce issues of authority, control, and discussions of who is first among equals. In general, a lover's involvement puts unnecessary pressure on the business. Instead, get your lover to understand what you are doing and recognize your pain, hopes, and aspirations. Lovers create excellent support systems, but do not make a lover your employee. If your lover ends up as your boss, you could lose your commitment to the idea before it has had time to become a reality.

For an organization in Courtship you want a leader who is a realistic dreamer, who knows what to do when he or she wakes up. Dreamers who can only dream end up moonwalking. On the other hand, doers who aren't dreamers can carry the flame faithfully into the future, but they cannot ignite the ever burning bush. They don't inspire others or even themselves to take the risks that starting something new demands.

If the founder doesn't embody both of those characteristics, the organization in Courtship should form a complementary leadership composed of a dreamer who prophesies and a doer who is ready to act. But because complementary leadership can mean conflict or difficult transfers of authority, when one or another member of the team doesn't work out, it is time to find a replacement to take that person's role.

Rewards

Just as structure is anathema to Courtship, discussion of rewards is also dangerous. Enthusiastic founders, in their exuberance for their ideas, often make promises they later regret. It is easy to promise ownership, positions on the board, representations in foreign offices, and the like. After all, none of that has any value because, initially, there is nothing but the idea. From the founder's point of view, the promises evoke people's support, and during this stage, every founder craves support, emotional as well as financial. Later, when they have to deliver on those promises, owners usually regret their generosity. Too late they realize that they gave away much too much and their promises were far too open-ended.

There are no real financial rewards at this stage, but people can nevertheless expect to work hard to start something from the ground up. The rewards are intrinsic to the process: camaraderie, friendship, and the satisfaction of committing to an idea with a future. Money must be a secondary consideration because there can be no assurances or guarantees. If people get involved only for the money, they may get discouraged and quit when doubts arise about the feasibility of making the expected money. Everyone involved must believe in the idea and its message rather than just its financial potential. Like people newly in love, would-be entrepreneurs thrive on the pleasure of being swept up by inspiration, a mission, and an organizing purpose in life. Later, in Infancy, the incentives will be less ethereal.

During Courtship, founders must be clear about their visions: That clarity attracts people who first and foremost share their vision.

Many founders make the mistake of recruiting people by selling them on the money the idea will make. Then, when the money is behind schedule, the founder redoubles his efforts to convince them that the money will be there. Disenchanted, the unmotivated recruits initiate a revolving-door employment pattern. In some instances, the founder "bribes" the employees to stay by making more promises that will haunt him later or by simply raising wages beyond the company's capacity to survive. Founders would do better to surround themselves with fellow revolutionaries—people who are willing to go to the mountains. I am certain that Castro did not promise government positions to the guerrillas he recruited.

PLANNING AND GOALS

Entrepreneurs at the Courtship stage need to be flexible and make sure their dreams are in working order before they expose them to a marketplace rife with dream-killers. The entrepreneurs must continually expand and test the viability of their plans. Because Infancy, the next stage, will require actual risk-taking, during the Courtship, entrepreneurs need to evaluate the true nature of their risks and their willingness and capability to take them. Those risks take many forms: quitting the secure job, signing a lease for office space, promising delivery of the first order on a certain date. When an entrepreneur takes those risks, a new company is born, and we move on to the next stage.

WHERE DO YOU STAND? A CHECKLIST

Normal Problems of Courtship

- The primary emotion of founders is excitement.
- Almost all energy is focused on the why.
- The how, when, and who take minor roles.

Abnormal Problems of Courtship

- Refusing to consider reality when involved in making decisions is blinding.
- The measure of commitment is not commensurate to the risk.
- By denying the need to analyze the future, the founder fails to give any heed to the who, how, or when.
- The founder makes irresponsible promises he or she cannot deliver, will not be able to deliver, or will not want to deliver.

Infant Cares

────────── *Infancy: A Parable* ──────────

A CNN war correspondent, whom we'll call Jack Galbraith, was a veteran observer of man's inhumanity. From Afghanistan to Sarajevo he had chronicled atrocity and anguish. On his thirty-ninth birthday he woke up in a Paris hotel room, numbly watched a TV report on a terrorist car bombing, and realized he had had enough. He was finally, indelibly, irrevocably sick of war. He quit CNN that same day.

Three months later, while renewing his battered psyche in sunny Grenada, he conceived a new magazine that would satirize the world's most ferocious generals, mercenaries, gun nuts, and war groupies. He called it *White Flag*.

With joy, anticipation, and a brilliant little prospectus, he shopped *White Flag* among a rarefied circle of very rich New

Yorkers who had all, at one time, been combat infantrymen. Three of them put up half a million dollars to run a test-mailing. The results—wild enthusiasm from too few potential subscribers to justify launching the magazine—were disappointing.

Undaunted, Galbraith called in all his chits, mortgaged his possessions, and proceeded. He only barely paid the printing bill for his first issue, but he loved what he was doing. He was positive *White Flag* was destined to become the country's most iconoclastic political humor magazine.

He was right. In fact, only one year later, Galbraith was pretty much drowning in success. He had set up shop in the Virginia countryside, about 30 miles southwest of Washington. He had rented a defunct farm with a big old barn, and he used e-mail to maintain close contact with his many sources in Congress and the Pentagon. As a tabloid bi-weekly with clever, biting headlines, *White Flag* was a hit: It had attracted 150,000 subscribers on the strength of Galbraith's dead-on reports on military delusions, pretensions, and absurdities. *White Flag*, for instance, reported that taxpayers pay tens of millions of dollars annually to maintain the Army's several hundred surplus generals in country-club luxury while they stoutly resist "another Vietnam," meaning any mission placing troops in harm's way overseas. One general angrily sued *White Flag* for group libel, and the case helped publicize the magazine and doubled its circulation.

Galbraith, however, was unprepared for success. Keeping the magazine going and growing was relentlessly hard work, and he did most of it. He wrote, edited, and designed most of the magazine's articles, sold ads, pursued subscribers, and got on as many radio talks shows as possible, all while he endlessly sought sources of cash and staved off creditors. He felt as if he were a single parent caring for a colicky infant on his own. He grew tired and resentful. He snapped at his colleagues for not performing as hard or well as he. Accordingly, several good staffers began living down to his estimation of them. On a single grim day he fired his production manager for incompetence, missed the printer's deadline, and lost two big advertisers. All of that happened just when Galbraith was desperate for cash to pay the bank, the Internal Revenue Service, and the law firm defending *White Flag* in the attention-getting but costly libel suit.

All that left Galbraith so drained and discouraged that he had trouble putting out the next two issues. Soon he considered folding *White Flag* while he still had his health and ironic humor. Business, he decided, was simply another kind of war.

But *White Flag* survived. The lawyer who represented Galbraith, a smart, funny woman named Charlene Noonan, not only rescued Galbraith from the depths of self-pity, she also got her firm to slash its fee by half. Soon Jack and Charlene were working closely together. Reinvigorated, Galbraith held fast to his magazine and to the life-purpose it gave him. He set up a 16-week forward cash-flow projection, which he monitored weekly, and he named Charlene Noonan his full-time publisher.

He undertook all that with the renewed commitment and exuberance of falling in love with his best ally. So *White Flag* survived Infancy and entered childhood in the strong hands of its partner-parents. Today, both the magazine and Jack and Charlene's marriage are thriving.

INFANCY

Founders of many infant companies almost immediately discover that they didn't have the slightest idea what they were in for. Every business baby is colicky, and every day brings unforeseen crises. The founder's role is to be firmly but fairly autocratic, fully confident about every decision, without stooping to tantrums or focusing on trivia.

Employees at infant companies look for excitement and stimulation. Founders shouldn't disappoint them. While an infant organiza-

INFANCY: A CLOSE CALL

As they say in baseball, it's not over until it's over. As they should probably say to would-be entrepreneurs, it's not a sale until it's a sale. One of the telltale signs of Infancy, however, is an entrepreneur committed to a brave new idea while struggling with the reality of getting the purchase orders out. Entrepreneurial dreamers often get discouraged when the realities of real life show up.

In 1981, Neil Kleeman launched Solution Systems, Inc., in Philadelphia. He had lined up quite a few potential clients, all of whom had assured him that they would bring him their business. After all, Kleeman was offering good deals for his proposed computer time-sharing service. Among his clients he counted many with whom he had dealt when he worked as a programmer for United Computing Systems, later a part of Sprint Corporation.

Much to his chagrin, when Kleeman went to close a deal with one of his strongest prospects, he found that the company had been sold. Not easily deterred, Kleeman and his partners approached the new owners, who were already planning to resell the company.

Kleeman ached for the business. He was completely committed to his idea, and he was confident that it could be an enormous success. Because of his background in the industry, Kleeman knew customers would line up for his service once the word got out. Convinced that his services would sell, he already had taken on a huge risk. To get Solution Systems up and running, he had borrowed a large sum from his parents, and he had already worked out a deal to lease a $300,000 computer. He had even recruited and hired a couple of his former cohorts from United Computing.

After months and months of relentless campaigning, Kleeman finally did win that business, and, in the process, he learned what all founders of infant organizations learn: Prepare to persevere. Commitment will be severely tested. You will face more than a few disappointments and close calls before your company emerges from its Infancy.

And that was Solution Systems, Inc., in 1989.

tion needs autocratic, no-nonsense, nuts-and-bolts leadership, that will not suffice to make the transition to the next stage in the lifecycle. An infant who stays small dies eventually. The energy to sustain it is, in the long run, prohibitive. Just as a baby needs to start sleeping through the night so that the parents can catch their breath, the organization needs to stabilize so that the founder can start dreaming about the next steps.

STYLE

The infant organization needs the dreamer-doer who brought it from Courtship to Infancy, but during the advanced stage of Infancy (when the viability of the company is not in question and the cash flow is predictably positive) the organization again needs the dreamer, who can imbue it with the impetus for growth. It is time to renew the vision that may have vanished behind the strain and frantic activity of fighting for survival.

How important is education for founders and company leaders? In my previous books I have written that capable leaders are not what they know but what they are. What they know becomes obsolete over time. But what they are endures. College degrees are not nearly as important as common sense, willingness, and commitment to getting the job done: I am, of course, referring to character.

Founder is not a job for a people-pleaser, a stickler for protocol, or a politician. The founder is the one who has to establish firm, unambiguous priorities. Will a one-day shipment delay endanger the baby's health? Probably not. On the other hand, a shipment of defective parts certainly will.

Babies do better with authoritarian, hands-on parents. Founders who start to delegate responsibility when their enterprises are still in their Infancy may be losing their own sense of dedication. The heartbeat of an infant company is the founder's commitment, and if it loses that, the enterprise will soon be a statistic.

The founders and their close associates must realize that infant companies will consume most of their waking hours. These demanding babies require close attention and nurturing. Entrepreneurs must explain to their doubting families just how much attention their infants require. It is difficult for most people who are not entrepreneurs to grasp the dimensions of the founders' sacrifices to ensure their babies' survival to the next stage in the corporate lifecycle. The wisest entrepreneurs decide with their families how much of their lives they are willing to relinquish. The families of company founders need to understand that entrepreneurs leave their homes before dawn and don't return until it is time for the late news—six days a week and many Sundays, too.

Infancy is, in most cases, mercifully brief: Even fanatic founders can't stand the intensity for much longer than a few years. By then, cash flow should be positive, most customers should be repeaters, brand loyalty should be rising, suppliers should be stabilizing, and production snafus should no longer be daily events. Founders should, at last, be able to stop and breathe: The baby is sleeping through the night.

STRATEGY

In its Infancy, a company's only strategy is to produce a stellar product or service that satisfies its clients and competes effectively in the marketplace. Sales are vital, but founders should not forget costs or neglect cash flow. Profits are unimaginable so far, but cash flow should top every founder's list of concerns. Founders fear and avoid cash crunches like the hounds of hell. Cash crunches lead to such fatal mistakes as overborrowing or suicidal price slashing. More sales, more production, more cash, more everything except overhead are the keys to success for the infant company.

Infant companies should prepare themselves to move quickly whenever the need arises. If they are mired down in systems and procedures they cannot respond to changes, whether external or internal.

Companies in this stage should work to generate cash and to maintain accurate cost accounting. I don't need to explain the importance of cash flow: All founders are aware of the bills they need to pay. Many, however, are not attuned to the importance of cost controls. Accounting and information systems in infant organizations are usually weak. Their budgets—if they exist—are usually inaccurate.

Because of the new founders' meager experience, their companies often lack systems to record income and classify expenses. With everything happening for the very first time, the novices make decisions by the seat of their pants. Those founders are not necessarily incompetent or unwilling to learn. In a new enterprise, it just takes time for discipline and methods to develop.

A company without cost accounting may appear to be doing well if its sales are climbing. But delayed or overdue cost data might hide losses, leaving everyone with a false sense of security.

The goal of Infancy is survival, and founders with strong perfectionist tendencies are in for a truly painful period. Nothing works well enough. There are crises every hour, every day, and every week. There is little time to think, plan, or strategize. This is a normal Infancy—as long as it is not prolonged.

STRUCTURE

Flexibility in the infant company is characteristic and crucial. Everybody does everything, and nobody requires titles or organization charts to tackle whatever needs to be done. In this stage it is normal and expected to have no organizational charts. General instructions or descriptions of expectations might work, but a company in Infancy should not yet carve anything in stone.

The infant must grow, and growth takes single-minded dedication and intense focus. An infant company intent on establishing a formal organization chart and implementing management systems is a company pointed in the wrong direction. The founder needs to create an environment in which producers, not administrators, can succeed. Sales, production, growth, margins: The infant company wants and needs more and more and more. Its appetite is insatiable. The prevailing attitude is, "Let's do it. We'll do it now because we must if we want to be sure of getting a paycheck at the end of the next pay period." A healthy child has a voracious appetite. Unless you feed it, it will keep crying or it will die.

In the Infancy stage founders must centralize authority around themselves. They should be unwilling to delegate authority that influences growth. Founders must approach every business function experimentally. Despite the overwhelming demands on their time, founders should delegate only sparingly. With more than one parent, an infant company gets confused and loses focus. That is when a founder's commitment (indispensable motivator of long hours of work) evaporates.

Centralized authority does not mean unfair behavior. Yes, founders must be autocrats, but they must, at the same time, establish their reputations for fairness. With difficult days ahead, founders need to build mutual trust with employees, vendors, and customers. Mutual trust exists only when each party considers the other to be fair and reasonable. Founders who fail to establish reputations for trustworthy justice will eventually pay the piper. They may achieve short-term success, but in the long run they create cultures that encourage political backstabbing. That can only threaten long-term success. Founders must be hard-nosed, but they must complement that quality with integrity and respect.

The infant company needs a board of directors, but the founder (presumably the owner) would do best to use insiders only. Why? Because outsiders have a stultifying tendency to advise prudence. Their interests are fiduciary rather than inspirational. They will, with quiet decorum, kill new proposals that stray from the beaten path: They will crush dreams. Insiders, closely allied with the founder and his vision, understand intuitively that the company must always progress toward Prime. Their livelihoods are on the line. They need the company to succeed. And at that stage they know what they are talking about.

STAFFING

Founders who don't have partners with complementary styles may do well to hire an excellent executive secretary, a nuts-and-bolts person who knows how to keep business orderly. If an infant organization suffers from anything, it is the lack of order. Surprises are the norm. Suppliers do not deliver, workers fail to show up, product quality is below expectations, customers pay late, accounts receivable are confused with accounts payable and prepayments, and accrual accounting and cash accounting get mixed up. A first-class executive secretary is indispensable for a founder who can't yet afford an administrative vice president.

For the time being, it is fine to hire people largely on the basis of their energy and enthusiasm. Avoid hiring anyone who needs a formal plan or strategy to be productive. Look for guerrillas and improvisers—self-reliant people.

What happens if a founder's lieutenants don't share the dream? What if they disagree with the founder's vision? They must leave the company, and the sooner the better. The infant can't survive if people are stretching it in opposing directions. Conflict during Infancy is a disease. Founders must be brave enough to remove divisive people, regardless of their capabilities, since their mere presence undermines direction and success. An infant company cannot afford dissension.

During that early stage founders should give serious consideration to subcontracting production of their service or product. Subcontracting can help lower fixed costs while enhancing the organization's flexibility. True, subcontracting production may cost more than in-house production, but having variable costs high in relation to fixed costs is preferable to the opposite configuration.

Infant organizations need self starters like the founder: people with initiative and drive who are willing to work for commission or on a piecework basis. While reducing fixed costs, that tactic also weeds out the unproductive.

Once a company has enough capital to expand its structure and reach, it is in a stronger position to allow its fixed costs to grow.

REWARDS

While founders must await their own personal payoffs, employees should receive immediate and compelling compensation: short-term bonuses for reaching measurable goals and generous sales commissions. Founders who are smart enough to bestow rewards that really fire up enthusiasm will reap the benefits of employee satisfaction.

Founders should reward employees of their infant companies with compensation plans tied directly to individual productivity. The rewards need to be short term—awarded on a monthly or quarterly basis—and they must reflect performance. A salesperson, for example, who exceeds budgeted sales by 50 percent should receive proportionately more than a salesperson who exceeds budget by 25 percent. And any salespeople who don't meet budget need to catch up quickly or leave the company. The infant company can have little tolerance for nonperformers.

We are not considering profit sharing here. Infant companies rarely show profits, after all. Stock options, however, whether or not the company is public, are appropriate for companies in high-technology industries. Those companies need highly qualified (unaffordable) people with advanced training. To lure those gifted talents and get them to put in the long hours that lift start-ups from obscurity to sunlight, infant companies ought to offer "a piece of the action."

PLANNING AND GOALS

The immediate goal of every infant company is to sustain cash flow to finance growth and operations. During that early stage of life an infant must prove to itself—and to the world—that it is alive and strengthening itself for the battles to come. Cash is the infant's milk. Without sufficient cash the infant will die. And that can happen even while sales are skyrocketing. An infant company is particularly vulnerable to cash-flow problems during periods of fast growth because expenses tend to outpace revenues and, more to the point, collections.

A related goal of the infant company is to break even. That alone verifies the baby's staying power, its viability. The young venture's customers must have faith in it: They must believe that the infant will endure and grow into a healthy adult.

Curiously, one great danger in the Infancy stage is that founders do lose their vision. They are so busily engaged in making ends meet and meeting commitments that the romance vanishes. And the more hours the founders work, the less time they have to see the big picture. In short, they lose sight of their beloved. And with that loss, they and their organizations start to drift. Innovation declines and goals turn murky.

Many founders find it difficult to articulate their goals, so they turn to advisers who can help them step away from the fray. With that small distance they can, once again, say, "Yes, here is what we're trying to achieve, and here is where we've veered away from the dream." They formulate a specific plan that outlines how the organization can get back on course for Prime.

It is still too early to focus on details and systems. There will be time for that later. The infant company should simply hit the market running, seize every opportunity, and avoid promising the undoable. The goal is to sell enough to cover costs and get the business growing. Offer excellent products and services. Sell, sell, sell. Watch cash flow. And when life seems rough, breathe deeply, take a walk, and get back to work.

An Infant Company That Failed

Typically, an infant company is vulnerable to a series of diseases: It sells to the wrong markets and runs out of cash during a heady period of growth. Clinging desperately and fanatically to the founder's original dream, the infant company ignores its customers' needs. It fails to provide the products and services customers clamor for. The dream that was critical for the success of Courtship becomes a liability in Infancy. Now that they have reached the Infancy stage, founders, who had to be uncompromising prophets during Courtship, must adapt to reality. They need to analyze what works and what does not, and they have to be willing to compromise their exclusive dream by waking up.

Founders who refuse to look reality in the eye may eventually succeed: They do, however, need more time to go through painful trial-and-error processes, and they need deeper pockets. Some do fail because their dream was not the dream of the market they hoped to address. Those who face failure feel misunderstood, hostile, or apathetic. They run out of energy and money, and their companies die without their founders' total dedication to protect them from the realities of the marketplace.

What follows is the story of a start-up that failed.

A budding entrepreneur approached me with an idea to start a car wash business that offered a service available at no other car wash. To understand his idea you must first accept that the car wash industry is outdated. Recognizing the enormous disparity between the love people have for their cars and the low level of service provided by almost all car washes, the entrepreneur had determined that California would welcome a network of sophisticated car washes. He would call his car washes Car Salons.

The entrepreneur was passionate about his idea. During the Courtship stage of the lifecycle, as we've seen, passion is an entrepreneur's most important asset. That fellow loved cars, and he had devoted a great deal of time to watching how people washed their own cars. He had also observed many car wash businesses, noting the quality of the wash, how much time they devoted to each car, the selection of waxes and soaps, and the owners' and managers' attitudes toward customers. There was no aspect of the car wash business he hadn't examined.

He planned to buy car-wash machines like the ones car dealers use to prepare new cars for sale. Those machines do away with the assembly-line approach and demand the manual contribution that guarantees a wash of high quality. His machines would apply high-gloss carnauba wax, which lasts about 12 months. His plan was to locate his car washes at high-traffic gas stations.

The entrepreneur had started to approach potential investors who would purchase the washing/waxing machines and have them installed at the gas stations he lined up. In exchange for providing the space, processing the credit cards, and handling the cash, the gas station owners would receive a percentage of sales. The founder's organization, which would hire part-time college students to operate the car washes, would take a management fee for staffing, advertising, and managerial services. The investors, the business plan showed, would enjoy a good return on their investment. The founder was confident he had a winner.

I was impressed with both the entrepreneur and his idea. I invested in the company and watched as he launched the business. Wasting little time, he quickly had two machines up and running at two gas stations. Car Salons was born with a solid infrastructure, and the founder was a credible businessman with other successful ventures.

That was the summer of 1972, perhaps the rainiest summer in 30 years. People do not wash their cars on rainy days. To make matters worse, when the rains ended, the energy crisis began. To get gas, people were obliged to line up at gas stations and wait for hours. Few were in any mood to have their cars washed. Their cars, at that point, were purely necessities of modern life, and nobody wanted to spend another minute thinking about them.

It wasn't long before the company's cash flow jammed. There was no money to pay college students, no fees for gas station owners, and no earnings for investors. Car Salons died.

Where did we go wrong? Why did our baby have to die? Our postmortem showed that we had not provided a cushion for contingencies. Who could have predicted the turn in the weather or the oil crisis? Still, we ought to have prepared for both negative and positive cash flow. We should have known that a company in its Infancy stage is much more vulnerable to shocks than a more mature company with ready cash reserves. We should have known that even when every factor appears rosy, even when the money and people are in place, there is always an element of uncertainty.

Normal Problems of Infancy

- Leadership is authoritarian.
- Because there is no delegation, operations become over-centralized.
- The organization is usually short of cash.
- Problems with quality are not unusual.
- On-time delivery is unpredictable.
- Infant organizations have no second tier, or any other tier, management.
- There are no cost accounting systems.
- All information is centralized with the founder.
- Everyone works hard and long, way beyond normal hours.
- The organization's insufficient tools, equipment, people, and communications make it vulnerable.
- There is no good work space.
- All management is management by crisis.
- The lack of structure means overdependency on the founder for survival.
- Job descriptions are ambiguous.
- Cost controls are loose at best.
- Budgeting is helter-skelter. Either there is no budgeting at all or a budget is prepared three months into the fiscal year.

Abnormal Problems of Infancy

- The founder is too arrogant to listen to anyone.
- Expectations for success have little relation to reality.
- There is much more dreaming than doing.
- Cash flow is perilously unpredictable.
- Inadequate funding cannot sustain the company.

- Demand for the company's product or service is shallow.
- By taking short-term loans for long-term investments, the company's investment structure is thrown off balance.
- Founders spread their product lines too thin.
- The founder's commitment is insufficient to support the risk taken.
- The founder spreads his or her interests too thin.
- A lack of support from the founder's family makes it difficult for him or her to devote adequate time to the company.
- The founder fails to take even preliminary steps to form a complementary team.
- The organization is characterized by an unresolvable lack of mutual trust and respect.

C H A P T E R

Surviving
the Go-Go Years

A company we'll call Zoom, Inc., found itself in a self-created mess. The blame was put by most people squarely on the shoulders of its charismatic founder. The founder, whom we'll call Inger Nielsen, following a career as a much-admired downhill racer, had designed the most popular downhill skis in racing history. Her design incorporated slightly hollowed-out bottoms that allowed downhill racers to go at least 20 percent faster than other skis, and she thrilled millions by giving them a way to ski infinitely better than the laws of fear and gravity ever before allowed.

Nielsen became a Wall Street darling the moment investors realized that Zoom had no serious competition. It looked as though her only problems would be keeping up with orders and deciding how to spend her profits. Although Zoom's skis were superbly engineered, they were so cheap to manufacture, since they used epoxies developed for spacecraft, that retail markups of 500 percent were common. Zoom stock went on the market at $18 per share, and within nine months, its price had jumped to $86. Following a three-for-one split, the price resumed its climb.

I know this hardly sounds like a mess, but that's because I have told you only half the story.

With her company tearing through what I call the Go-Go years, the bratty stage of business development, Inger Nielsen started to behave with a certain grandiosity. The world, she seemed to believe, had told her she could do anything. Already, her healthy face had graced the covers of five major magazines, including *Business Week* and *Sports Illustrated*. Encouraged by their plaudits, she went on a buying spree that astonished her colleagues at Zoom, Inc. She started with a whirlwind weekend in Austria, impulsively buying the second biggest ski-boot manufacturer in Europe. Next she purchased a half-developed ski resort in British Columbia's Coast Mountains along with a small airline that shuttled between there and Vancouver. It was, no doubt, a brilliant idea for the up-market future, but her purchases sent the company so deep into debt that Zoom's profits from operations couldn't service that debt. Sales were climbing fast, but so were expenses.

To compound the problems, it was difficult to analyze what was happening and why. The accounting for the new acquisitions was mixed with Zoom's numbers. Furthermore, inventory control was alarmingly bad, and the company was not well disciplined about systematically entering data. And although the quality of the skis was deteriorating, Nielsen hadn't visited the production plant for six months. The sales manager was complaining that the company had planned no response to the emerging competition, Zephyr Skis. Nielsen got terribly upset when people asked what they were going to do. "Zephyr is just a passing phenomenon," she would say. "It cannot innovate. It's a run-of-the-mill organization that will wither away."

Still, Zephyr Skis, Zoom ski clones, allegedly schussed just as fast for half the price. Zephyr was able to undersell Zoom by using abundant Brazilian balsa wood and fabricating its skis in Ecuador. Nielsen was concerned and upset, but she had no time to solve the problems. She expected the people she hired to take care of any glitches.

Nielsen's people tried to talk to her, but she had bigger fish to fry. She was busy making new deals. Nielsen continued to run around like an oversized toddler, testing the limits of her powers and the patience of her guardians, getting into trouble, and being rescued by her bravado and her past successes. The board's concerns were growing, but no one spoke out until Zephyr's stock began overtaking Zoom's. For the increasingly anxious investors, the final straw was Nielsen's unilateral decision to buy a 12-seat Gulfstream jet without getting the board's approval.

Her behavior was not unusual. In private, Nielsen expressed the view that the company was her creation, and she knew what was the best for it. She reasoned that she needed a company plane to inspect her far-flung outposts. She viewed external investors as people who had loaned her money rather than people who were owners of the company. She resented the investors and even questioned their right to intervene.

The Zoom board, however, did not see it her way, and its members promptly voted to ground the Gulfstream and appointed a three-person executive committee to search for a COO. In effect, they gave Nielsen a warning: Shape up or else.

Fast Food a Go-Go: A Case (in Disguise)

From My Clinical Work

Tim, founder of a fast-food chain, had teetered on the brink of bankruptcy before. In the early 1970s, he called on me to help. He was losing control of his fast-growing company, and he was afraid of another big surprise. In spite of the long hours he put in, seven days a week, and the time-management courses he had taken, he was not on top of things, and the problem was only getting worse.

When I looked at his company, I saw a marketing genius with a predictable and frequently encountered organizational problem. Tim was an entrepreneur with a simple, foolproof idea: Serve fast food in places where people want fast delivery. He started on military bases, delivering food in 30 minutes or less. If it took longer, he promised, the customer paid nothing. His was a good idea with a good future, and Tim himself was admirable. He jogged every day, attended church, nurtured strong values, and raised a supportive family. His wife was the accountant, and they worked well together.

Why couldn't he make a go of it? What was missing? Organizational accountability, the piece that is typically missing from the Go-Go puzzle, was jeopardizing his company's well-being. Tim had an organizational chart, all right, but it made him look like a three-armed paperhanger. He was doing everything. He was the marketing department and the advertising director. He designed the stores and chose the equipment. In short, Tim insisted on running all the company's creative functions. Of course, he couldn't do everything single-handedly. Instead of keeping control, he was losing it. Part of his problem was that when he finally sought help, he hired people who only made things worse. When he released control, they took advantage of him and his money. His most recent partner had stolen most of the company's liquid assets, and by the time Tim discovered the theft it was too late to collect, even if he could win in court.

Tim had to escape a founder's trap that he himself had set. Release from that trap required freeing himself from exclusive responsibility for the various entrepreneurial functions of the company: finance, marketing, store design, and public relations. But how? To do this in one fell swoop would have been certain folly. He feared losing control, a fear he had since the organization's Infancy, which experience only reinforced.

We coached the executives to structure the company's functions and the founder to delegate. Delegation started with those responsibilities that interested Tim the least. For example, he delegated activities like accounting, which is more suitably administrative, and manufacturing and sales, which are more production and performance-related. Then we coached him as he selected his team to head the new departments.

That accomplished, we sat back to await reactions from the rest of the company: Many employees complained that Tim was too busy and too often absent to manage the new structure. That was the feedback we were waiting for: It gave us the political will and organizational permission to bring in a COO. The new COO was an outsider who had long-term relations with the company. He had been the manager of the chain's external advertising company, and Tim trusted him implicitly.

The new COO got to work shaking up controls and systems. He established budgetary systems and control of the expenditures. Just as we expected, people started to schedule many more meetings to coordinate all the activity. So we established a system to regulate the meetings: frequency, length, agenda, and so on. Before long we had a culture of decision making far advanced over the former anarchy in which people literally ambushed Tim to get a simple yes or no.

Only after we had accomplished those changes and established a pattern of controlled delegation did we tackle the heart of the problem: the need to transfer leadership of the entrepreneurial roles that required discretionary decision making. Those roles, which included marketing, public relations, store design, and finance, have a strategic impact on the nature of the company and its direction. Founders retain those roles with almost fanatic zeal.

First, I coached Tim to release his hold on finance. As in other Go-Go situations, our task was to establish a system of controls that clearly separated the founder's personal finances from the company's. Tim was delighted to stabilize the company's finances, so we were able to move our focus quickly.

Next, we set up a good marketing department with him as vice president, adding to his other roles as president and chairman of the board. The marketing department included public relations and a store-design department. Since Tim was too busy to attend all the meetings of the marketing department, he asked the public relations manager to lead the meetings in his absence. It worked so well that his approval of their ideas became the norm. Tim allowed himself to miss more and more meetings, and eventually he decided to make the de facto situation official. He appointed Jim, the PR man, as vice president of marketing.

It did not take long to cure Tim of micromanaging, and the COO was soon overseeing all operations including marketing and finance. Tim was free—free of the founder's trap. And his company had successfully navigated the transition from childhood to Adolescence. Tim's baby had grown so independent that he dedicated himself to a new passion—football—and wound up buying his own team.

STYLE

To encourage a healthy, growing Go-Go stage, founders need to nurture a culture of mutual respect and trust. While the structure remains amorphous, a climate of listening, reasoning, and predictability will help systematize the organization in this stage of its lifecycle on the road to Prime.

Founders who reach Go-Go can be their own worst enemies—or best friends. Arrogance is par for this course, so founders must fight the urge to venture in directions that will excessively (and often dangerously) diffuse organizational energies. While it is too early to delegate authority, decentralize, or appoint a chief operating officer, it is essential that the company hold organized staff meetings and that the staff listen to each other. Those professionally run meetings should be scheduled in advance, with published agendas and well-prepared presentations. Too often, staff meetings in Go-Go companies are unannounced, called with no agenda, and poorly attended. And presentations are altogether too casual. Follow-up on decisions is spotty, and nobody challenges the people who fail to carry out their assignments. Such irresponsibility gives the undisciplined leader of a Go-Go company the license to be managerially promiscuous.

The big message for the Go-Go stage is: Get the company to stand on its own. Caught up in the chaos and excitement of growth, founders think there's no time to set up effective entrepreneurial, production, and administrative systems, and there is even less time to get them working together and to integrate those systems. They must make time or they will find themselves in such messes as failing to deliver on a big promise and selling bad products as a result of inadequate quality control or testing procedures.

Go-Go is a heady time when founders continually see new possibilities but may fail to perceive their attendant dangers. Founders must stay focused and stick to priorities. They need to decide not just what else to do but what less to do: They need to decide what not to do so that only priorities occupy their attention. They should keep tight reins on costs.

In the advanced stages of Go-Go, market share as a goal becomes less important than keeping profit margins up to par. In Infancy and early Go-Go, discounting prices helped to boost revenues and morale even when the company lost money. In the short run, that was okay, as long as losses were a marketing expense to build market share. In the later stages of Go-Go, however, losing money on volume sales can be fatal. The company needs a strong administrative or accounting person and eventually a COO to balance growth with controls.

Still, Go-Go companies can't move through the transition to Adolescence without a blowup or two. Their leaders are too excited with success. Moving from rags to riches, leaders grow infatuated with their own successes. They begin to believe their own exaggerated press releases. It usually takes a crisis to awaken everyone to the realization that boundaries are necessary, controls are indispensable, and discipline is of paramount importance. Those are enormous challenges for founders: After all, if they were self-disciplined, they would never have started companies in the first place.

As we have seen before, and we will see again and again as we study the lifecycle, what is an asset in one stage turns into a liability in another. Change prompts a crisis, and its significance to the company is directly correlated with the success the company has achieved. The greater its success and the more arrogant its leader, the larger the company's crises. You can't really get a child through the terrible twos without an accident, large or small, depending on the child's level of discipline.

If a company is not capable of institutionalizing the leadership of the founder, if the leader is indispensable, the founder is in what I call the founder's trap.

The trap can reach beyond the founder; in that case, I call it the family trap. It usually takes three generations for that trap to do the family in: That is when the family loses the business.

Where do those traps originate? Founders and the founding families create them when they fail to make the transition from entrepreneurial to professional management. In some situations we see the founder's style failing to progress in concert with the growing company. Family-run businesses get in trouble when promotion to leadership positions is based on family ties rather than on competence.

The founder's trap has two jaws: one, the founder's sometimes spastic, sometimes vice-like but always compulsive hand on the organization's operating machinery. To extricate themselves from that trap, founders have to work simultaneously to get a grip on themselves while loosening their grip on their companies. That is a process that needs to start in Go-Go and conclude in the next stage of the lifecycle: Adolescence.

Relaxing one's hold is hard. Sharper than the serpent's tooth, as Shakespeare cautioned, is the ingratitude of children. As parents, we focus all our love, intelligence, and time on developing a new person, fully capable of standing independently on his or her own feet. At least that's what we profess to do. When the time comes, and our children begin actually to make their own choices in the world, we parents experience floods of complicated feelings: Anxiety, pride, and bitterness do battle in our hearts. We know, however, that if we don't let go, our children won't mature. A healthy Go-Go company has to prepare for its healthy Adolescence: Its second birth will occur with the emancipation of the organization from its founder or the founding family.

To achieve a healthy transition, it is imperative to monitor the dependency syndrome. A Zen Buddhist story might help make the point:

A farmer walks holding a rope at the end of which is tied a cow. He meets a man who asks, "Why are you tied to that cow?"

"I am not," he asserts.

"If so, let go of the rope."

"I can't," the farmer says. "The cow will run away."

We like to control things because we believe that the more control we have, the more freedom we will have. The fact is, however, that whatever we control controls us by the same degree. We are prisoners of whatever we do not want to lose. And the more we want to control something dear to our hearts, the more we become its prisoners.

In Go-Go companies, founders' commitments can be so strong that they cannot let go. The more they try to control their companies (and control is a function of their commitment), the stronger their companies' hold on them. They cannot leave. Commitment, which was an indispensable quality for a healthy Courtship and Infancy, now becomes a barrier against progress. Founders who hold their companies back that way are like parents who love their children so obsessively that they cannot let them grow. When their companies reach Adolescence, and the founders need to transfer authority, they cannot do the maneuver. They are caught in traps of their own design.

To check whether a founder is prone to fall into that trap, determine whether the company's complementary team formed before or during the Go-Go stage. There should be a person with an administrative orientation: a person whose knowledge and style provide the organization with systems, order, efficiency, and process quality. Next, determine whether there is mutual respect and trust between the entrepreneurial founder (or entrepreneurial leader if the founder is no longer in charge) and the administrative person.

If there is no administrative leadership—or if that position is constantly changing due to the entrepreneur's lack of respect for the function and/or the person in that role—chances are high that either the

GO-GO: REACHING WITH CONFIDENCE

Joseph C. Walter's Houston Oil & Minerals Corp. began with his 1964 purchase of a tiny firm that invested in low-risk oil and gas royalties. After three relatively uneventful years, Walter embarked on a new strategy that put his company on the oil and gas exploration fast track.

Walter invested in proven properties, milked them a little harder than the major oil companies had, and pledged the reserves against loans for riskier exploration. Although most industry insiders had lost interest in Texas's coastal frio sands, in 1973 Walter struck rich gas deposits in those "spent" fields. Walter's company shouldered enormous risk, but, from year to year, it doubled its reserves through the mid-1970s.

With his self-assurance growing along with his successes, Walter continued to risk his resources, extending his reach farther and farther afield: He strayed from his Texas turf to try his hand in the Rockies. He poured money into Australian coal and into gold and silver mines. To fund that aggressive expansion, he borrowed heavily, running through capital at rates as high as three times annual cash flow. Long-term debt quintupled between 1974 and 1977.

Houston Oil & Gas, now far bigger, had spread beyond Walter's grasp, and in 1978, an annual appraisal revealed that reserves had fallen. The company's stock echoed that decline, crashing from a high of $42 to a dispiriting $13.50. As the company's glory dimmed, Walter suffered a severe heart attack.

Despite his apparent insouciance during the company's Go-Go years, Walter had, years earlier, hired F. Fox Benton, Jr., as chief financial officer, and the two had come to work as a smooth team. Walter was the wildcatter with a nose for properties. Benton insured a dependable supply of cash to propel company fortunes and underwrite drilling budgets. No one was surprised when, two months after Walter's convalescence, the entrepreneur named Benton became the administrator and chief executive officer.

Under Benton, the company took fewer risks, burned less money in exploration, and narrowed its focus on the most promising oil and gas properties. In 1981, despite debt of $450 million, the company merged with Tenneco, and by the decade's end, its stock, adjusted for splits, had rebounded by almost 5,000 percent.

organization will fall into the trap or that the founder will get squeezed out during Adolescence, the next stage.

Weaning is mandatory during Adolescence. Founders do not completely relinquish their passionate interest in their babies, of course, but they must step back and recognize that their companies' current needs may be very badly served by their interference. They may no longer consider their companies and themselves as inextricably related entities. It's a rare founder who at this point undergoes weaning voluntarily. More commonly, Go-Go companies grow too big and/or too complicated for one person to manage. Consequently, their founders make increasingly bigger and bigger mistakes that stem from their growing detachment from reality.

Snap goes the trap. Founders, stretched thin, tend to focus on the aspects of their businesses that they personally find the most stimulating. Their entrepreneurship overrules all other imperatives. An organization heading for Prime must serve three additional imperative functions—performance or production, administration, and integration—or face ruin.

Deprived of those functions, an organization will face ruin that can take many faces: Stockholders, customers, or employees sue; an employee embezzles significant amounts of money; quality deteriorates to the point that the company loses its markets; the company runs out of cash without knowing how or why; the company uses up its access to credit; or perhaps the company uses all its resources to develop a founder's folly, a product nearly no one wants to buy. In this situation, the founder is dangerously optimistic. Without the brakes a complementary team provides, the founder races toward disaster.

While a company in Infancy does best with a board of supportive internal directors, the Go-Go company needs the independent, critical contribution of an external board. If there are signs that the founder is heading for the trap, the external board can provide sanity and control.

In the classic Go-Go organization, the founder monopolizes the entrepreneurial function and hires manager after manager to handle administrative functions. Each administrative recruit joins the organization with a high probability of failing. Either the founder interferes, causing the new manager to give up, or the hired administrator's effort to succeed is so intense the founder feels threatened. Founder and recruit send conflicting signals that confuse the entire organization. Told to act more independently, beleaguered managers are chided if they do and chided if they don't. A highly charged office atmosphere and an emotionally tone-deaf leader create turbulence, nasty crises, or even insurrection. To avoid disaster, the founder must stop dominating and start delegating. Though still the garden's owner, the founder must let other flowers bloom: the more blooms, the better—for everyone.

The second jaw of the trap includes the founder's reluctance, inability, or refusal to distinguish between personal expenses and the organization's. Nothing could be more natural to, or common in, the Go-Go stage than this all too convenient lack of clarity about whose wallet is whose. After all, whose company is it anyway?

It is not at all unusual to see many founders grandly helping themselves to winter homes in Palm Beach, ski lodges in Aspen, fancy cars, or speedy airplanes. Before long, those founders find themselves engaged in conflicts with the stockholders. Mixing personal finances with the organization's is like mixing gasoline with hot barbecue coals: The result is spectacularly dangerous for the company.

Of course, spendthrift founders maintain that their new toys are good for business: The plane will improve connections with customers, the Aspen condo is intended for entertaining potential clients, and so on.

The problem, however, is much bigger than just conflict of interests or abuse of one's position. The problem is that the financial controls—and often even the statements—become meaningless. The freedom the leader takes with the company's money sends a signal to the rest of the company that fiscal discipline is not as crucial as the founder preaches. If the statements mix personal with corporate expenses, no one knows what is really happening, adding to the confusion over the highly flexible and ever-changing organization chart. Compounding the confusion is the tendency to set up an extensive array of legal entities for acquisitions. Founders instruct their lawyers and accountants to do what they can do to minimize tax liabilities while enhancing earnings and capital. But turning lawyers loose on a young enterprise virtually guarantees an impenetrable snarl of interlocking structures that can only impede accountability as the organization continues to grow. Now, the riddle no one can solve is: Who is accountable? Ironically, the founder gets increasingly upset at his or her inability to identify who is responsible for the company's results and messy information. Feeling that he is losing control, the founder starts shooting from the hip, moving people from one position to another and confusing the organization even more.

Another troublesome behavior of founders who are altogether too self assured reminds me of a seagull. Catching her first glimpse of success in her new enterprise is for a founder what swallowing a tasty minnow is for a seagull. The first taste of success sends her off, scanning the seas for yet another morsel, making deals, foraging for more joint ventures.

Some seagull behavior is normal, and we expect that. Anyone who has ever known the exhilaration of starting a new business is more or less bound to get bored when the challenges appear to subside and the baby seems ready to grow into a healthy teenager. If the founder does not turn his attentions to other business opportunities, he will focus on politics, trade associations, or other worthwhile causes: anything to bring back the thrill of first love.

But, as any boat owner knows, seagulls can make a real mess. They fly off, and when they appear they drop a smelly thing on the deck. Then they take off again and again, only to return later, unannounced, with more to unload. Founders, excited with their success or, as one of them told me, "feeling as if the world is on sale," disappear for a while on exciting trips or ventures. When they reappear and call a meeting, everyone gets worried: What now? What big new surprise or smelly new top priority are they going to drop this time? Whatever people have done until then is—for the forever creative entrepreneur—always insufficient, inadequate, and inappropriate anyway. They change their minds fast and expect everything to be achieved by yesterday. People cover their faces with their hands in a defensive posture: What now?

Founders' premature and unsuccessful withdrawal can create unwanted problems. Infatuated with success, they prematurely move on to other "love affairs." No business can survive founders who fly in, land on the company, fuss, fret, leave messes of absolute commands and half-baked ideas, and then flap off. For their managers, that behavior is intensely frustrating. They can't win. If they do what they believe the founders want, they can never do it well enough to suit them because such founders always manage to change their minds or expectations before you know it. If employees don't follow up on their founders' orders and wait for them to determine what they really want, they catch hell for ignoring orders.

The founder, an entrepreneurial type, hardly notices the havoc and dissension he leaves in his wake. Monday morning he is on a flight from Chicago to Tokyo. By the time he lands in Tokyo he has already hatched another dozen ideas, which he immediately faxes back to Chicago.

One way to change the seagull's behavior is to change the company's board of directors. The cozy, family-like coddling appropriate in Infancy and early Go-Go is no longer appropriate as the company moves into late Go-Go and approaches Adolescence. Outside advisers, executives of other companies, will bring new ideas to the company's board and will challenge both the founder and the status quo. Without those challenges there is nobody to stop founders when they embark on ventures that are not in their organizations' best interests.

If seagull-like tendencies do not respond to the discipline of the board of directors, investors and employees had better pray that the company has hired managers capable of guiding the daily operations. Entrepreneurs are not, by any means, always seagulls; many develop management teams with skills that complement their own. Nevertheless, those capable managers, like outside boards of directors, need the authority to challenge founders' decisions. Without that authority—and the responsibility that goes with it—managers cannot grow and become proficient in their own right.

As we've seen, some degree of letting go is essential once it appears that the company can stand without constant propping up by the founder. But the company must plan for the execution of that emancipation. Pure expectations are not enough. Entrepreneurs manage by expectations, and I repeatedly remind them that what gets done in a company is not what is expected but what is inspected. For that the organization needs structure.

STRUCTURE

The message is clear: When their companies reach the Go-Go stage, founders must define the boundaries between them and their companies. They must establish a structure and define accountabilities. Now is the time. Earlier, structure would have dangerously reduced necessary flexibility. In later stages, a company without established structure and accountabilities has no one to take corrective action when troubles arise. It is a company adrift.

In typical Go-Gos, job assignments are based on people's skills. With all the inward (founder-driven) and outward (market-driven) changes a Go-Go company must endure, the real requirement is for fast, responsive—even experimental—decision making. Go-Go companies structure themselves around quick-thinking, fast-acting employees: capable performers who bite off as much as they can. Often, unfortunately unaware, they bite off more than they can chew. The Go-Go company's structure is so amorphous and variable that the salesperson, for example, ends up being responsible for marketing, advertising, sales, customer service, distribution, and even warehousing.

As tasks emerge, with no one assigned to them, people are assigned randomly or based on their current availability. This is incrementalist decision making at its worst. There is no grand design: only reactive ad hoc decisions that remind me of an old joke. A guy goes to a tailor for a custom-made suit. When he tries on the finished suit, he realizes one sleeve is too long. The tailor tells him not to worry. He should simply pull his hand in a bit and bend his arm. Now he sees that the shoulder droops. The tailor tells him to lift that shoulder slightly.

"But the back feels too wide," the man complains.

"Look, just bend forward a tiny bit, and it will look fine," the tailor advises.

Satisfied, the man hobbles out of the shop in a convoluted posture: arm half-bent, one shoulder higher than the other, hunchbacked. Two women, passing by, see him leaving the tailor's shop, and one whispers to the other, "Look at that poor cripple."

"But," her friend answers, "look how beautifully the suit fits him."

The problem with ad hoc, incrementalist decision making is that there is nothing more permanent than continuous temporary. Ad hoc decisions on positions are good and necessary as long as people don't feel they own them. When the time comes to structure in an organized fashion, people might put up a fight and turn reorganization into a nightmare.

A Go-Go company organized around people rather than around tasks eventually develops an extremely complicated structure. People do not know who is accountable for what. The organization acts like a team of small children playing soccer: Every one of them goes for the ball, and, from the sidelines, they look like a swarm of locusts moving around the field. They all try to kick the ball and end up kicking one another in the shins and crying. Their coaches spend time lecturing the children on the value of teamwork. Stop fighting, they tell the kids, and help each other.

The coaches' speeches fall on deaf ears because the kids have no idea how to play as a team. Their coaches have to tell them what their positions are and that they must stick to those positions in a way that does not ignore the ball.

For me, a precondition of teamwork is that all individuals have their own well-defined roles: That means structure. Look at your hand: Each finger has its own definite role at which it excels, but all the fingers cooperate and back up the others. The examples of the soccer team and hand are analogous to the workings of companies.

Too many Go-Go companies, suffering from confusion, import coaches who lecture and preach teamwork as an attitude when they should be clarifying roles and interdependencies. It is better, I maintain, to hire truck drivers to drive a race car than to hire race-car drivers to drive a truck: Design your organization to function like a race car so that even a truck driver, or a mediocre manager, can excel. A messy organization, on the other hand, can survive only with exceptionally talented managers. As they say in the military, instead of having idiots designing organizations only a genius can run, geniuses should design organizations that anyone can run.

In discussing aspects of Adolescence, are we getting ahead of ourselves? Not at all. Think of the mother of the problematic teenager who asks the doctor when she should start teaching her son how to behave. The doctor responds, "Sixteen years ago."

Many have remarked on the terrible twos' uncanny foreshadowing of adolescence. In both stages, we see an unabashed appetite for life combined with a comical (or perhaps not so comical) inability to handle life properly. That's why parents and teachers forever reassure one another that what toddlers and teens really need are boundaries, that is, structure. "Actually," they say, "the kids want it."

Whether founders want it any more than kids do is doubtful, but Go-Go companies—with their ravenous appetites—do need structure. They lack organization strong enough to assimilate the new projects, products, or promotions that headstrong founders want to undertake. Effective decision making breaks down under those conditions. After all, to make effective decisions, everyone needs to know who is responsible for what and who has authority for what.

Solid structures assure those desiderata. The structure will be provided in Adolescence, but it cannot come all at once. There will be rebellion. No system changes abruptly from a total lack of discipline to system-wide discipline. Thus, in a Go-Go company, there should be the beginnings of structure, discipline, mutual trust, and respect for the functions everyone serves. If instead the company is allowed to continue growing as a spoiled brat, everyone will pay the price in the company's Adolescence.

STRATEGY

Having created exciting products and services that actually sell, founders at this stage should be seeking ever-increasing market share and stressing long-term prospects rather than short-term deals. They should pick their opportunities carefully, avoiding prematurely diffuse diversification. Focus on your core capabilities and stick to them. Conduct analyses: Is the new idea, project, or priority a result of carefully diagnosing your needs and capabilities? Or is it the result of an unwarranted sense of confidence in indestructibility? Are you making decisions like toddlers who, not knowing they cannot fly, jump from third-floor windows?

Leaders of Go-Gos should think big, but they must work hard to make their companies take off as companies instead of continuing as one-man bands. The strategy is to focus, to decide what not to do, to set priorities, to make those hard decisions about what to put on the back burner. Tom Monaghan of Domino's Pizza had a file he called new dreams. Whenever he came up with a new idea, he would slip it into that file, planning to check it out a few months later to see whether it survived the test of time. As it turns out, he rarely looked at the file, but he found it comforting to know that the ideas were there and there was no pressure to implement them. Go-Go companies should have well-articulated definitions of what they are, as well as what they do. State your values clearly. Establish what the company will not do; define the businesses in which it will not get involved.

Pursuing Prime, from the Go-Go company's perspective, calls for introducing discipline into strategic thinking. Strategy is not the accumulation of reactive decisions in response to opportunities. Disciplined strategic decisions define the desirable opportunities. The organization should be opportunity *driving*, not opportunity *driven*. That is a precondition for building structure in Adolescence.

Being a healthy Go-Go is not easy. At the same time that the Go-Go company, in its pursuit of Prime, keeps a close grip on costs, it must be increasing market share—sometimes at the expense of profits. Take care. Neither overdo nor underdo discipline. To achieve the right balance, a complementary team, which was a nice option during Infancy, becomes a need in Go-Go and a must in Adolescence. Do not overdo the profit orientation either. Why? A Go-Go company is a calf, not a cow, and it is, therefore, in no position to contribute profits to the stockholders or the corporate headquarters. To fund its growth, the Go-Go company needs to reinvest the surplus resources it generates.

Throughout the Go-Go company, the ethos of more-more rages. In addition to the marketing force and salespeople, everyone is crowing about, yearning for, and going for more-more, and that, inevitably, costs more-more. The company has to increase spending on sales commissions, parts, supplies, wages, new employees, and more space. As sales increase, so does the flow of outbound cash. Profit margins can easily shrink as money flows out faster than it comes in.

But here is the worst of it: Because the company is structurally challenged, so to speak, its accounting and related administrative functions are crawling at a snail's pace while the rest of the business is blazing along at the speed of light. Managers, free of restrictive procedures, do whatever it takes to get their jobs done. Discipline suffers as people make decisions they all may regret for years to come. Eventually, a company that is growing with such abandon will be undone by a project that demands more than its ad hoc systems can handle.

In essence, function outpaces form. The company loses either the capacity or the inclination to grow in a controlled fashion.

Poor inventory controls, for example, have demolished more companies than I care to think about. The typical Go-Go company does not do a good job of tracking its inventories. Its records do not reveal how much inventory is already accounted for in its products and services. When inflation is climbing, that can disastrously inflate inventory costs and valuation. Few companies can disentangle themselves from such a mess without first experiencing serious financial setbacks.

STAFFING

In successful Go-Go organizations, competent managers, confident and ready to take on additional responsibility, help make the transition from Go-Go to Adolescence. By hiring or promoting from within, Go-Go enterprises should cultivate administrative types who can complement the entrepreneurial founder. They should staff and organize around strong and capable managers who know how to deliver sales, production, or other key functions. To strengthen their boards of directors, founders need to recruit outsiders with diverse experience.

During this stage, founders need tough-minded criticism. Insiders on their boards usually become far too agreeable to dispute the founders' notions, much less hold their feet to the fire. Go-Go companies need outsiders who won't shy from slapping the founders down a mite, especially if they start cashing in. An external board of directors with significant ownership in the company will, to protect its own assets, cool the leader's unwarranted enthusiasm for taking on too many projects. Go-Go organizations need to invest in the discipline that prepares them to weather unpredictable storms.

The tendency to abdicate control prematurely to a COO is not at all uncommon. Many founders in the Go-Go stage have come to me, asking for help finding a COO: They feel they can no longer control their companies. But, I explain to them, it is still too early for that maneuver. It is impossible to bring a COO into a company that is accustomed to working around the idiosyncrasies of its founder. No one can fit into the founder's custom-made shoes.

If the COO asserts himself, the people complain furiously to the founder, who gets scared of losing the company. He becomes protective, returns to take charge, and fires the newly appointed COO. If the founder has already lost voting control, the COO—to bring order into the organization—will try to evict the founder from power positions. The COO considers the founder a source of continuous dysfunctional change. COOs who do not assert themselves devolve into benign entities, ignored, despised, and, eventually, discarded. The founders, meanwhile, return to their original positions, and everything is the way it had been except that everyone is a few years older.

What should happen is that the Go-Go company needs to establish a new unifying, articulated mission. With that mission, the company needs to develop a structure that institutionalizes the entrepreneurial roles personified by the founder and frees it of the founder's exclusive monopoly of the entrepreneurial functions. After establishing accountability—then and only then—the company should appoint a COO. Those changes should take place during a healthy Adolescence, and by the time they are all accomplished, the company will have attained Prime.

As a company approaches Adolescence, a love-hate relationship develops between founders and their managers. The love component is natural enough: Founders have provided their people with jobs and opportunities. The managers respect the role the founders' courage, drive, and value (if not indispensability) played in the company's success. They look to the founders to guide the company to further glory and themselves to greater satisfaction.

That's where the hate part of the relationship enters into the picture. The resentment stems from the founders' continuous change of direction, lack of guidance, expecting too much, demanding too much, and supporting too little. The founders either have not been attending to the company with the fervor and dedication of the early years or are continuing with a fervor that suffocates the people who work in their companies. They neither give their managers responsibility nor heed their advice. Perhaps they continue to insist on making every decision—small or critical—whenever and however they please. In short, they refuse to let the organization grow up. Children have hated their parents for less.

But emotions flow in two directions. Founders are close to their managers; after all, they hired them, worked closely with them through hard days, nourished them, and brought them along. Like their companies, the managers are their children whom they want to protect. Nevertheless, the managers hold founders back, away from their new interests, and that is a source of irritation. Founders ask themselves, "Why can't my managers stand on their own two feet?" "Why can't they take initiative, leadership?" "What," they ask me, "is wrong with the people I hired?"

The founders, to motivate leadership, design expensive reward systems that share profits and equity. That cannot work unless the company is structured for accountability, delegation of authority, and measurable, verifiable results. If the founder continues to control everything on the fly, the people cannot exercise initiative and survive. When they take initiative there is a chance they will get reprimanded for making the wrong decision. More than a few senior managers have heard their entrepreneurial founders second-guess their decisions, saying, "It's too late for you to disagree with me; I already changed my mind." Yet, when the managers grow gun-shy and simply stand by, waiting for instructions, the founders attack their lack of leadership. Managers simply cannot please the founders no matter what they do.

Frustrated and smothered by their own creations, founders find themselves unable to set out on what appear to be more rewarding and glorious adventures. Their own creations, "tyrannical tots," threaten to consume them just when they want nothing more than to escape.

Not only is the company unhappy with its leadership, its leadership is unhappy with the company. I call it the hate period. To minimize—or, better still, to avoid it altogether—founders must from Infancy on hire people whom they trust and respect. They must continue to nourish that trust and respect through the lifecycle. That, however, does not come naturally to most founders. On the contrary, the greater the change, the more challenging will be the task of keeping trust and respect at all functional.

REWARDS

Since market share is the Go-Go target, founders should continue to reward sales growth and production increases. Profitability is not a top goal. Founders need to reward sales increases, manufacturing improvements, product development, and whatever else it takes to establish a strong market presence and a viable organization.

If during Infancy most if not all of the reward structure was commissions (minimum fixed and maximum variable), now is the time to start changing the proportions: Cut the variable in favor of fixed, aiming for having fixed compensation, say, 20 percent below market rate. The bonus for individual achievement could be worth 33 percent of the fixed compensation, and then total income can exceed market rates. Be careful, though, to see that the bonuses are measured neither totally subjectively nor totally objectively. It is too early in Go-Go to have predictable, controllable results, and a bonus based exclusively on a formula of controllable and achievable results is a fata morgana. If you base part of the bonus on results to be achieved, another part can be subjective.

Planning and Goals

There are two types of goals: deterministic and constraint goals. Those in the first category, we strive to achieve. And the more they are like market share—or in certain conditions, the less like production costs— the better. The second group includes those goals we are determined not to violate. For example, 5 percent bad debt might be considered normal for mass marketers who include it in their cost of sales. Not to violate the 5 percent limit is in itself a goal. In this case neither more nor less is the goal. The goal is to have 5 percent and use it the best you know how. You made it a constraint not to violate that goal.

Another example: While in Infancy, because the deterministic goal should be survival, everyone has to watch cash like a hawk, and maximizing cash flow is often the deterministic goal. For that purpose, companies on accrual accounting systems must maintain cash and accrual accounting in parallel. The constraint goal is to avoid letting work destroy one's health. During Go-Go, the deterministic goal should be revenues and the constraint goal should be profitability. There can be no profit orientation yet because the calf needs feeding, not milking. The priorities for Go-Go are market share, market share, and market share. But be careful which markets. Focus, focus, and focus on core capabilities should rule the fight for market share.

WHERE DO YOU STAND? A CHECKLIST

Normal Problems of Go-Go

- Management by crisis characterizes the daily life in a Go-Go company.
- There are more priorities than the company can handle.
- The company prepares budgets—late—and there is a high variance between actual and budgeted figures.
- There are no regularly scheduled staff meetings, and when there is a meeting, there is no real or up-to-date agenda. If there is one, many people ignore it.
- Centralized management and a messy organizational chart make it nearly impossible to understand who reports to whom.
- Operating results are either extremely good or extremely bad.
- Management, such as it is, doesn't follow up on decisions.
- Results are king.
- More is better.
- The organization is sales- not marketing- or profit-oriented.
- There is no world-class inventory control, material planning, or cost-accounting system.

Abnormal Problems of Go-Go

- No budgets, of any type, exist.
- Management's arrogance precludes any meetings or attention to problems.
- The company has established a board of directors made up exclusively of company insiders who depend on the founder for their existence.
- People—not situations—are blamed for all problems.
- Elitist management generates a climate of fear and suspicion

- Access to top management slots is preordained and reserved for only those with the right blood type—family members.
- Negative cash flow or no control over cash flow threatens organizational survival.
- Everyone is spread so thin, it is hard to know "who is on first."
- The company is a leggy collection of interwoven legal structures. Wide-ranging joint ventures are interdependent and confusing.
- Strategy has lost its focus.
- The founder confuses personal interests with corporate interests and milks the company in exclusive self-interest.
- The missing founder, who is often absent (caught in the seagull syndrome), reappears from time to time, drops a "load" of new priorities on the organization, and disappears to follow other interests that have nothing to do with the company.
- The company makes unrealistic promises and commitments to clients without thinking about how it will deliver on them.
- Deliveries are unpredictable.
- Individual responsibilities are not clear.
- Goals are murky.
- Insufficient or monopolized access to information compromises quality.

CHAPTER 6

Adolescence: Struggling for the Sweet Taste of Independence

Adolescence: A Parable

Harvey Holmes should have known earlier that trouble was brewing—trouble that he couldn't handle. An electrical engineer, he had had a vision of bringing to market a set of unique laboratory instruments lauded by hospitals and freestanding labs. His customers snapped up his product, hungry to cut labor costs and slash turnaround times. But as he fed customers the products and services they yearned for, and as sales of Health Instrumentation mushroomed to $80 million, he didn't have the vision to see, or the humility to admit, that his management missteps had brought his company to the brink of insolvency.

For two years his management team had argued over the company's direction. Sales and engineering had maintained that the product line had become too diversified, with too few engineers to support too many models of products. Holmes did make an effort to clarify the company's direction: After enrolling in a three-day planning course given by the American Management Association, he had assembled his six top people for two 14-hour days to answer the critical questions: "Where are we now?" "Where do we want to go?" "How do we get there?"

But the planning meeting accomplished little more than confirming the disarray. Tempers flared as the level of disagreement surfaced. The company's engineering chief stormed out. Holmes ended up insisting on a set of six strategies that, in many managers' opinions, chiseled the current failed product strategy into stone. Holmes got his way all right, but in the view of his most trusted senior colleagues, he had tarnished his image as a strong leader. Three days later, Holmes later learned, the entire management team rented a suite in a local hotel to meet. He had not been invited.

The end run was near. And Holmes knew he had only himself to blame. As year-end approached, Health Instrumentation was running nearly $5 million in the red. Suppliers would ship only COD and required a 30 percent down payment on all orders. Because of archaic cost accounting, nobody was even sure which products, or customers, were the most profitable. Holmes's success in making all decisions based on his gut was failing him. The losses pressed the board of directors into action. In a series of three meetings, they agreed that, given the dire states of finances, Health Instrumentation needed new management. Holmes was sent packing. The board replaced him with Andrew Caine, a board member hired a year earlier as a consultant.

Caine, a former Motorola executive who had become an independent consultant, first dealt with the cash crisis. Over two weeks of meetings with senior managers, he put together a recovery and operating plan to present to Health Instrumentation's banker, Chemical Bank. After a five-hour meeting with the bank's health technology group, Caine persuaded the bankers not to call the loan, in spite of the fact that Health Instrumentation's was in default of five loan covenants. Caine coaxed Chemical to put up an additional $400,000, so that the company could pay its suppliers, and he pledged an expected tax refund as collateral.

With some time to breathe, Caine then set about preserving and raising cash from operations. He cut three expensive custom products, tightened internal inventory and accounting controls, reduced receivables from longer than 90 days to fewer than 70, and focused on getting suppliers paid in no more than 40 days. He then had time to bring in more specialists, particularly in finance and information technology, and send senior managers to a course that would help them improve inventory control, logistics, and marketing. Caine met resistance from some of the old guard, who chafed as he shifted the boundaries of their turf, but they couldn't argue with the success of Caine's measures in making Health Instrumentation solvent again.

Adolescence

Much like a teenager, the adolescent company struggles for emancipation from its parent-founder. The stakes are high during this wrenching rite of passage: nothing less than rebirth as an adult. Brave, teary-eyed, scornful, scared, the teenager zigzags into a new sense of self. Annoyed, admiring, fearful, loving, the parents' feelings are almost as incoherent as their child's. Naturally, their child is one day a cause for rejoicing and the next a reminder of their own indispensability.

Intellectually, at least, we accept the teenage years as a normal if sometimes unbearable passage from dependence to self-reliance. Nothing grows without struggle. Still, corporate Adolescence is an especially stormy time, and the founders' safe conduct of their creations through the tempest is by no means guaranteed. Everything seems at odds with everything else: Production exceeds or falls short of sales estimates, quality control is not up to customer expectations, old-timers fulminate against new hires, yesterday's goals are sales oriented to maximize revenues, and when the cost of sales mushrooms, profits deteriorate.

When the company tries to maximize profits while expanding revenues, everyone ends up frustrated. Fingers point in rounds of accusations. The board and the founder often find themselves at odds. As long as the company does well, expanding revenues and market share, the board regards the founder or the CEO as a genius with a golden touch. When, however, profits decline and uncontrolled activity brings about a succession of managerial disasters, the board starts to view that same leader as an unguided missile. Suddenly the leader, accustomed to the magic of adoration, is transformed into an unruly enemy of the company. Emotions are volatile, and organizational morale traces a jagged line: ecstasy in one quarter, depression and dejection in another. Throughout the organization, people are busy tracking the real and imagined injustices they have suffered, and they nurse them with great care.

What is going on? How did the company manage to struggle through Infancy and Go-Go only to arrive at Adolescence once again to do battle? The answer lies in understanding the dynamics of systems development. The situation is similar to those that absolute monarchs create when they turn their domains into constitutional monarchies. Almost invariably, they balk at the prospect of losing absolute power. Some do make successful transitions to constitutional monarchies. Some of them lose their heads to republics because power is addictive and exhilarating; it is difficult for them to give it up. When monarchs decide to take steps to change their governments, they believe that they will be willing to abide by the constitution. In practice, though, they can't bear to relinquish their perks and powers. Caught between noble intentions and the humbling reality of diminished authority, the erstwhile monarchs may be lucky just to keep their heads.

So it is for leaders of adolescent organizations who want law and order, predictability, acceptance, and "ownership" of decisions and policies. They want a constitution, but one that they can stand above—free to break the laws by which others must abide. Their predicament may seem so commonplace as to require no comment, but, as with most such commonplace occurrences, everyone can describe it, yet few know how to do anything about it.

STYLE

Confession may be in order here. At the Adizes Institute, I often establish rules and policies that I am the first to violate—not perversely, or so I tell myself—but because I'm operating in a time warp. The Institute has left Infancy behind, but I haven't. I still make autocratic decisions on the spot. Why? Because I once had to. I'm afflicted with organizational atavism. Now that the institute has reached Adolescence, however, my regressive behavior is a problem. For example, I recently computerized all our accounting, and, as a consequence of my frustrations with the transitional mess, I laid off the accountant—all much too hastily. Instead of enhancing financial clarity, this reorganization left everyone more confused than ever. Whenever I shoot from the hip like that, the sound resonates throughout the office. If I violate policies, my colleagues understandably feel they can do likewise. We wind up with unenforceable rules, unstable structure, and a founder nervous about losing control. Such insecurity feeds on itself.

Adolescent organizations tend to ignite crises, coups, and wars of independence. The road to Prime is littered with the wrecks of companies whose founders failed to negotiate the second sharpest turn. The first turn is birth; the second is a kind of rebirth: the company's weaning from its founder's overwhelming influence. Unless the founder resolves that crisis in the right way, the company may never gain the discipline necessary to reach Prime.

Founders must master the art of delegation without abdication—

ADOLESCENCE: WHO'S IN CHARGE HERE?

Back in 1985, John Sculley left PepsiCo, Inc., to join Apple Computer, Inc., as its new CEO in a position of "shared leadership" with legendary founder and entrepreneur Steven Jobs, who had taken the job of chairman. Although the two were said to be close friends, conflicts soon arose when it became painfully clear that they were engaged in a struggle to determine who would lead the company. With power plays plaguing the organization, Apple experienced many of the problems, normal and abnormal, of Adolescence.

As chief visionary for Apple's computer products, Steve Jobs had become a kind of mythic hero for thousands of loyal Apple customers, not to mention scores of young entrepreneurial types who dreamed of emulating his success. Indeed, in the mid-1980s he was an icon of the entrepreneurial spirit. Stories, most of them true, enhanced the image of the man who, with technology wizard Stephen Wozniak, had turned his garage into a computer company some ten years earlier. Jobs's reputation as a driven—some might say possessed—inventor was matched by his infectious charisma and ability to drive others just as hard as he drove himself.

Although no stranger to technology, Sculley had established his leadership credentials in devising various marketing successes including the "Pepsi Challenge." Accommodating yet tough-minded, he came to Apple as something of a savior, a person who could provide necessary managerial skills and know-how in running a large, high-growth company. The computer upstart had suffered two major fiascoes: the recall of 14,000 Apple III computers in 1981 and the disastrous flop in 1983 of Lisa, a user-friendly but extremely expensive ($10,000) and clunky computer that functioned better for video games than for word processing.

One of Sculley's first acts as CEO was to name Jobs executive vice president and manager of the Macintosh division, which at the time comprised fewer than 100 people and had no real responsibility for profits and losses. Over the next two years, Jobs gained more and more managerial authority, and the number of people reporting directly to him increased tenfold. Sculley described his own position as "sandwiched between a visionary chairman above . . . and an operating executive below." And both of them were one and the same person.

Like most companies in Adolescence, especially those embodying a strong entrepreneurial spirit, Apple in the early and mid-1980s suffered the effects of inconsistent planning. Even though the Macintosh commanded a loyal following, the industry perceived it as a system in isolation, unable to communicate easily (or at all) with PCs.

True to the pattern of companies in Adolescence, Apple witnessed the breakup of both a friendship and a management strategy. Sculley took control, forcing Jobs to leave the company that he had founded. Powerful administration-armed with balance sheets, P&Ls, and cost accounting systems-usually wins out over creative entrepreneurship.

And that was Apple Computer, Inc., in 1985.

the art of sharing power without losing control—or become increasingly obstructive to an organization's development. To make the transition from Adolescence to Prime, leaders of adolescent organizations must subject themselves, without reservation, to the company rules and policies. Their organizations cannot be subjected to their ad hoc decision making. Commitment to transform their organizations can lift great weights from founders' shoulders and their companies, freeing them to soar to Prime. Leaders of adolescent companies have to ask themselves, "Am I committed to the organization or to my own ego gratification?" They are like the parents of teenagers who have to decide to let their children grow up. Do the parents refuse to relinquish the joy of controlling their children's lives, or will they experience the thrill of seeing their children soar: free, mature, and independent?

In theory, all founders yearn to delegate once they realize that they can no longer run their companies alone. There just aren't enough hours in the day for one person to act as a booming company's production chief, sales director, bill collector, and morale booster. In the earlier stages of organizational development, there is nobody else other than the founder to make the decisions. So when founders do finally start to delegate, they have trouble holding their tongues when someone makes a decision they consider wrong. Big mistake. They should bite their tongues. When founders resume command with their heavy hands, people feel squelched, lose initiative, and become less fit for delegation. I claim that one can identify the successful leaders of companies in this stage by the depth of the scars on their tongues.

It is wrong to abdicate authority and let people carry out decisions you believe are wrong; but at the same time, you must avoid paternalism. Let people make decisions, and even let them execute their mistakes after you tell them why you believe they are heading in the wrong direction. They will develop respect and trust in your leadership. If you hold them so close they cannot make their own mistakes, they will rebel or grow apathetic. The love-hate relationship that ensues will waste your energies and those of the company. So it is critical in Adolescence not only to convince founders to share power but also to stop them from taking it back. If they relinquish only to renege, their companies will head right back to the paralyzing founder's trap.

The way to avoid that misfortune is to separate management from ownership and get serious about creating truly workable structures. Ad hoc job assignments, titles, or plans—amateurism of any kind— have run their course. The organizational emphasis must shift from what the founders want to what their companies need. The founders must begin by systematically delegating and holding people accountable. In Adolescence, structure should count more than leadership and strategy.

Now is the time to hire or promote a chief operating officer, a management specialist versed in organizational skills of the process of management. Again, this may not be easy for the leaders of adolescent organizations. While it is true that each stage of the lifecycle has its difficulties, the treatment of adolescent organizations is difficult in each of the treatments prescribed below.

Many founders fear sharing control, and the differences between entrepreneurs and COOs—in style, spirit, and substance—are notoriously deep. Founders do what they do by breaking rules, defying conventional wisdom, and ignoring systems, protocol, and the ordinary cautions of managerial expertise. COOs, of course, do what they do by making rules, respecting convention, observing systems and protocol, and deploying specialized knowledge. It's the familiar drama of the technician versus the romantic, and a happy ending ultimately depends on their cooperation.

Disrespectful of their new managers' rules, founders often ignore them, setting a poor example that oldtimers are only too ready to follow. In response, the COOs hire people to police their rules and strengthen their political base. If things worsen—as they often do— oldtimers and newcomers find themselves at an us-versus-them impasse. The oldtimers, battle-scarred sales- or production-oriented veterans, are tough and shrewd, and they have worked with the founders since the beginning. The newcomers are management professionals hired by COOs to bring systems and order to disorganized companies. They consider the oldtimers undisciplined amateurs. The oldtimers, for their part, consider the pros desiccated number crunchers who couldn't survive five minutes in the real world. Such tensions can turn companies inward, distracting everyone from emerging opportunities and precluding the teamwork that seizes those opportunities.

And so the drama unfolds with the departure of the new chief operating officer, who either quits out of frustration or gets fired when the managers (oldtimers) undermine his or her authority. Next, replacements arrive amidst anarchy: There are no objective rules or rewards. Oldtimers, each of whom seems to have private deals with the founders, set a tone reminiscent of an undeveloped country run by warlords.

The drama repeats itself, but this time as farce. Quite properly, the second-round COOs assert themselves, telling the founders that they will not allow the managers to subvert them. They attempt to set rigorous policies and procedures. The oldtimers chafe under the new structures. They especially dislike the new expense account forms: They are demeaning. "Mickey Mouse" is the mildest of their epithets. When the news of conflict reaches the founders, they can't help expressing sympathy for their old comrades in arms. Worse, when their COOs produce carefully honed budgets—more often than not, the organization's very first—the founders exercise a line-item veto.

The newly hired controllers raise questions about the founders' vacation condos or airplanes or speed boats. Why do corporate funds cover mortgage and lease payments? Founders often ignore those queries and rewrite new rules to suit their own needs. The oldtimers smell blood. Before long, they openly violate the rules and make wisecracks about the new regime. And who gets blamed? Not the violators. More likely, the founders reprimand the COOs for imposing needless rules on their extraordinary companies. Behind the backs of the beleaguered COOs, the founders often confide their own discomfort to their oldtimers.

Now the conflict gets down to the bottom line. There are only two ways to increase profitability. One (an MBA's or COO's likely choice) is to cut costs; the other (more attractive to entrepreneurial types) is to increase revenues.

When the bottom line is an issue, the stakes in the conflict are very high indeed. One or more of the players will have to leave. Who goes and who stays depend on who controls the board of directors or the capital investment. Founders who have lost or given up controlling ownership are, almost invariably, sent packing. Boards, in many cases, agree that cutting costs is the surest way to enhance the bottom line. The impact of revenue increases is not, however, as predictable, so many boards vote for caution and the COO. Off goes the founder, as Steven Jobs and countless other entrepreneurs have done, to found new companies.

Holding on to their controlling interests, the founders who stay have a messy impact on their companies. You might expect that they would automatically fire their COOs, but they have already gone that route and may be embarrassed to retrace those steps. So the founders make their COOs' lives miserable, and rather than dismiss them, they ignore them and belittle them behind their backs. Eventually the COOs obligingly quit.

Another entrepreneurial type—the compulsive salesperson—dictates an alternate scenario. Adrenaline is the salesperson's drug of choice. Though they head Adolescent organizations, the sales experts remain addicted to the joys of Infancy. Their companies offer so many products in so many markets at so many prices that cost accounting often lags sales by six months. Painfully, the truth emerges: Their companies spend far more to reach all those markets than they reap in profit. Morale slumps, good people eye the exits, and some leave. Desperate to stop the exodus, founders hand out all sorts of equity- and profit-sharing deals. But precisely because there's so little profit to share, the recipients take the bribes as cues to harass the founders who are endangering everyone's holdings. The directors' response is to urge the founders to hire new COOs to create structure and bring stability.

It takes only a few months for the new, professional executives to calm the company. Their boards are thrilled, and the COOs take their cues: They make allies of their boards in not so subtle bids for control. The founders, sensing danger, invoke their past successes while their boards review their current failures. Without support, the founders angrily exit their board meetings, and the directors vote the founders face-saving settlements. The COOs, left in control, become CEOs when they make it quite clear that they defer to their boards' authority.

What's wrong with these pictures? For one thing, they tell bitter tales of blind egotism, runaway conflict, and missed opportunities. For another, they depict founders missing the whole point of corporate Adolescence.

The essential goal of the arduous transition from Go-Go to Adolescence is a new culture that optimizes entrepreneurial energy by professionalizing the company with administrative stability and operational (producer) strength. This requires a change in style, which is achieved either by changing the style of the leader or by replacing an exclusively entrepreneurial leader with one who has an administrative style. When leadership is held jointly, they should not try to solve the problem by replacing each other. Rather, they should switch roles—the navigator should, for example, take over the driving. They will continue to work together because the company needs both of them. If they decide that one must lead instead of the other, the company will either get stuck in the founder's trap or start premature aging.

The ideal time to pass the baton—to change who is in the driver's seat—is when events are going well and the company can absorb major leadership changes with minimal strain. Of course, during smooth sailing, founders are less eager to welcome a newcomer. On the other hand, these are the times when founders are at their strongest. If they postpone the change until disaster looms, they will be forced to act from positions of weakness.

Adolescent companies need skilled executives at their helms, leaders who are firm yet tactful and who can establish rules that make everything work more effectively. The new executives ought to be quite different from the Go-Go organization's leaders. Their skills should complement the founders'. While the contrast of their styles may introduce stress, COOs whose abilities mirror the style of the Go-Go leader have little to contribute to the future of their enterprises. To be a true leader, a person must take the organization to the next stage of the lifecycle by behavioral modeling: showing what that next stage is supposed to be rather than reinforcing the organization's existing style and behavior. To mature, children need mature parents.

The newly hired executives should be smart, confident, and sensitive, and they need enough political talent to challenge the founders with compelling arguments that win the founders' respect. The COOs should compose social contracts for their organizations—policies that apply equally to everybody. Fair rules, fairly enforced, introduce a new stability with universal benefit. COOs with the strength to prevent war between the oldtimers and their own new people often embody the integrity to resist playing games with the directors. Even boards that have wearied of founders' vanity are wary of new COOs who conspire to depose their bosses.

When companies reach Prime, their challenge is to manage diverse people and projects: The requisite leadership is not the hard working producer of results, the hands-on manager of Infancy, the charismatic, extroverted entrepreneur of Go-Go, or the administrative, organized, thoughtful leadership of Adolescence. An organization in Prime needs an integrator who can get the most from all the other styles. Those people now have roles that correspond to their styles. Founders who train leaders and decentralize during Adolescence will be prepared for Prime. Their style should be administrative as needed for Adolescence and integrative as needed for Prime.

During this period those CEOs should establish structures that include executive committees with well-defined responsibilities for oversight. This is a critical aspect of the institutionalization of the professional process of management. Organized, systematized meetings, with agendas and preparatory documents distributed, take place on time. Participants recognize and adhere to rules of discussion. The leader does not dominate teamwork. This is a management style that complements the strategy of Adolescence: It introduces the long process of developing a managerial cadre capable of running day-to-day operations long into the future.

The team works together with the leader guiding the process toward a decision that is truly owned and supported by the team. Every decision is reached by consensus of the team as a whole.

A word of caution: What works to bring an organization from Adolescence to Prime is seriously detrimental after Prime. The functional, well-ordered meetings of Adolescence become stale, depressing, and impotent when the company has moved beyond Prime. What is functional in one stage of the lifecycle is dysfunctional in another: To every thing there is a season.

This is the time to eradicate all traces of ruinous us-versus-them mentalities. It is up to founders to pay heed to how their managers interact, and they must put an end to all backstabbing.

STRUCTURE

During Adolescence, founders need to relinquish their absolute control and release the reins they have grasped so tightly during the early stages of their companies' growth. Their companies' future management needs to exercise both authority and responsibility. But how to do that? Adolescence calls for inaugurating the arduous process of separating ownership from management. This is the appropriate sequence of separation and of building a structure of responsibilities that can be translated and interpreted into a structure of authority and eventually into a system of rewards that reinforce desired behavior.

First, conduct a diagnostic workshop to relieve tension. People need to understand that what the organization is experiencing is not significantly different from most organizations' experiences in the adolescent stage of the lifecycle. Everyone will find that reassuring. That process will also temporarily arrest the love-hate relationship between the leader and the followers.

The diagnostic workshop cannot and should not involve sensitivity training: There should be no hot seats, no be-honest-and-tell-it-all confrontations. It should in no way, shape, or form focus on people. The focus should be on the organization independent of the people that compose it. I have designed a three-day diagnostic workshop that promotes teamwork through a carefully directed process. Once we release this energy, the process immediately focuses on the next workshop: mission definition.

This workshop provides temporary respite from the organization's warfare. We use that brief period to generate a new excitement within the company. It is crucial, however, that the mission not create a vision of fewer chairs around the table: When we are ready to start reorganizing—when the game of musical chairs starts—people will fear that there are fewer and fewer positions. The mission should be to remove distractions while revealing the enormous opportunities of growing up and up rather than sideways and nowhere. The people need to regain their confidence in the future of the company while releasing those activities that sidetrack it.

Now we are ready to tackle the next step: organizational design and architecture of responsibilities. This next step is treacherous: Up to Adolescence, the organization structures itself around its people, hiring tomorrow the people it needed yesterday. Because it makes assignments according to its people's availability and talent, the organization grows unwieldy, confusing, and debilitating. Now is the time to reorganize around tasks. Rather than compromise the task to fit the people, as was desirable during Infancy and suitable during Go-Go, during Adolescence, we need to compromise the people to optimize the task.

Doctors don't do surgery on their own children, and lawyers don't represent themselves in court on important cases: They are far too emotionally involved. Their moral, historical, and legal obligations interfere with their clear thinking. Similarly, the founder of an organization should not do its restructuring by himself or herself. It takes an outsider skilled in the technology of organizational design, conflict resolution, and team building to bring about staffing changes and facilitate the transfer of responsibilities and, eventually, of powers and authority according to the managerial structure. Our goal should be to design an infrastructure—when the company is still at $400 million in sales—that will serve it when it is, say, a $1 billion company. That goal restores the leader's confidence. Leaders who have brought their companies up through Go-Go want to be sure that efforts for development do not detract from the efforts for growth. Furthermore, that approach assures the COO and the rest of the company that there is a future, that all will be part of that future, and that their problems are temporary.

Of course, if we cannot honestly envision such a future, it means that the organization's problems are abnormal problems of Adolescence. Such abnormal problems may take the form of irreversible lack of trust in the entrepreneurial and/or the administrative leadership of the company. Or perhaps the organization cannot make the transition from a more-is-better approach to a better-is-more approach, or from an exclusively functional approach with little or no attention to form to a balanced process that optimizes function and form. In those abnormal cases, a psychologist from the Adizes Institute team deals with the personalities involved. Personal coaching comes into play in situations where organizational change is not sufficient to make the difference. People as individuals have to change. I do not support psychotherapists who attempt to change organizational cultures only by coaching individual leaders. That is frequently necessary, but it is insufficient. Coaching's place is to facilitate new structure, rules of conduct, and realignment of power bases.

We aim for a structure that exceeds the current needs of the company. We focus, I like to say, on hats rather than on heads. Heads, as you have no doubt heard before, can wear several hats. As the company grows, one by one those hats become full-time jobs, the multi-hatted people shed extra hats, and new people take over those responsibilities. A well-designed structure prepares the organization for growth and does not require reorganization as the organization grows.

In designing the structure, we coach the organization to identify as many key profit units as they can. This prepares the way for later decentralization and permits reorganization that takes into account each profit center's location on the lifecycle. At this stage, I work hard to avoid a structure that has a single vice president responsible for both sales and marketing or a single vice president responsible for both process engineering and production or—in accordance with the fad of the chief financial officer—the controller, treasurer, and director of finance all reporting to a single person.

Uniting sales and marketing into the same red box, or under the same overhead function, eliminates the true role of marketing. The organization that takes an intense sales orientation loses its sensitivity to market changes. A CFO who controls all the financial resources usually ends up too powerful for the company's own good. That person threatens the position of the Go-Go leader in transition, developing politically dangerous alliances with board members. The company loses its flexibility.

Next, we design the accountability system, and we illustrate it by a chart with colored boxes: Green boxes are profit centers; blue boxes are internal profit centers, which, because they have no sales costs, provide products and/or services at discount market prices to internal clients; brown boxes are service centers that provide services at fully loaded cost; red boxes are overhead units that share costs among users so there is no transfer price from reds, as there is from browns or blues.

In setting transfer prices, the accountants provide a formula and advise, but the users negotiate and accept responsibility for their share: no taxation without representation.

The color system clarifies the structure. Before implementation, the color system acts like a wind tunnel test, representing the structure in a way that brings all potential conflicts to the surface. During this phase of the program, we set transfer prices, determine who has authority to make decisions, and clarify who is in charge of what. We define responsibilities, clearing away possible contention in the design room rather than waiting to handle discord on the fly.

The participants themselves, coached by a certified Adizes organizational therapist, conduct the restructuring process. We next coach the leader in the transfer of authority. Note that we do not even approach the question of authority until the participants have clarified and stabilized responsibilities and until they establish an information system to monitor application of responsibilities. Now the leader, accustomed to individualistic decision making, might be positioned to consider transferring authority. But what is the best way to do that?

Initially, people will not believe that the leader really intends to transfer responsibilities and authority. After all, they have been witness to earlier declarations of intent to transfer power. The hapless souls who took those words seriously ended up being punished. They have reason to doubt the new promises. Furthermore, leaders who want to transfer authority are scared. They have experienced how wrong their subordinates can be. Of course they are afraid to delegate.

I respect those fears, and in the beginning I refrain from delegating authority to any individual. Instead, I delegate to a complementary team that at the start most probably includes the doubting leader. I do not appoint that leader to direct the team's discussion even though he or she has the authority to make final decisions. A person we have trained integrates, that is, leads, the discussion.

Over time, leaders of companies gain confidence in their teams and recognize that the teams work well, and the teams make better decisions than the leaders could make alone. To achieve that, we conduct five-day workshops to train people to make decisions as a team with mutual trust and respect, to handle conflict constructively, and to accommodate decisions correctly without compromising. Eventually, the leaders (after developing confidence in their lieutenants) start to beg off and skip meetings, and we gladly accept their absence. Nearly painlessly, delegation takes place.

We are now positioned to redesign the reward system, which until this point most probably focused on sales. All attempts to tie rewards to profits have failed because people had no authority to manage profits. Now, with structure, mission, accountability systems, and information systems that specify who creates and spends how much and why, a profit-centered reward system becomes meaningful.

STRATEGY

Adolescent companies frequently suffer from a temporary loss of vision, due to extensive internal fighting. Their founders grow gun-shy. Perhaps their failure during Go-Go that prompted the transition to Adolescence has put their boards of directors on their back. Leaders of the emerging adolescent organization lose their old confident assurance that they have the magic touch. Every day the administrative types remind them that their fears are not without grounds. Since the administrative people focus not on what more to do but on what less to do, and the entrepreneurial people are languishing in the penalty box, the company is in disarray strategically.

What is to be done? The therapy should be as follows: First, you, the leader of the company in transition, must get rid of whomever you do not trust. Clean up shop. It is extremely difficult to make repairs using parts and pieces you do not trust. But watch out. I said fire the people you do not trust, but I did not say to fire everyone at once. I have dealt with more than one case where the CEO fired all the vice presidents one afternoon. Keep whomever you can, and do not hire new management until the company's structure, as I describe it above, is set. Strategically, you should turn your energy inward. This is not the time to do more outside your organization. As the leader of a company, you need to recreate its visions to ensure that your COO's plans adhere to your visions and directions.

During Adolescence, because companies experience disintegration, their founders' strategy should be to provide integration forces: mission and vision.

My experience is that the strategy that emerges from the founder's review of the adolescent company's activities should be a strategy of convergence. The adolescent company is like a young tree that has grown leggy and shapeless during its Go-Go stage. If nobody prunes the extraneous branches, refocusing energy upward, it will continue to grow as a small, squat bush. Adolescence calls for redefinition of the real business of the company.

Courtship was characterized by anticipation, dreams, and expectations that sustained the reality tests of Infancy. During Go-Go, the company pushed boundaries to see whether the company could achieve more than anticipated: The company diversified, expanding into a miniconglomerate. Now, in its Adolescence, the company is ready for convergence: It must dispose of those ventures that, in retrospect, are not within the company's main core competence.

The pruning is not easy. Some founders resist, refusing to accept what they consider to be defeat. They believe that if they have succeeded in one endeavor, they should be able to succeed in all endeavors. The more those founders fail, the more they redouble their efforts, raising the stakes so high that only a detached outsider who has neither planted nor watered the tree can prune it. The founder loses the political battle and is eased out.

Which founders endure Adolescence successfully? The successes are those who have installed a complementary team around them—a team they trust and who provide the founder with reality, analysis, and controls.

STAFFING

Unlike organizations in Infancy and Go-Go in which individuals' capabilities defined functions, adolescent organizations must professionalize: Founders need to redefine job structures to reflect functions rather than individuals. No longer may flexibility take precedence over control. The decision to define functions makes it easier to recruit skilled outsiders. This staffing phase of the program has its own problems. Leaders from the Go-Go stage or even the Infancy stage have loyalties to the employees who were with them through the tough times. There are all kinds of written and unwritten commitments. Even to think about violating any of those codes creates an emotional episode.

To get to Prime, though, the business needs diversity in its organizational structure, in the reward structure, and in the leadership of the company. Each role should define its own levels of flexibility and control, productivity and integration, and the personalities of the people who fill those roles should reflect the definitions. Diversity of styles was not necessarily the characteristic of a Go-Go organization or a source of its success. Rather it had an almost exclusive dedication to penetrating and expanding its position in the market with deals and joint ventures. Go-Gos usually ignore their companies' internal systems. The diversity in staffing that Adolescence requires is alien to its older culture, and people resist incorporating those whose style is different. That is why an organization in Adolescence has a tendency toward cliquishness.

When I help companies navigate through this stage, I insist that they make no appointments to the structure without first consulting me. I am trying to avoid two common problems. Left on their own, the lobbyists work overtime, and the leaders, caught in webs of loyalties, respond to pre-reorganizational political constellations. Afraid that they may rock the boat too much, the leaders end up altering the structure we've designed to accommodate the existing staff. The result? The more it changes, the more it stays the same. The other common outcome of leaving the leaders on their own is that they head in the opposite direction, discarding the whole or most of the existing leadership team, claiming they need totally new crews for the new realities of the new structure.

My job is to hold the leaders' hands during this difficult period, which should not take long. We get together and we discuss who could fit where. I encourage the leaders to give their current people a chance. Even people who have never demonstrated the desired personality traits might nevertheless excel in the new reality.

I tell them a true story that illustrates the importance of giving people a chance. When my son Shoham was quite young, I bought him a globe. He asked me why the earth was tilted. I told him that if the earth were not tilted, we would not have changing seasons. If the earth had only the North Pole's season of continuous winter, only the polar bears would survive. Then it occurred to me that if a camel wanders to the North Pole, it either has to die, get out, or adapt by developing a polar bear's skin.

So, I tell the leaders, many of their people might be camels in polar bear skins. Now that their companies have established a diversified structure, it is as if the earth has been tilted to allow diversity. Some camels who parade as polar bears to survive will, given the chance to live in the Sahara, hurry to shed their fur, and they will start to act like the camels that they are.

Many times, I have seen people who had been labeled as bureaucrats respond to new positions in marketing jobs by turning into full-fledged entrepreneurs. True, we did have to change the reward system, clearly define their new roles, and empower them, but that was all part of the program.

To keep the leaders from adapting the chart and compromising it to fit individuals, I insist that only people with good chances of success get appointments to the new structure. Occasionally the CEO has to fill a senior position temporarily. True, some people who are accustomed to reporting to the CEO will feel demoted, but they should not feel so: Wearing their vice presidents' hats, they are still reporting to the CEO. That approach helps stabilize the changing situation. It enables the CEO to see whom he has and how good they are. People start to get used to their new roles, and, over time, they create space for new people to come in and take over the hats the CEO has been wearing temporarily.

As adolescent companies progress through this challenging stage of organizational life, they need more outside directors to provide objective guidance. During the Go-Go stage, an external board was at what I call the need-to category. During Adolescence, an external board moves to the must-to classification.

REWARDS

In earlier lifecycle stages, founders use bonuses and commissions to increase revenues. In adolescent companies, a diversity of rewards recognizes different kinds of performers. Frontline supervisors and managers should get salary along with bonuses for individual achievement. Middle managers should get proportionately lower salaries with more profit sharing and stock options. Top management needs compensation packages that motivate them: conservative salaries supplemented by extensive opportunities for profit sharing and stock options. By entwining employees' personal future with their companies', leaders of the organization can secure their workers' support during the restructuring and decentralization that accompany Adolescence. Because those changes to the reward system are revolutionary, some will express tremendous resistance. Some people will resign or stir up trouble.

Of course, none of the program's transformation processes is easy or without pain. The pain here stems from withdrawal of rewards that are individual in nature and focused on only one side of the profit equation: either the revenues or the costs. The new system intertwines everyone's success and requires managerial judgment to evaluate the impact of costs on revenues. Such individual achievements as reaching a sales quota or cutting costs are emotionally less taxing than achieving profits by juggling the value of costs against the revenues they will generate. Achievement of the latter is dependent on others' performance. Profit sharing—in effect, a motivating force rather than a windfall—requires a climate of teamwork, mutual trust, respect, cooperation, and intellectual and managerial maturity. Many companies, because they fail to give their people the power to affect profits, make the transition badly. The leadership does not share information, delegate authority, or build meaningful teamworking communication patterns. Although they share profits, they see no impact on productivity, sense of ownership, or loyalty—the legitimate goals of profit sharing.

In these circumstances profit sharing is meaningless as a motivating force. It is merely a windfall for those who benefit from it.

Another danger is that the leader's largesse is not supported by structure, direction, controls, or boundaries. Profit sharing based on good intentions may make employees consider themselves entitled to second-guess the owners' actions. While they usually do not dare to challenge the leader's decisions, employees nevertheless can, and do, feel cheated when they don't receive what they believe they should. If only the leader would stop making decisions they don't support. In the end, the profit sharing backfires: Instead of motivating, it makes people cynical.

In my practice I have worked with many clients who wanted to establish profit sharing prematurely. Oddly enough, I made the same mistake myself at the Adizes Institute. It's best to establish a solid structure before papering the staff with profit sharing or equity. To have profit sharing that is motivating, first make sure that the structure of roles and expectations is operational and correct. By correct I mean that the structure reflects the requirements of the tasks and the mission of the organization. Furthermore, the distribution of powers should not create a plethora of control-oriented power centers or change-oriented centers. Be sure to distribute power correctly.

But even a well-designed structure is not enough to support reward systems. The flow of information—and information is a source of power—has to reflect the organizational structure. I should have a dollar for every organization that computerized without redesigning its structure. Designing information systems within a bad structure reinforces the bad distribution of powers and further erodes the organization's ability to remain flexible. I personally helped an organization discard a software system that had cost $200 million to develop. Its information delivery system had a built-in detrimental effect on the new structure we had designed.

Once the organization's mission is clear, known, and owned, and once people's roles are clearly balanced to achieve flexibility and control, information distribution systems should provide the decision makers with the data they need to plan and correct directions. Now the rewards are meaningful because they reward and concurrently reinforce the desired behavior. And those rewards are attainable.

Finally, if the salary scales and the bonus systems are balanced and aligned with the structure, conditions are right for meaningful profit sharing. Profit sharing is the cherry on the pie. Putting a cherry atop a pie made of horse manure will not make it a cherry pie.

Planning and Goals

In Infancy, companies focused on producing results for cash. In Go-Go they fought for market share. Adolescence brings organizations closer to the payoff: predictable profitability. To net a profit requires drawing boundaries that define lines of business, discount structures, sales approaches, and so forth. Go-Go companies get into trouble because they assume fixed profit margins. Their exuberant founders believe that the more sales they make, the higher profits they will reap. In reality, to increase sales, the Go-Go companies offer more discounts, more deals, more advertising, higher sales commissions, and more concessions to customers. Their weak information systems and hopelessly outdated cost accounting cannot possibly track cash flow. Predictable profitability remains a distant dream.

During Adolescence, management decisions should focus on what to do and what not to do. By doing so, the organization converts itself from being characteristically Go-Go—that is, opportunity driven—to being an organization that drives opportunity. I am describing, in other words, an organization in Prime. At this stage, the organization should write policies and manuals and departmentalize to decentralize. Set constraints: Define the ten *Nos*, the ten things the company will not do. Identify and derive those Nos from past strategic mistakes. For example, one company I know found that the time demands of government contracts far outweighed potential rewards. Its leaders set "We will not bid for government contracts, period," as one of its Nos. Other Nos I have come across are: We will ship no product unless we have fully met the production release criteria for ramped-up production, we will make no sale until the customer's credit has been approved, we will sign no new deals above a certain value without board approval, there will be no salary increases without approval from Human Resources.

Management of an adolescent organization should be carefully trimming the branches of their overgrown trees. Deciding not to engage in certain activities and businesses calls for a virtual change of religion: No more will they succeed simply by acceding to demands for any price and getting sales by doing whatever it takes. The factors that, in the past, translated into success will mean failure in the future, and what caused failure in the past will (if handled correctly) be the future's source of success. Cold is hot, and hot is cold. Growing up is both stressful and scary.

In Infancy there was no planning. The goals were clear: Sell, sell, sell, and remember to collect. For an infant organization, serious planning with econometric models and supply-and-demand and competitive-market analyses is as premature as the proud young mother who introduces her newborn baby as "my doctor."

The company in Go-Go might have started to do some organized planning, but at that time it would have been mostly wishful—but valuable—thinking. For a Go-Go, nothing is impossible so long as its people want it badly enough. Positive thinking, expansive thinking, and daring to be what its leaders want it to be are vital at this point. All that thinking and daring contribute to the successful Go-Go mentality until the company dares too much and falls off one of the leggy branches of the tree. That's when goals have to change, when it is time for the Go-Go leader to ask, "What do we want to be when we grow up? What do we have to *stop doing* to get there?"

Turning inward, the leader must examine the organization to determine what it is, not just what it does. What a company does is easy enough to copy. Defining what it is—its values, culture, meaning, and purpose for being—is more difficult. Planning must focus on who we are, what we stand for, what our values are, and what our vision is. The organization has to reinvent and recreate itself. That cannot and should not be done by so-called consultants-content experts from the outside. The people in the organization must tackle the difficult task of recreating themselves by themselves. If members of the organization are caught in the web of their past successes and want to return to what they know is secure and proven, they might need the assistance of an organizational coach to make that transition. In such situations, people think that they can regain childhood's relative freedom from responsibility. They want to revive the times when they could indulge their curiosity and make impulsive decisions. "It was our lack of structure, our daring, our passion, our creativity that made us succeed. We lost it all with the structure, organization, rules, policies, and limitations that were imposed in Adolescence," they lament. And they rebel, returning to Go-Go and the founder's trap.

It is not easy to escort companies over the difficult road to Prime: Quite often, the leadership fails to appreciate what we are urging and coaching them to do.

"If you want to be hated, try changing someone." I can't remember where I saw that sentence, but it resonates in my memory. Many founders and managers have accused me of being the cause of the company's difficulties rather than a healer who is doing them any good. Their animosity reminds me of the bad feelings people have for their dentists whose repairs to their rotting teeth cause pain. I have learned that only an enlightened leader can see what is happening and realize that the transformation is necessary to get the company to Prime. I am careful to analyze the style and values of the leader in Adolescence. Unless the company's leader is enlightened, able to see the big picture, and has the style to make the transition through Adolescence to Prime, our work as coaches has very limited impact.

A CAUTION

The pain—for parents, teachers, and teens themselves—of human adolescence is so intense that it is easy to ignore or forget the bright creativity, energy, and, yes, even the romance of those difficult years. That same forgetfulness afflicts adolescent companies, at their peril. Even—no, especially—under reconstruction by an MBA, young companies must hold fast to their entrepreneurial assets: the creative people who give them vision, vitality, and drive. Under the new regime of the COO, those free spirits may feel blocked or irrelevant. "The fun is gone," they may grouse. Everyone, including founders and COOs, must fight to keep those people engaged and on board. The so-called bean counters may constrict creativity by choking innovators with procedures and paperwork. Without dynamic talents immersed in exciting projects, adolescent companies age prematurely. They may turn profits, but such profitability, unsupported by new products and services, is doomed to be short-lived.

If founders, like good parents, help their companies mature, they can avoid that fate and progress to Prime.

WHERE DO YOU STAND? A CHECKLIST

Normal Problems of Adolescence

- Although there are internal conflicts among the partners, mutual trust and respect are still strong.
- The confusion that started in Go-Go over who is accountable for bad results is becoming an acute problem.
- Because it is unclear who the real leader is, leadership struggles and power plays plague the organization.
- The company expects to increase both sales and profits.
- There is no consistent planning.
- Meetings are generally useless, and it is not clear who should be attending them. Although the meetings do have agendas, no one follows up on the decisions because they are not enforced.
- The founder is easily irritated by the staff, and the staff resents the founder.
- The cost accounting systems are useless.
- The company devotes resources to developing computer systems that do not serve the organization because they are based on a poorly defined structure.
- Reward systems are either inconsistent or nonexistent.
- Decisions with regard to promotions, titles, salaries, benefits, policies, and rules are inconsistent and easily forgotten.

- When there are problems, management's response is to hire additional people to solve them.

Abnormal Problems of Adolescence

- The leadership team cannot stand one another. They have lost all mutual trust and respect.
- Oldtimers fight guerrilla wars against newcomers.
- There is no cost accounting system.
- The company changes leaders frequently and impatiently, not waiting long enough to see any impact. Everyone wants a do-it-now savior.
- Witch-hunts focus on the leaders.
- Tremendous amounts of time and energy are wasted on internal politics.
- The frustrated leader announces intentions to resign but soon reverses the decision and takes over again.
- Partners, who can no longer work together, split up. The administrative type buys out the entrepreneurial type.

7

Prime:
Ready, Willing, and Fit
for Success After Success

Prime: A Parable

George Anders, the founder of Belle Image, had perished in a helicopter crash two years earlier. Until his death, he was the creative, inspirational spirit of his rapidly growing cosmetics empire. He had chosen fragrances, penned advertising tag lines, even tinkered with in-store promotional setups. To his last breath, he had devoted all his creative powers to the company. The news of his tragic death stunned employees and investors alike. Belle Image stock crashed from $81 to $62 per share in one day.

But amid the panic, savvy outsiders emerged who understood that the depth of Belle Image's management ran deeper than Anders. The next day, in fact, investors bid Belle Image stock back up to $75 per share. What they knew is that Anders hadn't carried the entire management burden for the company. Several years before his death, he had searched the world for a partner and successor. He found it in Claude Bournet, a jolly Frenchman, who was running Asea Brown Boveri's U.S. operations.

The choice of Bournet had confounded analysts at the time. How could an executive who cut his teeth selling electrical turbines and subway cars find the next fragrance of favor? But Anders had been unapologetic. As if scolding the analysts, he had snapped at them, asserting, "He knows the managerial process well."

Bournet brought to Belle Image 25 years of experience compressing inventories, tuning manufacturing, and streamlining development processes—many of the skills that Anders felt would make or break Belle Image as it continued to grow. No longer could the company tolerate heaps of unsold product coming back from stores. Those skills, it turned out, were crucial to the company's good health. Five years later, Bournet was in a position to declare that he would have had to borrow an additional $190 million and pay $19 million more in interest had he continued to run the company as it had been before his tenure.

Bournet instituted not only strict inventory controls but also hard-nosed manufacturing standards; tight, detailed budgets; more sophisticated distribution; and marketing that more sharply defined target customers. The days of unrestrained entrepreneurship were gone. The company couldn't rely on just fat margins to cover up slipshod operations.

While Bournet tightened controls, George Anders turned to the company's industry veterans to concoct new fragrances and lipstick colors. He was acutely aware that product lifecycles in cosmetics can be as short as a few months, a far cry from the years or even decades in the heavy-machinery industry. Cosmetics fads change faster than hemlines. The company had to stay tuned to changing tastes, demography, and social habits. If women joining the workforce wanted clean, transparent makeup that looked as if they were wearing no makeup at all, Belle Image would provide it.

Bournet and Anders then divided Belle Image into five divisions to foster more freewheeling decision making. Although the units—fully supported and coached by the founder—had to adhere to corporate standards, they retained responsibility for products, packaging, and advertising. A corporate marketing division did marketing research and media planning among other functions. It took over more and more from Anders, and its decisions reflected his style and judgment.

The manufacturing/engineering unit was well established and respected, and eagerly awaited recommendations from marketing. With good reason: Bournet and Anders established a reward system based on profitability and increases in market share. As those two measures improved, the value of employees' stock options climbed. The company had a structure of responsibilities, authority, and rewards that kept each person focused on individual responsibilities and simultaneously kept everyone pulling in the same direction for the benefit of all.

Anders saw that his role was not to do but to create an environment in which people make the right choices and perform effectively. Bournet fully supported him in his effort. The two enjoyed working together, and although they frequently disagreed, they always learned from their disagreements and arrived at conclusions they both supported. Those two managers knew that they would not cross one another. Once they made a decision, both of them would defend it.

While the units followed psychology and fashion in each of their markets, Bournet and Anders pushed innovation across markets. The company introduced its products to new channels—supermarket shelves, for example. And it launched its own Belle Image stores, catering to upscale shoppers in high-traffic suburban shopping malls. The company even diversified into skin-care products, building on knowledge gained from product development with oils and emollients used in cosmetics.

Each profit-center unit had its own capable leader, motivated and rewarded by the unit's results, which were in concert with those goals of the larger totality. They worked like fingers on a hand: different but united. Under Anders and Bournet, the company was on a roll and never in the same place.

When Anders died, people were sad, but they did not despair. The company had a culture and a group of leaders who were able to take his place and continue the nurturing that he had started.

PRIME

Prime is an ever-changing condition, a segment of a journey, not a haven at the end of the road. Companies in Prime are recognizable: All aspects work well together, all operations thrive, and all members of the organization know where it is going and how to stay on track. Prime is a state of balance: flexibility and control, function and form, imagining and producing, innovation and administration. But companies in that exultant equilibrium—so hard to achieve, so easy to lose—continually risk sliding back to childish habits or stumbling into the rigidity of old age.

An organization is no less vulnerable in Prime than it is at any other stage of its lifecycle. The cash shortage of Infancy, the founder's heavy hand in Go-Go, the infighting of Adolescence—those are challenges it has overcome. Now the complacency that comes with a surfeit of success looms as a potential and significant threat.

I have a rule of thumb by which I judge an adult company: If it does not produce significant new products or spin off promising start-ups within any three-year period, it is either decaying or on the brink of decline. Ask yourself what percentage of your revenues come from products you were not selling three years ago? Be honest. There are enhancements, changes that are cosmetic in nature that make old products look new. Pharmaceutical manufacturers are well known for introducing tiny changes to products to establish their legally defensible claim that they have a new drug. That is what their customers—doctors and patients—expect and pray for, and that is what the pharmaceutical companies provide. Nevertheless, if the companies are not introducing truly new products, and only their executives know the truth, those companies will grow without developing. They will start to age, and they will eventually decay.

Why do I specify the need for new products or services within three years? In fact, this rule of thumb varies by industry. In the aerospace industry, the cycle is much longer, whereas in the fashion industry it is much shorter. In the restaurant business, you must offer a new special every day, and you must change the restaurant's concept every five years or so. Consider Domino's Pizza. Its original innovation was fast delivery of pizza. But the fast-food industry has a lifecycle too. I pointed out that hot dogs were enormously popular, but they yielded first place to pizza. Pizza, too, would peak. I warned that unless Domino's introduced the next new rage, it would age. From our vantage point in the 1990s, we know that bagels have outpaced pizzas. Today, three years is an extremely long life for almost any product or service you can think of. In certain industries that are evolving at a breathtaking pace—electronics, biomedical research, or telecommunications—product lifecycles last only six months to one year.

A company in Prime predicts trends correctly and is not attached to a single product line or market to the exclusion of any other. It develops and changes. I wish that Domino's had redefined itself, not as a pizza company but as a company that delivers quality snacks quickly. It could have opened a new chain for bagels as pizzas were declining: It should have transferred energy to the new endeavor.

A company in Prime has goals it meets, regularly and predictably. Its people are poised to seize the right opportunities, but they also know how to handle an inappropriate turn of events. They focus on results with a ferocity that ensures that they will meet and exceed customer needs. The entire organization shares a vision, encourages creativity, and performs with excellence. The company realistically and successfully pursues growth and profitability. One no longer precludes the other.

PRIME: LIFE AT THE TOP OF THE CURVE

Walt Disney died of cancer in 1966, leaving an extensive legacy of creative, entrepreneurial genius and a wide-ranging enterprise with neither a capable successor nor an enduring management structure. Disney, fueled by an infinite gusher of ideas, had led his company through a thrilling Go-Go era, but he had not prepared it to advance without him. In the terminology of corporate lifecycles, he had failed to institutionalize himself.

The company seemed to have lost its keen understanding of its customers and their tastes. Without its founder's autocratic leadership, the company floundered, releasing a puff of unmemorable films between 1972 and 1984.

Investors on Wall Street began to lose patience. They fretted that Disney managers weren't getting the most out of the company's unique and valuable assets: cartoon characters, films, theme parks. During the takeover boom of the 1980s, corporate raiders-the likes of Saul Steinberg and Ivan Boesky-hungrily eyeing those assets, drew Disney into a series of takeover battles. They wanted to split the company up and pocket the untapped value for themselves.

Finally 18 years after his uncle's death, Roy Disney, Jr., cobbled together a plan to keep the company intact. In 1984, he and his allies gained enough strength to hire an executive team: Michael Eisner, formerly with Paramount, and Frank Wells, a longtime executive in the film industry. Eisner, a strong entrepreneurial force, and Wells, a strong force for professional management, formed an outstanding team, complementing each other's best qualities. Long-standing friends, they mutually trusted and respected each other. Together they introduced structure and strategic leadership, hiring top creative talents to lead various business units, directing the company to focus on customer needs and financial results, and pursuing an aggressive strategy to spur growth of both traditional and brand-new businesses. In short order, they launched such enterprises as Hollywood Records, EuroDisney, and Disney retail stores.

Now, more than a decade after the arrival of new management, Disney represents far more than its founder's original concept for the company. Inspired by the legacy of Walt Disney's creative imagination, the company is in Prime, combining flexibility and control, creativity and discipline, rapid growth and fast-paced business innovation.

And that was the Walt Disney Company in 1995.

A Prime company acts aggressively. Its systematic approach to growth and development extends beyond product or market strategy. It pertains to corporate strategy and policy, and deals with the processes of management, structure, staffing, rewards—the variables I am discussing in this book. Those variables are not an accumulation of historical happenstance. They are integrated strategies for continuous maintenance of the portfolio of products, markets, leadership, and so forth. Prime manages its market environment: now with flexibility, now with control, now with a nicely calibrated measure of both.

Success hides danger. It creates a false sense of security. Prime companies are growing in many ways, starting new subsidiary companies and churning out more new products every year. The new products create new market niches that garner sales. But because they are growing so quickly, those companies don't have enough well-trained employees to take advantage of every opportunity. Clearly, the major problem of an organization in Prime is not cash flow, setting of priorities, or internal conflicts. The Prime organization suffers from a dearth of managerial depth and talent to match its opportunities for growth.

Rather than confront the instability and challenge of Prime, too many companies ignore the signs of their degeneration. They enjoy and appreciate the results as they appear on the balance sheet and the income statement, but they ignore the process of management that produces those results. They fail to recognize that they are in dire straits until they are already slipping away from Prime. Their management introduces restructuring efforts, but often those gestures are so late that the company faces hopelessly expensive, nearly incurable problems.

Note that, in my diagnostic assessment of companies' lifecycles, I don't mention their financials. That's because the financial picture may appear rosy: rising sales, growing profit margins, and encouraging financials. In short, the financials paint a wonderful picture for the potential investor. Remember, however, that financial statements show only what was. A company's financial statements capture individual moments in its history; they do not at all indicate the future unless the company is in deep trouble. In that case, the prediction is almost trivial. Financial statements are no more prescient than a urine test or even a cardiogram. They can tell you only whether there is any evidence of disease. They cannot tell you if you are healthy. One has to look at eating patterns and lifestyle habits to predict diseases before there is evidence in the urine test. Like Yogis who can control their heartbeats and blood pressures, a company in Prime controls all of its functions.

So, then, you might ask, do we judge a company only by its fertility? Not at all. If you can get in close enough to examine it, you'll also get a look at the company's culture. Do its managers search out the problems and opportunities of the future? Do they understand where the company is, where it is heading, and where it ought to be in the next five years? If they do, then it is a reasonable guess that at least they comprehend the exigencies of remaining in Prime. They know that they must set their sights on new markets, develop new products or services, and exploit new technologies. Again, be careful. Having a five-year plan can be a sign of a disease rather than a sign of health. It all depends on who is doing the planning, how conscious the company is of those future developments, and how flexible it will be in dealing with them.

Certain companies with large staffs of corporate planners tend to overdo the planning. Those are the aging and decaying companies. Their strategic planners spend enormous resources on econometric models, portfolio analyses, and overhead slides for special presentations. A whole forest disappears with the bulk of their paperwork. Still, the rest of the organization ho-hums along, giving the planners the nod, and nothing happens. It is as if they all believe that by making sacrifices on the altar of corporate religion, they will guarantee their places in heaven. The role of corporate planners should never be to plan. Instead, they should be making sure that the rest of the corporation—from the workers on up the line—is planning. All units—even individuals—should have plans that in the aggregate yield a total plan for the company.

A Danish company called ISS is the world's largest custodial-services company, providing its services in office buildings, airports, factories, you name it. One of the company's vice presidents, Jan Rassmunsen, who was at one time vice president for international operations and a senior associate of the Adizes Institute, heads the ISS training center, which systematically focuses the company's managers on the future. When managers from ISS subsidiary operations around the world come for training, Jan requires each trainee to complete a questionnaire. In it, the managers describe their own unit's culture, whether it follows a culture of Prime or is before or after Prime. Like a doctor who checks your attitudes and lifestyle to analyze the condition of your health, the test confirms or denies the diagnosis. With encouragement and direction from Jan's organization, trainees from those units that are lagging formulate new plans that will bring their organization to Prime.

Like athletes at the top of their sporting events, companies in Prime face a questionable future: continued triumph or decline. Of the two directions, decline is the more likely. That's because, with the onset of success, the entrepreneurial spirit that infuses companies during their heady growth years seems to vanish. Managers learn the tricky process of balancing flexibility and control, but as they enjoy success, they increasingly invoke controls rather than the changes necessary for continuity of that success. Energy, reflecting the style of the leader, declines. Over time the structure loses its power balance. The chronological age of the movers and shakers has advanced to the point where they prefer to protect what they have rather than risk it to create more.

Customers of Prime companies are content, but, as we might expect, management continuously resorts to more and more controls to sustain predictable results. The dynamics of the system are not desirable, however, and as the organization loses its internal flexibility, outside changes are occurring rapidly. The company starts to lose touch, and it begins to age.

Many of the most successful companies are those most susceptible to failure. Managers' delusions about their company's dominant position in its markets can bring about aging. Simply believing that their company has locked up all the customers their market has to offer is enough to fuel a dangerous fantasy. Or they might simply assert that the market segment their company serves is the market. After that, everything falls into place—or rather, apart. Managers argue that any efforts to increase market share are impossible or too costly. Complacency follows, as night follows day.

That particular downward slope, however, presents its own correction. For example, a company that has traditionally defined its business as the paint business can learn that it is actually in the business of providing protective and aesthetic coating services. With that adjustment to their perspective, the managers can now visualize the possibility of adding wallpaper to their product line. By expanding the definition of the company's markets, its managers dramatically enhance opportunities to increase market share.

Managers at many companies are not receptive to the idea of broadening their sense of the business they are in. Just think of the railroads or IBM. They recoiled from businesses that appeared to be less profitable than their core businesses, and they hesitated to scatter their resources: After all, every company has only so much capital to work with. Focus is the name of the game for a Go-Go company, not one that has passed Prime. What Prime companies need to do is to open their eyes to other possibilities while remaining within the range of businesses they know and understand.

Another hazard Prime companies risk relates to responsibility. In the growing stages, as we've said, everything is permitted unless specifically forbidden. In aging organizations, everything is forbidden unless specifically permitted. That difference represents a major shift in organizational culture. In the growing stages, managers seize responsibility because there is nobody to restrain them. In aging organizations, managers ritually observe all functional boundaries, including those they create themselves. It is true, of course, that managers in young companies have both authority and responsibility. In aging organizations, staff members have the authority to impose regulations, but they bear no responsibility for the aftermath. By the same token, line managers are responsible for following the recommendations from their headquarters staff, but they have insufficient authority to achieve the results for which they are responsible. I am describing the moment when disintegration starts and the structure starts to crumble. What to do then?

STYLE

While it was critical to have a process-oriented, control-oriented individual to bring the company from Adolescence to Prime, that style of leadership will not keep the company in Prime. Now it needs a strategically oriented leadership or it will lose energy, coherence, and fertility.

The founder's passionate vision and enthusiasm carried the enterprise through its early stages, generating the crises that inspired structure and controls. Now, as a fully developed enterprise it is making its mark on the economy. Swelled with success, however, the leaders of the company occasionally grow a little too big for their britches. They lose sight of the roots of their success: raw entrepreneurial passion. Living on Park Avenue, the founder may forget the formative early days back on the Lower East Side. Unless the organization's leaders work to renew those entrepreneurial roots, its soaring trajectory will dip, then dive.

I do not expect parents who already have many babies in their homes to be excited to conceive again. Nor do I expect that enthusiasm from elderly people with money but no energy to support a baby and change its diapers. Giving birth to new businesses is the task of companies in Prime. Although a lone person can not remain in Prime forever, families can. Part of the family conceives, another raises the babies, and another finances its growth. A company in Prime is a portfolio of units at different stages of the lifecycle that work together to maintain the company's capability to remain in Prime.

If a leader of the business-generation units wants to follow one of its conceptions into business growth, that is fine so long as that leader shows a propensity to change his or her style of leadership from conceptualizer to hands-on manager. May that person lead the organization into the Go-Go stage? Again, my answer is yes, so long as that leader shows a capability to plan strategically. Once that person's style becomes dysfunctional—the unit's growth has outpaced the leader's ability to lead it—that person should move to manage an emerging unit that is in an appropriately earlier stage of the lifecycle.

That practice is common in the hospitality industry's management of hotels and restaurant chains. The leadership style that can develop a new restaurant concept is quite distinct from the style that excels at opening restaurants, stabilizing and institutionalizing discipline and controls, or managing an already mature establishment.

A Prime company has a portfolio of markets and products consistent with its position in the lifecycle, and its leaders have a range of management styles that permit managing different lifecycle locations. It needs also, as we shall see below, a portfolio of reward systems. A company that has reached Prime has developed a correctly diverse portfolio. To stay in Prime, that company has learned to maintain and manage the diversity correctly.

What are the danger signs? Creeping bureaucracy, an intensifying tendency to go by the book, and a drop in the inclination and ability to improvise are some of the obvious signs. Remember: For an entrepreneur, everything that is not specifically forbidden is permitted; for an administrator, everything is forbidden unless specifically permitted. Leaders who want to keep their companies in Prime need to resist warring temptations to boost profits by discarding highly paid creative stars or, conversely, by granting excessive powers to those who control expenses—the bean counters, lawyers, and efficiency experts—without being responsible for the revenues.

When I observe a company to identify where it is in its lifecycle, I want to see how its managers conduct meetings and how they resolve problems.

In Courtship, founders and their managers meet anywhere, anytime. They could get together in the middle of the night or at any other hour of the day. In Infancy, there is no time to meet. If the staff of an infant company does meet, it is because there is an emergency or a crisis. In that case, the meeting takes place right on the production floor, by telephone, or in the parking lot.

During the Go-Go years, it's hard to hold any kind of meeting. The company's managers are dispersed all over the map. Sam is in Salt Lake City selling the Jones account. Jane has been in Kansas City for the past three days, sweating over the Samson Distributorship renewal. Harry is attending a manufacturing seminar in New Orleans. When they finally manage to get together, they meet at the boss's office over the weekend. Sunday night, everyone is back on the road. No more meetings until the next crisis.

In Adolescence it is the rare meeting, indeed, that accomplishes much: The different interest groups are busily backstabbing and infighting. Back-corridor whispers between two vice presidents carry more weight than a dozen formal meetings.

Companies in Prime hold regular meetings that start at 9:00 a.m. sharp in conference room C. Nobody would dare come late. Every attendee has an agenda and a scheduled time to discuss his or her latest project. Order is the rule. The group explores issues carefully and thoroughly, reaches consensus, and makes assignments.

The meetings of companies in Prime are orderly and productive, showing none of the rigidity that indicates incipient aging. Before Prime there are conflicts, and there is no structure to help reach constructive solutions. After Prime the meetings are still orderly, but the content has lost its magic. The company goes through the rituals, but there is no dissent, no disagreement, and no constructive conflict. In Prime, there is dissent and a structure to channel it constructively.

Now let's examine how managers in companies at different stages of the corporate lifecycle approach problems.

In Courtship there are no problems: There are only opportunities. In Infancy there are more than enough problems to go around, but managers have no time to solve them. They are too busy chasing sales and trying to organize production. The only problems companies in Infancy bother to solve are those that erupt into crises. Then and only then does the organization stop, catch its collective breath, and do something. You might define Infancy as management by crisis.

Companies in their Go-Go years no longer manage by crisis. They are simply trying to endure crisis by management. In Go-Go organizations, management precipitates its own crises, one after another. In that stage, you remember, management has too many priorities. Founders, in particular, believe they are capable of starting and succeeding at businesses of any kind. That illusion generates untold headaches for their companies as managers rush around trying to keep all the founders' projects under control.

In Adolescence, everyone is always asking, "Who is responsible for the problems?"

"Oh, the cost accounting manager is blocking the deal."

"No. Isn't the sales manager building an empire?"

"Come on. It's got to be the production manager who is fed up with all the changes."

Adolescent companies are in turmoil, struggling to move into Prime. There are too many transitions, too many secret meetings, and way too much inconsistency in corporate goals. Is it any wonder problems seem to linger interminably? Managers spend so much time in impromptu meetings that they have difficulty doing their jobs.

As you might expect, the managers of companies in Prime know how to deal with problems. You can identify them easily: They are people who bide their time. They don't react to crises; they anticipate them. They have the self-discipline to approach problems calmly and deliberately. That discipline comes only with years of experience, systematized into a continuously scrutinized system of planning and implementation.

Aristocracy is the first stop on the downward slope that beckons Prime companies. In aging companies that are nearing Aristocracy, problems grow increasingly opaque. Even the most attentive listener will find it difficult to follow the befuddled discussion among managers of such companies. Clarity is rare; and, it is rarer still that managers find solutions to their organization's problems. Managers know and use the stock phrases that get them off the hook: "Well, yes, I think that might work in some companies, but will it work here? That might fly under different circumstances." Managers have mastered the process of hedging.

STRUCTURE

Management teams of companies in Prime must strive to build a family of profit centers. Those should comprise one or more units at each of the developing stages of the lifecycle. Economies of scale justify the existence of corporate units. Companies in Prime must configure themselves to manage and nurture the diversity of their entrepreneurial and their administrative aspects, which naturally conflict. If one side dominates, the company can easily degenerate and lose its Prime condition. Integrators will monitor and control that conflict to conserve Prime.

A company in Prime is prolific, continually spinning off new companies and developing new products that fill the voids left by those businesses and products entering the death throes of their lifecycles. The revenues the newer product lines generate often exceed their predecessors'.

Brinker International has a portfolio of eating establishments. It has strategic alliances with creators of new concepts. It has the right of first refusal to use stock to buy any of the new, tested concepts. Brinker's structure lets it expand a concept until it runs its course, and then Brinker sells it.

The dangers for the emerging businesses, of course, are the same as those that confront any company in Infancy, Go-Go, or Adolescence. A company in Prime generates start-ups, and it has to spin them off, managing them in a nursery-like environment until the unit can survive on its own. At that point the parent integrates the offspring into the structure of the group that—in terms of market, service, product, or technology—suits it best. The company's vertical structure gradually gives way to a new horizontal structure.

A company in Prime might establish a business-generation unit charged with conceiving new businesses. I discourage calling these strategic planning units. Conception, I believe, requires more than thinking and planning. The business-generation unit's success is a function of the number of operational business plans it generates and the number of those the company implements. The unit ought to have a seed money budget to develop those plans.

A second unit, the business-development unit, performs a nursery function. Its responsibility, once it accepts a business plan from the business-generation unit, is to bring the start-up to viability (defined as break-even operation when costs include fully loaded overheads and depreciation for invested intellectual property) within a specified period. In other words, one unit is responsible for Courtship to Infancy and another for Infancy to Go-Go. Once the new business has attained the Go-Go stage, it joins the existing group that best corresponds to its markets and or product line. That is how a Prime company controls its growth and prevents any single unit from using its existing power base to suffocate newborns or to neglect them.

The solid structure of a company in Prime should equip it to act as midwife to those wailing bundles of vital energy. As we have seen, newborn entities require a broad range of organizational systems and management methods to get them through their early stages. Their needs force the parent to build deep reservoirs of talents, skills, and management styles. A dynamic momentum emerges: Ideas and exciting possibilities are always percolating. By generating continuous, successful rebirths, a parent in Prime may conceivably maintain the family forever young.

STRATEGY

Leaders of Prime companies should spin off new businesses. They need to look for opportunities to diversify. Those opportunities— preferably generated internally rather than acquired externally— should fit within the capabilities of their companies. Diversification for its own sake is a mistake, and diversification—even when well planned and justified—will not produce the desired results unless it is followed by a structural redesign. Diversification, expansion of the product line into new markets, is more than just adding more revenues and people. It is like expanding the family with a new child. One has to prepare a room for the baby correctly positioned near the parents' room, babyproof the house, and make sure there is someone caring for the baby at all times. Corporate diversification, whether by internal growth, acquisition, or merger, requires restructuring of the company.

Consider the difference between sales and marketing. During Go-Go and Adolescence everyone's focus is on sales. Whatever the customer wants, the company provides. Never mind shrinking margins. Every opportunity is an excellent opportunity. The company fears that any opportunity it passes up will cause it to lose market share and perhaps perish. Opportunities drive the company in its earlier stages.

In Prime, however, marketing dominates. Careful, conscious consideration of every customer need, its potential for revenues and long- and short-term impact on costs, precedes action. Unless the market's demand for a particular product is in line with the company's marketing plans, the company in Prime lets the opportunity go by. In its earlier growth stages, the company had to be utterly opportunistic and flexible. Companies in Prime, despite the distress of their founders, who have focused with single-minded determination on the customers and their needs, rein in opportunism with selectivity and control, flexibility with strategy.

The equilibrium of flexibility and control is anything but constant. Always battling a certain instability caused by the perpetual change, the company in Prime is always listing to one side. That is why it is so easy to slide into the declining stages of the corporate lifecycle.

How do you verify whether a company is operating at Prime? Just open its annual report. What is its growth strategy? Is it growing, for the most part, through acquisitions? I can tell you that such a company is not in Prime, regardless of the proud claims of its annual report. Growth purely by acquisition and doing more of the same signifies expansion but not development. Those mergers and acquisitions may be pumping up corporate revenues, but it is evident that the company has lost vitality. Corporate vitality depends on continual renewal of entrepreneurial spirit and commitment to generating and creating a company's own new products and services.

STAFFING

Staffing of every unit should reflect the location on the lifecycle and its requisite leadership style. The business-generation unit, which calls for imaginative leadership, needs people who, uninhibited by pressures to make a success of the unit, can both dream and convince those who will execute their plan that the dream is worthwhile.

Companies in Prime need a team of leaders with a diversity of styles and skills. They need people who are able to lead businesses at their various stages of development. A diversity of businesses at different stages of the lifecycle should be staffed by a diversity of styles and reinforced by a diversity of rewards. Prime calls for systematized diversity. Prime companies should always be training their future leaders. Luminaries on the boards of directors can help with strategic and global insights.

Prime companies ought to have their full complement of entrepreneurs, administrators, integrators, and producers balanced in such a way that no one group controls any of the others. To maintain that delicate balance, management and human resource specialists who understand Prime must direct their attention to the staffing function.

REWARDS

Like adolescent companies, Prime companies need to peg management's rewards to the type of work their managers do and their ability to influence results. Diversity is called for: stock options, profit sharing, and individual and group bonuses. Workers should earn the largest part of their compensation in the form of salaries, a small part as a percentage of their earnings in the form of bonuses for individual achievement, and a smaller part as a bonus based on their immediate teams' achievements. The smallest part will come from stock options. Top management's compensation, by comparison, should comprise primarily appreciation of their stock options, followed in size by a bonus for corporate results, and salary should be the smallest part of the total. Compensation for the rest of the organization should be combinations of those two extremes.

When companies make the transition to Prime, they need to strengthen the reward systems they established during Adolescence. Reward systems are as significant during Prime as at any other stage of the lifecycle: Properly constructed, reward systems point the organization in the right direction, helping to attain the delicate balance between flexibility and control. Founders, the original entrepreneurs who still own a certain portion of their companies, should continue to earn rewards based on the overall success of their companies, often measured in terms of return on investment (ROI). The rewards system for the people in producer, administrator, and integrator functions should be structured so that succeeding levels of each earn lower salaries and increasing levels of incentive compensation.

Producers measure their accomplishments hourly and daily: sales, production, delivery attainment, quality, and costs. The incentive portion of their compensation packages, which is tied to sales, production, delivery attainment, quality, and costs, should be short-term, measurable, and verifiable. A compensation package based on ROI would make no sense for producers since the factors they affect are measurable in the short term. "I did it, now pay me for what I've just accomplished," is the producer's refrain.

Administrators want to earn decent salaries, but they also yearn for job security, fringe benefits, and health insurance. Compensation based on measurable results is not as meaningful for cost accountants, results that are equivalent to a producer's sales or production measurements. In fact, a measurement in the case of, say, cost accountants, could backfire. Its failure is that it follows the street lamp fallacy:

A man walks down a dark street in the middle of the night. He encounters a friend looking for something under a street lamp.

"What are you looking for?" he asks.

"I lost my keys," the friend replies.

"Where?"

"Down there, at the end of the street."

"So, why are you looking over here?" our guy asks.

"Because the light is better up here," he responds.

Some managers who try to avoid making subjective judgments devise quantitative systems for determining rewards. Such systems are about as rational as the guy above who lost his keys. When people use a formula as a replacement for thinking, they invite the beginning of their exit from Prime.

So beware. Other than the number of reports completed on time and error-free, there is little to measure. Reports do not have the same relative impact as sales and production on company profitability. I like to tie accountants' rewards to the profitability of the units they serve.

Entrepreneurial types other than founders want to know what they must do to earn stock options. They all want a piece of the action because they know their contributions ensure their companies' longevity. They focus on building business: Their long-term success is their companies' long-term success. Entrepreneurs want to become owners and partners.

Integrators need team-based rewards since their essential task is to bring their companies' disparate functions into harmony.

Why is a company like Minnesota Mining and Manufacturing (3M) so successful? That company pegs much of its reward system on the introduction of new products, enterprises, and ventures. Its executives earn compensation packages commensurate with the revenue their organizations derive from products introduced within the most recent three-year period. That, of course, is a great motivator, and 3M's executives spend considerable time focusing organizational resources on building new and improved products and opening new market niches.

PLANNING AND GOALS

Companies in Prime focus with single-mindedness on enhancing both profits and sales. They do, however, take time out to develop future resources, most notably the company's managerial staff. Sustaining Prime is the overriding goal.

Planning is not reserved to top management. It is spread throughout the organization, and at the top, all planning is integrated. Each unit has a goal that (if it is a profit center) reflects its position in the lifecycle. We measure the success of organizations in Adolescence by how well they control their budgets; in Go-Go, by market share; and in Infancy, by chances of survival. The success of organizations in Prime is a function of the number of new units they create. And I don't mean units they acquire. The success of Prime's business-generation unit is measured by how many of its plans get approved for implementation. The goals in those Courtship units in the aggregate will produce an organization that can remain in Prime. The business-generation unit conceives the future, and business development secures attention for the newborn. Go-Go aims for market penetration and later cost control, and eventually that organization reaches Prime.

WHERE DO YOU STAND? A CHECKLIST

Normal Problems of Prime

- The company never seems to have enough of the kind of talent it needs, and it is engaged in a continuous search for more and better people.

Abnormal Problems of Prime

- The headquarters staff gains more and more authority, which it takes from increasingly disempowered staff on the line.
- The finance and legal departments become more powerful than marketing and sales.

- The finance department makes budgets, which top management approves and then delegates to the heads of divisions.
- Rewards are based on short-term results only.
- Only a minority of the company's stockholders, if any, are company employees.
- Relying on past successes, the company depends on its tried and true lines. Only a small portion of revenues comes from products that did not exist three years ago.
- Decision making is centralized in the leader.
- The organization depends on a single leader for its development and growth.
- With no clear mission, the company repeats the past rather than inventing the future.

CHAPTER 8

Aging: Getting Old Is Forgetting Your Customers

—————— *Aging: A Parable* ——————

During a recent cross-country flight, I struck up a conversation with the elderly gentleman sitting next to me.

Charles: We've a proven track record in our industry.

I: How are your profits?

Charles: Great.

I: Your prices?

Charles: We just raised them.

I: Had you improved your product?

Charles: Customers love the product. You should see our new offices. They are built around a three-story atrium. We have an executive dining room with our own French chef. The boss loves art: He's even got the board ready to buy our own Picasso.

I: You sure you're still in touch with your market?

> Charles. Absolutely. We just acquired this cutting-edge young company. Dynamite energy. They have given us a real shot in the arm.
>
> I sighed. I knew Charles's company was in for some troubled times.

AGING

Any time a company's office decor becomes more important than its product, you can assume that the company is declining from Prime.

Companies slip into middle age when they start to lose their flexibility. Performance plateaus. Then it starts to slide. Declining companies lose their appetite for innovation. Business seems to be going so smoothly. Nobody wants to rock the boat. Any change, people worry, could jeopardize what looks like true success. So management institutionalizes its shortsighted focus: The goal is to maintain the status quo rather than to draft a blueprint for expansion.

Despite its failure to continue innovating, a declining company's sales may continue to rise for a few years, thanks to residual momentum and its good name. But the entrepreneurial spark is dying, and creativity is sapped. People spend more and more time fretting about internal issues, leaving little energy for working with clients.

Meetings lengthen because no one cares that time is being stolen from productive work. Form supersedes function. Office decor, decorum, and attire are very serious matters. Where a meeting is held and who attends it are more important issues than what the meeting accomplishes. Achievements cannot easily be attributed to an individual because in an aging company the authority and responsibilities are disconnected, and people do not understand their responsibilities, much less their authority. So even though everyone who attends admits in confidence that little if anything actually happens, people go through the rituals of meetings. It is so difficult to assemble and bring all those affected by and all those who affect a particular decision into agreement that it takes numerous meetings to accomplish anything.

After one particularly notable aging company restructured to clarify accountability, it was able to disband 200 permanent committees. How could that be? In an aging company, committees take the place of normal hierarchy. That structure promotes rigidity over flexibility. As its reflexes grow creaky, and too slow to respond to market developments, the company loses its edge.

Still, for awhile, the company remains profitable, and business appears to be thriving. The truth is that those earnings reflect price increases rather than rising sales. Eventually those high prices will consume the market share, and the company's neglected research and development will have no new products or services to offer. The finance department, with its focus on return on investment, has more sway than marketing, research, or sales. Everyone looks more to past or ongoing achievements than to real commitments for the future. People earn rewards for doing what they are told to do because they recognize a clear disincentive for initiating change.

The picture is pretty glum, characterized by massive denial of what is happening. That denial is organizational rather than personal dishonesty. Individually people do speak about their fears and worries, but when they get together, their behavior changes, and they act as if there is nothing to worry about. As the environment changes and results deteriorate, the organization's rigidity interferes with prompt corrective action, and paranoia sets in: It must be someone's fault; there must be someone to blame. Because communication is formal and indirect, even substantive ideas get lost in obfuscation.

The company's product lines are dying, and it has allocated insufficient funds for research and development. The company spends its money unproductively on benefits, buildings, and dividends. The climate is not, to paraphrase President Kennedy, one of what you can do for your company. It is, instead, what the company can do for you. It is the time of milking, not feeding; the time of entitlement, not sacrifice or investment.

Like aging men and women who, as they grow older, also grow increasingly selfish, people throughout the organization know their days are numbered, and they fear there won't be enough for survival. They aim to wring as much as possible out of what is left. They know they have neither energy nor time to replenish what they have lost. Everyone feels a lurking sense of unease.

People recognize that the company has lost its vitality, but they are afraid to speak out. Panic sets in when, as has been inevitable, sales start to slip, and cash flow turns negative. Suddenly everyone is desperate for a quick fix.

Most companies, when they first slip into old age, are flush with cash. Their managers make desperate bids to regain vitality by throwing money at the problems. They buy a dynamic young company and quickly stifle its entrepreneurial enthusiasm with their sclerotic management style. Its bright stars flee to companies that promise creative freedom, leaving the adoptive parent company with another dying limb.

THE FOUR STAGES
OF AN AGING ORGANIZATION

Companies that are aging (eventually dying) go through four warning stages: Stability, Aristocracy, Recrimination, and, particularly in those organizations that don't rely on a customer base for survival, Bureaucracy. We will discuss the ultimate condition, Death, in the next chapter.

Stability

In the stage that follows Prime, companies still seem strong. The first signs of aging are only barely perceptible. Profit margins are high but flat. Managers yield to the dangerous temptation to boost revenues or profit margins by raising prices. They welcome new ideas, but they receive them with suspicion. With its early entrepreneurial spirit pretty much depleted, fewer and fewer of its people expect they can get the company to grow and expand by exploring new markets.

In short, the company can no longer maintain the dynamic balance of flexibility versus control: Control is gaining the upper hand. Power drifts from marketing, research, and development functions to finance and administration. Managers grow increasingly narcissistic. They are much more absorbed in their company's politics and procedures than in their customers' satisfaction. They try to keep Wall Street's enthusiasm alive with short-term results rather than with long-term appreciation of stockholders' value.

An organization's inability to approach the future aggressively diminishes its ability to respond to short-term problems and opportunities. A sure sign that an organization is slipping out of Prime is, therefore, its lack of aggressive, explicit, and constructive conflict. Where there is little change, explicit, constructive conflict is rare.

Managers who once competed for resources and ownership of ideas no longer fight those battles. Their growing inclination to remain silent is, however, temporary. During the advanced stages of aging, there is conflict, but people do not express themselves openly. Controversy and discord in the corridors become more prevalent. Eventually, when the company reaches Recrimination, the atmosphere will have grown so destructive that people feel they need to undermine one another to protect their own jobs.

As long as creativity remains dormant, the company will lose its ability to discover and respond to its market.

Aristocracy

A company in Aristocracy is in the early stages of its slow disintegration. It is cash-rich, but its managers are afraid to invest that cash creatively. Instead they take shelter in the safety of overnight Treasury bills, and they spend their time meeting with one another in the luxury of well-appointed offices. They avoid risk. Rather than hatch new

AGING: THE SLIPPERY SLOPE

The current chief executive of Sears, Roebuck and Co., Arthur Martinez, has turned his company's direction back toward Prime, but its slide from Prime during the 1970s and 1980s still serves as a textbook example of an aging company.

Sears, founded in 1886, had for years been one of the lions of American business. It had vanquished key competitors, notably Montgomery Ward, and reached the top of its industry. At one point, Sears's merchandising revenues were four times the sum of its four closest competitors'. In 1972, only four U.S. companies (AT&T, Eastman Kodak, General Motors, and Exxon) commanded a higher stock market valuation. Its premier retail position appeared unassailable.

The remarkable, long-lasting success must have deadened the senses of the company's managers, buoying their confidence in the status quo. They devoted themselves to preserving the fortress that had served so well for so long. In that complacency and arrogance, they built the Sears Tower, then the world's tallest building, which opened in 1973 in Chicago.

The construction was a monument to the company's slip from Prime. Inside, Sears executives gloried in past successes. They seemed to wall themselves off from customers. Managerial control replaced flexibility; tradition supplanted innovation. The decision-making process became more important than decisions that made results. The company maintained a library of instructive management bulletins that covered every eventuality.

To expand the company's sagging results, management went on a buying spree, looking for youth and growth somewhere else. Sears acquired Dean Witter and Coldwell Banker, reasoning that the company's retail magic would work its wonders in the worlds of stocks, bonds, and real estate.

But true to the pattern of companies in the aging phase, Sears failed to recognize how the marketplace had changed. Even into the 1980s, Sears's marketing documents failed to mention that retail juggernaut Wal-Mart. By the time Sears acknowledged its true competition, discounters and specialty retailers, it was no longer strong enough to catch up. In one year alone, Sears reported a loss (including special charges) of $3.9 billion.

And that was Sears, Roebuck and Co. in 1992.

products and services, they purchase them from other companies or buy those companies outright. Ironically, their company is itself an excellent candidate for a takeover. They are immobilized by their confidence that past successes will carry them into the future. But individually, they acknowledge that deep inside they know that the past will not and cannot create the future. They know for sure that change is coming, and it will be change for the worse. They want to move, but their inability to get their acts together immobilizes them. They measure every move for its internal political dangers rather than for its external market opportunities. The company judges managers by their conformance to dress codes and conservative behavior. Agitators who make waves are fired.

Recrimination

Inaction finally brings about the inevitable loss of market share and negative cash flow. The witch-hunts start, as project after project fails to meet expectations. The rot begins to permeate the company's structure. People don't ask, "What caused the problem? What can we do to fix it?" They are much more prone to ask, "Who is to blame for this disaster?" Conflict among the company's executives and managers intensifies. Backstabbing and infighting are commonplace. The prevailing attitude is that customers are nuisances who demand too much attention. People are all busy protecting their backs. The company is flirting with collapse, and most of its executives feel powerless. It will not survive this stage unless people turn it around or put it under a protective umbrella. Protected from the market, though, it becomes a Bureaucracy.

To become a Bureaucracy, a company does not necessarily pass through all the previous stages. Some organizations are even born bureaucratic. Companies become bureaucracies when organizational survival does not depend on the satisfaction of customers: Organizational resources are a result of the ego gratification of a fund-raiser or, perhaps, not-for-profit ideological or religious enthusiasm.

Bureaucracy

Organizations in public service bureaucracies are ruled by so many policies, systems, and procedures that they choke themselves. Meaningful activity exists only at a tremendous cost. Rather than working to achieve results, people expend way too much energy on measures that aim to protect individuals or the organization from making a politically dangerous move. Such protective behavior is common in bureaucracies that are public service oriented. In not-for-profit companies like volunteer, religious, or arts organizations, inaction is a result of following a goal other than client satisfaction. The goal might be the religious intent or the gratification of the artist who heads the organization. It is not strange then that what is ignored behaves as if it has been ignored, and the organization loses its effectiveness in the marketplace.

In business organizations that became bureaucratized through nationalization or government ownership, the managers in sales and production are so tied up in paperwork, or so mired in office squabbles and difficulties, that they have little time left to attend to their jobs. What's more, they believe that their jobs are secure because they are treated like public servants. When people are secure in their jobs, and they know they will be rewarded regardless of their achievements, we can expect little from them. People in such positions don't seek rewards: They avoid punishment. Employees fear to extend themselves beyond the call of protocol: They know such initiative will invite criticism from someone who interprets the excursion as an affront. They know it is easy—and dangerous—to step into someone else's domain.

Meanwhile, the company continues to ignore its troublesome customers. It focuses energies on pleasing revenue sources other than customers: politicians, volunteers, or fund contributors. And, the competition attracts the company's neglected customers by serving them well. You don't need to listen very hard to hear the echoes of the organization's imminent Death rattle. And Death comes when the revenue sources decide that the organization is a liability rather than an asset.

There is a story from the ancient Middle East about two thieves who had been sentenced to die. One of them had the wit to send a message to the sultan saying that if the sultan would grant him another six years to live, he would teach the sultan's favorite horse to speak.

When the other thief expressed surprise, the first thief explained, "Six years is a long time. The sultan might die. The horse might die. And, who knows, maybe the horse will speak."

Executives of a moribund company subscribe to the same reasoning. The company is not yet dead, and while it is true that it might die six years from now, six years is a long time. Maybe the company's distressing problems will disappear. Maybe the competitors will go bankrupt. Maybe the company will have new products and services available by then. They usually specify external solutions supplied by forces outside the company. In those cases, I use a joke to make my point. A Mexican businessman told me the joke, but it applies to every situation where people passively await salvation. There are two potential solutions to the Mexican economic problem," he said. "One is logical; the other is a miracle. The logical solution is that Santa Guadalupe will come from heaven and solve the problem. The miracle is that Mexico will get off its rear end and do something."

In my work, I try to impress the client with the need to take initiative: There is no outside solution. Here is another story I use to illustrate the need for action: There was a righteous man who always worshipped God by the book. When terrible floods threatened his house, he climbed to his roof and waited calmly. "God will save me. I have always been a righteous man, and I have lived by God's word." A rescue team came by in a boat and offered to take him off the roof, but he refused the help saying, "God will save me." The water continued to rise until it was touching his feet, but he remained calm. "God," he repeated, "will save me." When a rescue helicopter came to take him to safety, he again refused to leave because he trusted God. The waters continued to rise, and eventually the man drowned. When the man arrived at the gates of Heaven, he faced the Lord with a complaint: "Why did you not save me? Have I not always been a righteous man? I followed the book word for word." The Lord's voice thundered His reply. "What do you mean? I sent you a rescue boat, and you refused to get on board. I sent you a helicopter, and again you refused to leave your roof."

What causes such paralysis of action? Another story might illustrate the reason.

When I was a high school student, my friends and I—about twenty in all—took an all-night train from the border of Spain to Paris. We took a single compartment, which, under normal circumstances, would accommodate eight to ten people. Two people slept on the bunks. Some slept on the floor. Some slept on one another's laps, a hand here, a foot there. After about two hours we had finally arranged ourselves, and we settled down to get some rest. It didn't take long before one of the group decided it was time to go to the bathroom. What a commotion. The rest of us had to unfold ourselves and clear a path. To get out, the person had to wake and inconvenience the whole group. He had to get permission to go to the bathroom from almost every one us.

In aging companies, it generally is easier to relieve yourself in your pants—to learn to live with your problems—than it is to go to the bathroom—to cause change that affects the interests of many others. Change, making waves, comes hard. The benefits of change are quite uncertain, while its political price is certainly high. Why take chances?

The executives of companies in the aristocratic stage have no incentive to upset their colleagues. If they lie low long enough, they may earn promotions. Those executives who attempt to try to do their jobs, stepping on too many toes in the process, find that their names are scratched off the promotion list.

Introducing change usually means having an impact on other people. If there is no system for cooperative change, it will be a real or imaginary threat to others. Anyone who feels threatened will try to discredit the impetus for change and its carrier. Experienced people understand that dynamic: They do not disturb the silence. They discuss change, but they do nothing. Instead they search for signs of hope—real or imaginary.

Prior to the civil war in Bosnia, I met with Slobodan Milosevic. The Serbs and the Croats had already started shooting. I had been invited to help keep the war from spreading. Obviously, my mission was not successful. I tried to reason with the cabinet, explaining logically—and, as history has shown, correctly—that the Serbs would be isolated and other governments would impose sanctions. The cabinet responded, "Don't worry. The Russians will not let that happen." At that time, Russia was weak, begging for foreign aid, and politically quite isolated. It was inconceivable that Russia would use the little political muscle it had to assist Serbia.

Whenever I work with bureaucracies, people always explain to me that solutions will arise from outside their effort. They challenge me to get them to consider reality. I need to restore or reintroduce leadership that is solidly grounded.

Leaders of bureaucratic organizations are always politically astute. They have a nearly infallible ability to say what people want to hear while doing only what is without political risk. In the political world, frequently what people say is not what they mean, and it is rarely clear who the real decision makers—the people who can make things happen—are. There are both real and imaginary centers of power.

I was so lost in the case of crumbling Yugoslavia that I called on my dear friend Ken Adelman, a former United States Ambassador to the United Nations, and asked him for help. What I learned was that people in bureaucracies are extremely pleasant, unlike people in Go-Go organizations who show no respect, fail to come to meetings, and challenge each other. In Go-Go organizations, you really find out what's going on. That is not the case in political bureaucracies. The Serbs worked hard to make me feel welcome. I felt that I should be able to get the parties to agree and cooperate. Like all other bureaucratic organizations, people came to meetings prepared, smiling, politely agreeing. But nothing happened. I discoved that I had wasted a significant percentage of my life on nothing.

It's easy to stand pat during Aristocracy, because, for the most part, the organization's results—the residual effects of those heady days when the company was in Prime—still look good. But those effects eventually dissipate. That is when the company tries to improve operating results by raising prices and cutting expenses. On the surface, the company looks robust. But if you take a look at the number of units shipped, the broad-based decline will be obvious. Everyone is counting on higher prices to compensate for the shortfall. That behavior is accentuated when inflation is in play. Even accountants have difficulty differentiating real change from changes caused by inflation.

Because the company continues to feed the dog its own tail, the dog will eventually disappear. Executives are justifiably terrified of the real possibility that their customers will balk at the price increases and that sales will fall even more, but, because the political price of interfering with the organization's direction is so steep, no one even tries.

During aging, life progresses from bad to worse. The company starts to experience negative cash flow, a condition it hasn't seen in years, possibly since its Infancy. At first nobody believes that the situation could have deteriorated so badly. Then panic takes over. Everyone knows downsizing is next, and everyone dreads getting a pink slip. In periods of crisis, employees focus on survival: They cannot give work their full attention, and their company slips inexorably deeper into the hole. Shoddy quality and repeated failure to deliver on time further irritate customers who have better and better reason to question the price increases. The competition looks good to those customers.

The drive to hold down costs during the aging stages of a corporation's life has its consequences: cut, cut, cut. In their frenzy to reduce costs, eager executives cut away sinew and muscle along with the fat. By then, the company will have pushed the limit on price increases. With costs pared to the point where the company can no longer provide the services and quality that customers have come to expect, profits will tumble. The company has entered its Recrimination stage. Witch-hunts start in earnest.

SPOTTING THE SIGNS

When did the decline begin? What were those first almost imperceptible signs? Decline commences when everyone least suspects it: in Prime. That's when complacency sets in. Slowly but surely, instead of aggressively initiating new products, services, and ventures, the company's executives begin to narrow their focus to today's products and services. Their goal is to maintain profitability by reducing costs, and so they discover 100 ways to shave the costs of research and development, manufacturing, sales, and support functions like marketing. Their chintzy inward focus is the first sure sign of decline. The company has lost its adventuresome, aggressive character. Instead of finding ways to increase revenues, they look for ways to cut costs only.

Do not misunderstand me. I am all in favor of cutting unnecessary costs, but after all attention has been focused on increasing revenues. Nobody can evaluate costs in a vacuum. Certain costs support the planned increases in revenues. Too many companies have paid enormous amounts in severance packages. Then, slim and trim, they redouble their push to expand sales. They need to hire people just like those people they paid dearly to fire.

Moving from Aristocracy, you can easily recognize a company in the Recrimination stage: The atmosphere is thick with managerial paranoia. There are fierce witch-hunts to locate someone to sacrifice for the greater good—your job and mine (mostly mine).

The first targets are the entrepreneurs who have been knocking their heads against a wall trying to get the company to initiate new ventures. Those entrepreneurial types are the managers in strategic planning, marketing, and research and development who have been frustrated by the inaction and paranoia. Their fighting for change did not endear them politically, and when the time comes to downsize, they are high on the hit list. The company's executives accuse them of having the wrong attitudes, having made bad decisions, having placed the company in the wrong markets, and having developed the wrong mix of products and services. This is a typical witch-hunt where someone has to pay the price for the company's condition.

Such witch-hunts do not stop at the vice presidential level. They can go all the way to the president's office. Even a new president who has made all the right moves will get fired if those moves have not yet borne fruit. The board needs someone to blame for the investment community.

Recrimination can continue to worsen: Backstabbing, infighting, and political maneuvering rule the day. No holds are barred, and colleagues who used to work as members of a team now feel threatened and compelled to explain their positions. Others interpret those position statements as attacks on them, and they, in term, have to present their own position. They start around the same circle.

If Recrimination does not end in corporate bankruptcy or turnaround, Bureaucracy, the next stage in the downward progression, takes over. In Bureaucracy, top executives are free to play the endgame of the dying corporation. They set out in search of salvation. That can mean frantic lobbying in Washington for legislative or regulatory relief. The executives, who can no longer remember what it means to be in Prime, resist Death the only way their limited imaginations allow: with artificial life-support systems.

Like animals gravitating to water, the executives search out money from those who support them for political, social, or ideological reasons. But those who provide the money are not necessarily the clients who benefit from the company's services. Consider, for example, the case of one of my clients. For three years, I worked with a children's services department, part of a division of social services. The clients are the abused children, but they are not the source of the money. The funding comes from the government. Guess where top management spends its energies and time: caring for children or lobbying the government? Doing social work or filing papers and reports? The top goal of management is to avoid becoming a political liability—especially in an election year.

The same dynamic is at work in artistic and cultural organizations that receive the bulk of their funds not from operations (box office sales) but from the wealthy members of the community and the government. Guess who will earn the attention of those organizations? The attitude of an organization in Recrimination is in stark contrast to that of one in the Go-Go stage. Once, during a visit to a Go-Go company, I saw a plaque on the desk of the vice president of sales: "The only source of our revenues is our clients. Cherish them."

When a company exists despite its detachment from its clients and their needs, it will eventually find itself in the Bureaucracy stage.

Unless it redirects its attention to the changing marketplace, that company will continue its direct approach to its Death throes.

But strange as it may seem, incipient rigor mortis is not inconsistent with a great deal of confusion. The aging company grows increasingly disorganized. Systems that once helped guide the company's procedures fall into disarray. Everyone is closed-mouthed. Managers defending their turf do not communicate well with competing fiefdoms. They withhold useful information. Employees do not know what they must do to earn incentive compensation. Salespeople are not up to date on the company's marketing plans. Production managers are unaware of the customers' quality problems. And, most important of all, customers do not know to whom they should take their problems. They have lost confidence even in the CEO.

Aging companies run on ritual rather than reason. Ask almost any employee for an explanation for certain processes, and the reply is likely to be, "I don't know. It's company policy. Don't expect me to violate it."

Like grandparents who adore their grandchildren—in small doses—the aging organization considers its customers nuisances and its vendors relentless irritations. More and more, its executives isolate themselves from such distractions. They rationalize their withdrawal, claiming they are simply following established procedures.

In many such situations, the executives restrict the company's means of communication with the outside world. The aging company conducts its correspondence by fax, e-mail, telephone, and letter. Seldom do insiders and outsiders meet face to face. The barricades do nothing more than further isolate the company from reality, its markets, and its customers. Disintegration prevails. The organization degenerates into decay

Reversing the Aging Process

What's the answer? What can executives do to rejuvenate their aging companies? They need to go on a diet and get more flexible. To get their companies back in shape, they need to cut management layers, decentralize, hire talented people with fresh ideas, make risk-taking a cultural tenet, banish as many control systems as possible, sell off secondary businesses, and, most important, refocus every person, every process, and every ounce of organizational energy on the company's products and customers.

I heard that when a new CEO took over SAS Airlines, he called in all the top managers, put all the company manuals on the table, and, in one swing, cleared the table, sweeping the manuals to the floor. "Now," he said, "let's start from the beginning."

Back in the 1970s, when I worked with the United States Postal Service to make it professionally managed rather than politically managed, one of our first tasks was to cut the manual's thousands of pages down to a few hundred. People did not like it at all. It was as if someone had snatched their security blanket. They told me that they felt naked and exposed. Many of them took early retirement because their world had become too risky.

Still, that is what needs to be done, and the why is obvious. In my experience, the place where many organizations fail in rejuvenating aging companies is in the how and the when. The situation is analogous to gourmet cuisine. It is not enough simply to have the right ingredients. One needs a recipe that tells the when and the how. A recipe that details the entire sequence spells the difference between success and failure. To insure success, the chef adds the correct proportion of every ingredient at the correct time and in the appropriate manner.

I once saw a cartoon that showed a lobby of a medical building. The directory on the wall lists all the doctors and their specialties. The last doctor's specialty is listed as "side effects." I worked with a company that had tried to rejuvenate itself using a long, expensive program that, for more than a year, focused on vision and values. The managers discussed to death what they wanted the company to be, but they did little other than festoon the hallways with platitude-studded posters. No one should have been surprised by the staff's resulting cynicism. People could muster no enthusiasm for the next attempt to change their company. I wish I had a dollar for each company where people have assured me that "we hate consultants."

I have come into companies that are suffering the effects of consultants' recommendations to downsize. They imposed a new structure without getting the opinions or benefiting from the experience of the people involved. No wonder everyone in those companies feared and resisted change. What happened? Rather than unearthing and dealing with reasons for potential resistance to the proposed rejuvenation in the planning stages, the consultants had proceeded with their implementation and waited passively for resistance to come to the surface.

The prolonged change process was unnecessarily painful, and while the company was preoccupied with its reorganization problems, its competition did not stand idly by.

What, then, is the right way to proceed?

The first, exceptionally challenging step is the most important. Like the first step in Alcoholics Anonymous and other well-known change programs, the first step must be to stop the denial. The company has to recognize that yes, it is aging, and it has lost its once golden position in Prime. People feel incredible relief when they can finally remove their masks. After that first workshop, the participants feel emancipated from the lies. Truth, like sunshine, is with them. With the truth on the table, people sense that, finally, there is a chance that the company's real problems will be addressed and perhaps become manageable.

What do I mean by manageable? We start with a workshop, a synergistic diagnosis, that I have dubbed Syndag. It is composed of the leadership of the company, the people who are in a position to make a difference: CEO, COO, vice presidents, and, occasionally, members of the board of directors. When I have worked with organizations in Germany and Israel, the leaders of the labor unions took part, too. The group identifies and analyzes only those problems that the participants believe they, themselves, are able to manage or control. We avoid discussion or analysis of them. We focus only on us.

The purposes of that workshop, then, are to remove denial and to empower the group by putting problems squarely in their court. The group accepts responsibility for the problems. At the end of the workshop there is a specific plan of action detailing the problems that require a specific person's attention and those that call for a team effort.

Following that initial diagnostic workshop, the team reconvenes to learn how to manage meetings and deal constructively with conflict. The subsequent workshop focuses the team's attention on learning how to empower the rest of the organization to solve problems and deal with change. That series of three workshops takes about three months. I designed them to give the organization a sense of potency—a sense that one can deal with change and problems without endangering one's career.

During this period, people test the limits of authority and delegation. Once everyone feels the confidence to make change, however minuscule, we progress to work on the organization's mission, assigning people responsibility for analyzing the market and clients and determining the benchmark for the industry. The goals of this period are to open and sensitize the organization to its environment. Executives from production analyze client needs, and marketing executives analyze the technological capabilities. Cross-functional learning enhances mutual trust and respect.

Starting and ending the rejuvenation with visualizing and mission statements, as many other consultants recommend, is, in my opinion, a hopeless exercise. Why? If the mission or the vision indicate change, the organization also must be structured to deliver that change. In my experience, organizations that haven't effected power changes cannot progress beyond their vision and values change workshops. Without an organizational power change, there can be no behavioral change. Commitment commands a price. People have to be willing to change positions. Positioned for defense, it is impossible to mount an attack. Just as a change in military strategy requires rearrangement of the forces, a shift in mission requires organizational changes.

Thus, the program next addresses organizational design. We establish that units responsible for change will be operating independently of units needed to produce results. For instance, we separate marketing from sales. Whenever marketing and sales are under the same vice president, marketing suffers because all the energy and rewards are dedicated to sales. Short-term goals easily supplant long-term goals.

The organizational design will emancipate process and continuous-improvement engineering: Install a business generation unit and a business development group, set up profit centers as strategic business units grouped by market or product, and establish the accountability of support groups and the power and authority of profit centers. In aging companies, power lies with the so-called support groups: They are in reality the controlling groups. In Prime those responsibilities coincide with authority. When we restructure, we reestablish the authority of those with responsibility over those who support them. The redesign creates a political revolution because it reunites responsibility with authority.

Once we have reordered responsibility and authority, and people feel honestly empowered with the ways and means to effect change, we can reorganize information flows and start working on detailed strategies. Rarely does the rejuvenation process require us to change leadership. As the system changes, so does everyone's behavior. The organization's indigenous entrepreneurs simply had had no arena in which to act. In the course of creating that new arena, the full force of entrepreneurial spirit emerges from people who seemed like useless deadwood. We can revive the entrepreneurial life that lies hidden in aging companies.

That brings me to my distaste for the current managerial vogue: mechanistic downsizing and reengineering. Cutting off a foot is no way to trim one's weight. It's so easy to cut muscle as one tries to cut fat. To get in shape, one must both diet and exercise to build muscle. Using my program, we are able expand the sales and marketing forces without hiring additional personnel; we take people who had been in administrative roles. If they cannot change over time, we replace them, but first, they get a chance. We increase revenues and profitability without hiring or firing. We reallocate resources and give people time to adapt. Healing often calls for treatments other than surgery, treatments that take time. These days people's impatience sometimes leads them to undergo unnecessary surgery. Similarly, too many companies have submitted to unnecessary downsizings.

Trained and certified coaches for organizational transformation (such as those coaches who graduate with masters and doctoral degrees from the graduate school I established) can help management proceed with effective diagnosis and transformation. Only people of true humility can acknowledge the inadequacies of their own leadership. All CEOs take a measure of pride in their accomplishments. So, an outsider's periodic assessment helps management ascertain the company's stage in the lifecycle and the direction it is taking. An outsider's objective, unbiased point of view can help CEOs who want to make sure that their companies pursue Prime, stay in Prime, or return to Prime.

STYLE

A company in Aristocracy needs a leader who is entrepreneurial and task oriented. A leader who is exclusively an entrepreneur will cause much ado with few of the short-term results the company needs. A leader who is only task oriented may make life look good in the short run, but before long, the company will find itself in arrears. When a company falls into Recrimination, it needs a strong, production-oriented, short-term-focused leader. Unlike a company in its Aristocracy, the company in the Recrimination stage has no need for visionaries. It needs hands-on doers or hatchet men like Margaret Thatcher, the Iron Lady. The company in Recrimination has little room for strategies. First and foremost, the company is simply trying to survive.

During wartime in the days of the Roman Empire, democracy was set aside and a dictator took over. The company in the Recrimination stage needs a strong autocratic leader who can both pull the company together and make the hard choices that cut out what is unnecessary.

Such a person will be a liability in the next stage of decay. To rejuvenate a Bureaucracy, one needs a politically oriented person who knows how to keep the politically sensitive powers at bay while maintaining a clear vision of reality and courageously leading the process of change. Notice that as we rejuvenate a company, its leadership needs change just as they do during the growing stages.

STRUCTURE

The big problem for aging companies is their growing overhead. In spite of excessive expenditures, those companies are neither productive nor innovative. It is crucial to decentralize. To reverse the downward direction, executives should assign staff to groups that are profit centers and excise functions the profit centers will not support. Public service companies, with no profits to serve as the measure of success, need to be structured around the needs of their true clients. These needs become the surrogate profit centers. Aging companies rejuvenate through decentralization, but note that decentralization is not the remedy for all ills as some consultants religiously recommend.

For a growing, developing organization that has not yet reached Prime, decentralization is inappropriate. With no control systems, decentralization of a Go-Go organization only aggravates its lack of control. Diversification in Adolescence only emphasizes the diversion and disintegration an adolescent company already experiences. In Prime, diversification makes sense because there is a unifying direction, structure, control, and leadership.

In aging companies the process of decentralization is the cure because it leads to delegation of authority and to diversification. IBM, in my opinion, did the right thing when it reorganized. Unfortunately, John Akers, who orchestrated the change, didn't get to stay and see the results of his effective reorganization. Robert Allen at AT&T applied the right strategy for change by spinning off divisions.

STRATEGY

A company that has aged beyond the Prime condition has lost focus and drive. It's time to redefine the business, spin off what doesn't fit, and crank up the company's rusty skills and neglected strengths. In Go-Go the strategy focused on what less to do; in an aging company the focus must be on what else to do. I find aging companies to be like the sands of Saudi Arabia: What looks barren and dead hides incredible resources beneath the surface. The aristocratic company has, over the years, developed intellectual properties, networking assets, and technologies, which, although extremely valuable, have lain dormant for years. The organization has failed to exploit its resources.

Customers and the competition of a client of mine in that stage of the lifecycle said fearfully that all my client had to do was to wake up. Another client with a worldwide presence was organized into regional fiefdoms. Within a year of globalizing its structure, the company raised its bottom line by more than any one of its individual regions had ever earned.

When I face an Aristocracy, I examine its intangible assets: locations, unexplored and unexploited technologies, underutilized sales force, and the like. In my work with a very large retail company, I discovered that the company operated thousands of branches. Every year, billions of people visit those outlets. I had to ask myself what is the best use of the time those people spend there. To explore its hidden assets, we had to redefine the company's business, a task that was much more difficult than it might seem.

People get attached to names, definitions, and titles. They are all part of their identity. In another company, because the marketing reported to the sales department, there was no functioning marketing department. Nevertheless, it took almost three years to separate marketing from sales. That move provided more room for a marketing division that would lead rather than simply report on sales efforts.

The name issue was so highly charged in one of my cases, that people were literally willing to fight a war over it. That was my work with the Macedonian cabinet and prime minister. Because years earlier, I had worked with Constantine Mitsotakis, the prime minister of Greece, I knew government members from both Greece and Macedonia. I offered to facilitate a resolution to the dispute over the name of the newly established state of Macedonia.

The Greeks objected to the name because it expressed, in their minds, intentions of the Macedonian government to extend its boundaries into Greek Macedonia. The Macedonian government's resolution stating that it had no geographic aspirations beyond the existing boundaries didn't help. It also made no difference to the Greeks that even if Macedonia had territorial aspirations, it was hopelessly underpowered to realize them.

Greece imposed an embargo that badly hurt both nations. When I was able to convince the Greek side to consider the appellation New Macedonia, the Macedonian prime minister rejected it, telling me that such a change would send his country into civil war. "How," I asked myself, "could three letters have the power to bring war?" But, it turns out, he was right. To lift the embargo, Macedonia did raise a new flag unlike the one the Greeks objected to. That very day, Kiro Gligorov, Macedonia's president, was ambushed and nearly killed.

To redefine a company's business is tantamount to redefining who it is, and the transformation is emotional and painful. To redefine, one must undergo a change of the third order. Let me explain what I mean by order change. Assume you want to change and lose weight. The first order change calls for you to go on a diet and reduce your intake of calories. Starving yourself (with intermittent binges) will work only for awhile. To achieve a more permanent weight loss, you will need to change your eating habits. That is order change number two. Note, however, that even that will not work in the long run.

For a more permanent loss of weight, you will need to go through change order number three: altering your perception of yourself. No longer can you hate being fat; instead, you must love being thin. That is a change in self-perception, in self-image, in self-esteem.

Many people try to achieve results of the second order or third order while making only changes of the first order. In my opinion, that is why Sears, Roebuck failed in its attempt to diversify. Management added real estate (Coldwell Banker) and insurance (Allstate), assuming that the existing retail outlets would be able to handle those sales efficiently. The power structure, the definition of who the company is, remained strictly retail. Compare it with the following case.

I tried to rejuvenate a large bank by changing its definition: making order change number three. Banking was a dying concept: Competition on both the demand and supply sides made the business of making money on money—paying lower interest on savings than the interest charged for loans—barely profitable. The bank had to emulate investment banking and brokerage services, making money from fees. That is, the bank had to change from being a bank to being a financial services institution.

Such a change, I found, is as difficult as a religious conversion. Jealousies run amok. Top bankers make in a year what an average investment banker can earn in a single week. Traders don't want to work for old-fashioned bankers who do not understand their artistic flair and business creativity. What was admirable to one group was detestable to the other.

An aging company needs to diversify, but it is wasting its time and money unless cultural diversification accompanies the business diversification. That calls for a new definition of self.

Back to Macedonia. If Macedonia is for the Macedonians, what are the Albanians in Macedonia? Or for that matter, if Israel is a Jewish state, what are its Arab citizens? If one of the components dominates in name, rituals, recognition, rewards, and so forth, you cannot lay claim to a concept of equality. But, if you call your country New Macedonia, both Macedonians and Albanians can be New Macedonians.

Transformation is difficult, I find, because people want a new strategy without yielding the old one. Everyone wants more rather than instead.

STAFFING

Aging companies need to reduce employment, but it is important to establish which people can contribute to growth. To regain Prime, aging companies need energetic, passionate people to nurture new businesses. Be careful whom you let go during this stage.

All too often, the people who are fired are those who got themselves into the political penalty box. They might very well be the people whose caring and passion can save the organization. In Hebrew we say: Friends go and come. Enemies accumulate. By the same token, entrepreneurs come and go, bureaucrats accumulate. It is important to give people in the new structure opportunities to show their true colors. Some bureaucrats may be entrepreneurs in disguise, and the effects of the new structure on responsibilities, power, and authority may help them reveal their dormant capabilities. Israel's Negev was a barren desert until it was irrigated and transformed into a gorgeous oasis exporting exotic fruits no one dreamt the desert could produce.

REWARDS

The appropriateness of the reward system depends on how far the company has advanced in its aging. For organizations in Aristocracy, I strongly recommend the stock option system for top management. The more insider stock, the better: That puts pressure on management to wake up and perform. During Recrimination and Bureaucracy, a bonus system will enhance short-term results. In one aging company we determined that to survive, management needed to cut everyone's salary by half. If, however, the company achieved its sales and break-even goals, people would earn bonuses that would, in effect, double their salaries. Sales bonuses are more effective than profit sharing, which may encourage harmful cost cutting. Golden parachutes encourage the best and brightest to leave.

PLANNING AND GOALS

Rejuvenation through expansion and innovation is the key to reversing the downward trend. Measure growth in terms of units shipped to customers and revenue from products that are less than three years old. Fix internal problems. Then find new businesses and markets.

Normal Problems of Aging

Aging by definition is not normal.

Abnormal Problems of Aging

ARISTOCRACY

- The organization is characterized by what I call the Fitzi-Contini syndrome: Individually, everyone is scared, but as a group, people are complacent.
- The organization is cash-rich.
- Meetings with detailed agendas fill the daily routine.
- People have a religious respect for overviews.
- Reams of paperwork and documentation require people to dedicate enormous amounts of time to saying it right while offending no one.
- True production engineering—for improvement and technology advancement—is buried, powerless, and ineffective within the manufacturing power base. It functions primarily as maintenance engineering.
- Elitism takes over the corporate culture.
- People hesitate to share information, and timely market information is not available to those who have authority to act.
- People in the field are detached from managers at headquarters, who show little respect for their distant colleagues. As a result people in the field harbor animosity for the managers in the home office.
- The finance, accounting, and legal departments dominate decision making.

RECRIMINATION

- Witch-hunts and mutual suspicion dominate decision making.
- Nobody trusts anybody.
- Many competent people are fired.
- From management's defensive mentality of denial, it is impossible to tell who is good.
- Leadership, getting the blame, changes frequently and continuously.
- With no good analysis of what has happened, cash flow starts to run dry.
- Clients feel the company has disenfranchised them.

BUREAUCRACY

- The atmosphere is peaceful and quiet.
- People are neither hard working nor well paid. They are outwardly satisfied, however, because there is little pressure to perform.
- There is no accountability for results.
- The company has lost touch with the market and its clients.
- The daily routine is highly predictable: Tomorrow will not differ from today. Plans, procedures, performance, rewards, staffing decisions—all are predictable.
- Because of a religious adherence to the written law, firings are few.
- Tremendous expenditures of time, energy, resources, and paper produce the most meager results.

C H A P T E R

Rescuing a Moribund Organization

—— *Rescuing the Moribund: A Parable* ——

For years, an executive—let's call her Janet—had watched her career blossom at a major life insurance company. Her many innovative marketing ideas had helped the company; people respected and appreciated her contribution. At a time when women executives were rare in the insurance business, she attained her company's top marketing position.

In recent years, however, the life insurance industry had encountered fierce competition from the financial services industry. Janet's once-confident company gradually lost its edge and turned feeble. It had been some time since the company had introduced new products, and the public had taken notice: The company's stock plunged 70 percent in only a year. There was takeover talk, and damaging rumors were rampant. After a year of standing by while her company continued its decline, Janet called me, somewhat furtively, from home:

Janet: I dread going to work. The atmosphere there is poisonous. Half my department is gone. I'm expecting the ax to fall on me any minute.

I: Isn't there someone you can talk to?

Janet: Sure. You.

I: I mean in the company.

Janet: I'm afraid I've already talked too much. All anybody wants to talk about is who's to blame. If I make any more suggestions, people will feel threatened, and they will accuse me of trying to take over. It's cover-your-hide time. Nothing constructive is happening. That's why it's so painful to be there.

I: Have you considered looking for another job?

Janet: I'm a 55-year-old single woman in a dying company in a problematic field. I need the employment benefits. I'm damned if I go and damned if I stay. What would you do?

I: Stay and fight. Whatever there is to lose you've already lost; you have nothing more to lose. The company needs you. Go right to the top, and tell it like it is.

THE REALITIES

Janet did stay, and she did fight. Her story—like too many others—did not, however, end happily. When the directors of the company finally acted on the situation, they did too little, and they were too late to ward off the apocalypse. They had failed to notice that management's lack of response to hard times in the insurance industry had destroyed the company's future. Management had suffocated the dissidents—the creatively entrepreneurial staff—and promoted those who knew how to follow the party line: "Make no waves." There was nobody willing or encouraged to revive the company's outdated line of products and services.

Eventually the company was sold for less than its breakup value, and it has since been subdivided out of existence.

Janet had no chance to save her job or to apply her marketing skills to the company's sagging product line. As she discovered, a company in sharp decline, especially in the Recrimination and Bureaucracy stages, has a difficult time making a turnaround happen.

Paranoia paralyzes. It is much easier to blame people for causing a problem than it is to solve it. The polite formality of Aristocracy gives way to the brutal combat of civil war during Recrimination. In an atmosphere of frenzied backstabbing, everyone forgets the customers. Ignored and alienated, it doesn't take long for customers to give their business to more attentive competitors. Market share slides, revenues wane, cash flow turns negative, and profits disappear. Those who attempt to fight this culture, rather than adapt to it and excel, receive pink slips—not rewards.

In my experience, no individual, no matter how charismatic or heroic, can resuscitate a company in extremis. The role of such an individual is to mobilize, harness, and direct the efforts of the many people needed to resow the seeds of entrepreneurship and restore creative energy. A company on the edge has to transform its corporate mind-set.

The further the company has advanced into the aging stages of the lifecycle, the more difficult is the rescue mission. The tendency for an aging company is to do less: Its management discards operations, products, divisions, and facilities in hopes of reducing costs and conserving capital. But the company shouldn't be doing less. It must be doing more. It needs the infusion of new ventures, new products, and new services that only a broadening of the company's horizons can provoke. The solution to obesity is not anorexia but exercising and developing a positive self-image.

Once the company has identified new opportunities, it needs to restructure operations, decentralizing wherever feasible. The parent company should grant the new endeavors the chance to market their goods and services without the overwhelming burdens of its entrenched systems, procedures, and overhead structures. A new venture neither needs nor wants the inflexible demands of a parent company ruled by bureaucrats. That kindness could overwhelm and undermine its future.

I have participated in attempts to rejuvenate many aging companies, from small family-owned companies to some of the largest in the world. My role is to enable companies to take initiative, act, and add new opportunities. We build potential new successes. When the company's employees observe that—when they see it for themselves—their initial reaction will be fear. They will question whether they "are up to it."

It does not, however, take long before excitement replaces anxiety. People's focus shifts from surviving to building new opportunities for the company and for themselves. When that happens, entrepreneurs are reborn and flourish. Except for those who had been in control and now find themselves in a different relationship to power, few mount resistance.

No one can predict for sure whether the future includes a return to Prime. The world is too cruel and complicated for easy optimism. One can hardly guarantee that an aged, infirm company has a serious chance of rewinding its lifecycle without professional intervention. Still, I can testify from personal experience that some companies have made that difficult return to Prime.

THE CHALLENGE

In a stable organization, form is just beginning to overtake function. The change is not sudden; it is gradual. The company, one step removed from Prime, is still decentralized, but the administrators are taking over, slowly, inexorably nibbling at the authority of the company's entrepreneurs.

As an organizational therapist, when I work with a stable organization, I have time to carry out my intervention. During more advanced stages of the aging process, there is little time, and the organization has less tolerance for the intervention itself. As profits decrease, impatience for results increases.

The therapist will notice that in the company's culture, how is becoming a more important question than what. The company places more emphasis on how its employees dress and behave. Management allots considerable attention to strict—often written—codes of dress and behavior. It pays considerably less attention to the results the individual managers achieve. It is not indifference that causes that behavior. It is that accountability is diffused, and individuals cannot be held accountable for their results. The focus shifts from function to appearance and form. Executives, for example, watch how managers behave in meetings and rate them accordingly. Decorum rather than performance earns rewards.

In a stable company the entrepreneurial spirit is declining so slowly that the company's executives may not even notice what is happening. What should be done to return the company to Prime?

First, make sure that all members of the organization are aware and open about what is happening. Denial is the biggest enemy of change. You cannot move to a new place in your life if you are spending all your energy disavowing your situation. If the company's managers do not realize that incipient decay poses a potentially serious problem, I can predict the company will move inevitably into its Aristocracy stage. Acknowledgment of the company's true condition is difficult to achieve because the company at this stage is doing fine, and there is no pain to cause change. How many overweight people change their habits before they suffer a heart attack?

One of the most negative characteristics of a stable organization is its monochromatic perspective. Too many employees agree on too many issues. Diversity cannot prosper in this environment. The company's managers must understand that lack of tolerance for different points of view threatens the company's health. It is up to the CEO to ensure that diversity pervades every level of the organization.

But let's be clear: I am not talking about uncontrolled diversity. The system needs controlled flexibility and disciplined diversity. The unification of differences (opposing forces) produces Prime: form and function, diversity and unity, discipline and freedom. Clients, management, workers, and stockholders are part of a system that unites their diverse interests.

The next phase of the recovery calls for looking into the future: peering a few years down the road and examining how the company should position itself in relation to the market and its competitors. This crystal ball exercise awakens management to the dangers and opportunities ahead. In the ensuing phase managers can establish stretch goals for every aspect of the organization.

This phase is not at all like the classic planning exercise that involves analysis of numbers and trends. Here we look at the big picture and general trends. I was recently engaged in revitalizing a major industrial company. People suspected that its operations polluted the water and earth under them, and its plants visibly polluted the air. The company's efforts to improve efficiency by cutting costs, improving advertising, and even expanding its product line were nearly overshadowed by a socially, environmentally, and politically motivated boycott of its operations. The company had to ask itself: If we are not an industrial company, what are we? The situation called for a conversion that involved thousands of people.

Many stable companies hire new chief executives to shake up their organizations and get them back on the rails. Management transplantation during aging—Stability, Aristocracy, Recrimination, and Bureaucracy—has its difficulties. The management of an organization, well set in its ways by the time it reaches the aging stages, may consider a new CEO too intrusive. CEOs who are entrepreneurially inclined will inspire deep resentment because an entrepreneur introduces a vastly different culture that will certainly clash with the style of a company in Stability. When that happens, it's a race to see who survives.

What causes a company to lose its entrepreneurial drive? Any number of factors can contribute: the mental age of its leaders, perceived relative market share, a dysfunctional leadership style, and a dysfunctional organizational structure.

If the cause is the advancing mental age of its leaders, those managers need to go. Mental age is not the same as chronological age. There are 70-year-old managers who embrace change with enthusiasm, and there are 25-year-old managers who can't abide change.

Perceived relative market share is the share of the market as the managers see it. They could be defining it too narrowly to claim the significance of their share. The paint company I worked with had for years asserted that it was in the paint market, of which it owned a major slice. A relatively large market share breeds complacency. When the company redefined its business as aesthetic surface protection, its market share declined miraculously with no decline in sales. Simply by widening its horizons, the company made a market-expanding move into the wallpaper business.

Companies that undergo continual redefinition never reach, nor should they ever, the horizon. They are like athletic champions. No matter what the achievement, they seek out new, increasingly challenging competitors, always heightening their chances of losing. They know it is the only way to stay in winning shape.

When structure is the problem, companies should strengthen their ability to deliver new products and services by emphasizing entrepreneurial functions. They should strengthen marketing by emancipating it from the control of sales, free production engineering from the authority of production dominance, free finance from the culture of controlership and audit, and free true human resource development— like organizational development and internal consulting—from the claws of human resource administration, which masquerades as human resources development. The company should explore new horizons, new products, new services, and strategic alliances with other companies.

If the leadership's style brought about the decline, the remedy is not less complicated. The American cowboy culture is to shoot first, fire the guy, and ask questions later. But the Wild West is long gone. Ask questions first: Was the leader's style dysfunctional for the life-cycle stage the organization is leaving? Will that style be dysfunctional for the organization's next stage on the lifecycle? For instance, if the

REVERSING A TERMINAL CASE

The recession of the early 1980s nearly killed Elyria Foundry, an 85-year-old metal-casting business located 30 miles outside of Cleveland. The company had logged sales of $17 million in 1980, but only two years later, revenues had plunged to $7.7 million. By late 1983, Elyria was losing $3 million per year on annualized sales of $4 million. The foundry was running at only 15 percent of capacity. Employment was down to 107 from nearly 400 in 1980.

The recession of the mid-1980s wasn't the only reason for Elyria's failing health. Managerial and manufacturing practices had grown stagnant and old to the point of ossification. Only the financial support of its parent company, Chromalloy American, kept Elyria alive. And Chromalloy was aching to sell.

In August 1993, Gregg L. Foster, an outsider, looked at Elyria and pledged his entire net worth to finance its purchase.

Foster saw bloated overhead: There were 38 salaried staff, most of whom seemed to have lost touch with the company. He fired 15 of them immediately. He saw too much free spending: He sold six company cars, discontinued three country club memberships, and made a show of bringing postage stamps from home for any personal mail he sent from work.

He saw a rigid union structure, where senior workers performed single-function jobs and earned special treatment that irked other foundry workers. He shut the plant down for three days. When he re-opened for business, he rehired, for ungilded base pay, the 100 workers who had the best attendance and performance records. When the union raised calls for a strike, Foster's take-charge speeches, in which he described the initiatives the company was going to take, so impressed workers that they voted for union decertification. He saw with the help of a new costing system that the metal-intensive jobs so prized for their profitability in the past did not yield such great margins after all. He convinced his workers that it would be more profitable to take the labor-intensive jobs that allowed Elyria to leverage its people's experience and skills.

Foster's radical steps reversed the company's aging. A year after the acquisition, net sales rose nearly $6 million. By 1990, they soared to $28 million, and sales per worker jumped from a disappointing $21,000 in 1983 to over $100,000 in 1990. Employment began a steady climb as Foster hired the cream of the labor crop from other aging foundries shuttered by bureaucratic managements. And that was Elyria Foundry in 1990.

leader is an entrepreneurial visionary, and the company is in its Recrimination stage, it will need leadership that is more hands-on, more impatient, less thinking, and more doing. It needs a leader who uses instincts more than mental exercises.

That style of leadership is inappropriate—dysfunctional—in certain stages. For a stable organization to move to Prime, for example, its leader must be able to keep sight of the big picture. That was my debate with the journalists, in the case of the bank I described above. The media pundits were calling for the ouster of the CEO at the time. They maintained that he was producing bad results by failing to show strong leadership. I disagreed adamantly. The bad results were not the results of current operations. The results were the consequences of too many agriculture, oil, and real estate loans that went sour. None of those loans had been signed on that CEO's watch. Those were the legacy his predecessor's campaign to grow the bank's asset base to the largest in the world. And what are a bank's assets? Its loans.

The next CEO was trying to clean house. His leadership style imitated the duck theory of change. It was the perfect match for the bank's needs then. It is a mistake to make big waves when one's profile is high. The impact on the industry can be enormously damaging. The duck theory calls for looking unperturbed and calm on the surface while paddling furiously under water. The paddling, in the CEO's case, was extensive.

The bank's aging was due to structural problems and an inaccurate market perception. Structure comprised a patchwork collection of piecemeal adjustments that had accumulated over the years. The corporate computer division that needed to serve the wholesale division and the trust department, among others, reported to the retail division due to historical happenstance: The bank had acquired a computer company with a retail orientation. The international division had no real identity because it conducted both retail and wholesale business. Neither was the domestic wholesale business coordinated with the wholesale business in the rest of the world, nor was the domestic retail business coordinated with the retail businesses in, say, Italy or Argentina. The disjointed structure prevented similar concerns from sharing accumulated knowledge.

The CFO function was pretty much in ruins. The preceding CEO had shattered its controls to increase the bank's assets, the loans it had made. Because internal audit powers were so weak, we had to reestablish those functions. Real estate loans and related activities had been scattered throughout the organization, and there was no central authority for professional real estate managers' decision making. I met executives who had no idea who their supervisors were. The trust department had little authority, and it had all but disappeared in the course of various power shuffles.

For all practical purposes, the bank had become, according to one newspaper account, "the smallest big bank you have ever seen." The manifestations of the bank's problems were shrinking market share and plummeting profitability. The situation was so bad that the Office of the Controller of the Banks in Washington, D.C., expressed its deep concern.

We were working to clear the table: The bank was recognizing bad debt, increasing reserves, selling buildings to raise funds that would raise the reserves, and restructuring as an organization that offers a broad range of financial products and services. In addition to expanding services to include investment banking, we established the world's largest payment-systems division that covers payments between individuals, between corporations and individuals, and between corporations.

We consolidated all the computer operations and strengthened its user interface to achieve central coordination, standards, and client-friendly services. Until then, each division had had its own computer development, and there was no communication among those independent installations. Because they were incompatible with the new global interdependent outlook, we had to discontinue certain software development projects on which the bank had already spent millions of dollars.

We established a unit that addressed the neglected needs of the middle market. We restructured a division that had included all kinds of loans (focusing on specific markets) to differentiate leasing from agricultural loans. Determining correct levels of a bank's bad debt and reserves is a judgment call, and as the reorganization progressed, the judgment improved. The new head of the professional real estate division gave one look at the portfolio that greeted his arrival and announced his intentions to clear the decks. Until then, the real estate portfolio had included aerospace, agriculture, and oil exploration. His good judgment did not, however, sit well with Wall Street. The more bad debt the bank recognized, the more reserves it needed, and the worse the beleaguered CEO appeared. Even though operational profits were climbing, bad debts instantly consumed them. "While we are collecting peanuts, the elephants are stepping all over us," one vice president complained.

Market analysts look at numbers, not at processes that produce them. Journalists write things that people can read and easily comprehend: They usually avoid such complicated topics as management theories of organizational transformation. Stories with heroes and villains are much more accessible to readers. The CEO's status degenerated from hero of organizational change to loss-producing villain.

While all that underwater paddling was going on, the directors' impatience grew, fueled by ongoing attacks from the media. The directors' desire for faster results eventually led them to vote for both my own and the CEO's dismissal. What's more, the board determined to recall the CEO's predecessor—the man who I believe created the problems in the first place. Shortly thereafter, the bank began to show excellent results, and he was hailed as the rescuer.

THE RESPONSE

Over the years, I have worked with managers from many companies. Together, we conduct diagnostic sessions aimed at uncovering deep-rooted organizational problems. Managers learn to share information so that everyone can understand and agree on the need for change. To make sure that all of its members understand the present state of the company and the challenges that lie ahead, we hold diagnostic sessions throughout the organization. Without that crucial consciousness-raising step, a return to Prime is highly unlikely. The farther the organization's aging has advanced, the deeper are the requisite interventions.

In the case of the bank, to generate enough impact to cause sufficient cross-organizational cooperation, I insisted on the simultaneous activation of a minimum of six different divisions.

The traditional consultant's approach is to meet with the company's executives and ask them to define their goals. In my opinion, if the organization doesn't start out with an honest assessment of its condition (in that case, Aristocracy), it is in no position to define its goals. Goal definition is useless because all the executives can do is contribute platitudes that are culturally secure. Just like any program that helps people get over bad habits, the participants must first stop denying before they can change.

Company managers need to acknowledge their interdependency. They must recognize the necessity of working together to redirect their organization. They must also develop a sense of their collective potency. Only then can they tackle the company's imposing problems and define goals.

Unlike companies in the Go-Go stage—bursting with energy, aggressively addressing their problems and opportunities—companies in Aristocracy are complacent, and their people begin to sense a disquieting impotency. The diagnostic process helps management develop group consciousness. They learn that by being open with one another about their problems, they can develop mutual trust that lets them address strategic problems. The united commitment entails energy that repositions everyone for the long and arduous journey back to Prime.

Only after completing the diagnosis and team problem solving to enhance mutual confidence can management confront the definition of its organizational mission. Teams of managers with diverging perspectives work together to do that. If people attempt to approach this assignment as they addressed the problems of Aristocracy—individually rather than collectively—the company's aging might well accelerate its slide into Recrimination and then Bureaucracy. Companies in

Aristocracy have wide-ranging problems, and they need various points of view to regain their competitive stance.

Decentralization is a crucial discipline in the process of regaining Prime. Based on the strategies it developed during the mission phase, the recovering Aristocracy takes all its start-up operations, along with operations in their Infancy or Adolescence, and sets them up as separate entities. Although it is hard to do, the company must resist controlling its offspring, lest it smother their ability to function. This process of divestiture imposes a horizontal structure on the parent company and prevents a vertical, colonialist structure ultimately doomed to fail.

When the spin-offs are firmly established, the parent can redesign its management information systems to support the decentralized operations, which will then be accountable for their results. Next, the company allocates resources to nurture the growing operations, and it designs reward systems that will motivate employees of the spin-offs. Both steps, which are financial in nature, let the managers of the new operations focus on market share, sales, return on investment, and profitability.

The leader of an organization in Aristocracy should take all necessary steps to keep as many entrepreneurs in its management ranks as possible. Usually the entrepreneurs are fired first. They stand out like sore thumbs. Because of their entrepreneurial spirit, those people have established long histories of bitching and moaning: They have been wanting the company to change for a long time. They refused to be benignly quiet, and that refusal made them unpopular. Nobody is surprised that they are the first fired when the new executive arrives.

Entrepreneurs come and go; bureaucrats accumulate. My approach is to hold on, for as long as I can, to the people the entrenched powers have recommended firing. The restructuring is tantamount to changing the environment: We change responsibilities, authority, and power as well as the incentive systems. Invariably, as I treat an Aristocracy, I find that the gadflies of the old structure are much sought after once the new structure is in place.

The entrepreneurial employees are easy for me to spot. They are the people who continually promote new products, new services, and new ventures. They will support the agenda of a similarly entrepreneurial leader.

During the next phase the entrepreneurial people need to identify a product or service that they can introduce in a short time. The success of their first venture encourages other entrepreneurs to step forward and request placement on other new and exciting ventures. Volunteers will appear to pepper the organization with many spin-offs, each with the potential to provide the company with expanding revenue streams and profits.

Downsizing

Recrimination, an ugly phase characterized by infighting, political bickering, and backstabbing among managers, calls for prompt removal of the troublemakers and a no-nonsense directive to cease and desist all unproductive behavior. Employees who fail to respond to this directive must leave the organization along with incompetents and employees who have negative attitudes.

Don't try to make those changes incrementally. Surgery should be thorough, if drastic, but it must be done all at once. A never-ending sequence of dismissals cripples any organization. A massive dismissal, inappropriate during Go-Go, is justifiable in an extreme case in Aristocracy or in Recrimination.

Since the behavior of companies in their Aristocracy is, by definition, very civilized, those companies trickle—fire people and downsize salami style, one slice at a time, prolonging the pain until people have no idea what will come next. The so-called treatment, in other words, may be worse than the disease.

Managers, afraid to stick their necks out, are easily infected with indecision. Managerial paranoia may swell to proportions that paralyze operations. No one risks taking responsibility for decisions that may not work out. As a matter of fact, most of the decisions don't work out.

A major aging organization moved its production facilities to another state. The transition was costly, and it turned out to be a bad decision. No one took responsibility; still many were held accountable, even those who believed they were merely bystanders.

The manufacturing vice president asserted that he had been told to do it by the president, who claimed that he had nothing to do with it. The president said that the executive vice president, who was very powerful, wanted the move. The president, for his part, did not want to use up his meager political power to stop the move. The executive vice president emphatically rejected the attribution, saying that the president had taken full charge of the matter. Accountability had so disintegrated that people who were responsible and had authority to act knew there was neither reward for acting correctly nor punishment for applying authority incorrectly.

In Recrimination, managers need to focus on survival, cutting back operations to a sustainable level that serves as a base for improvement. But there must be a floor. To stop losing money, managers must eliminate unprofitable operations and reduce costs in all but the most essential activities: those that are still producing profit and those that are potentially profitable in the short term.

In that stage, total authority and responsibility for the company must be vested in an individual. A team approach cannot help a company in Recrimination: It would only accelerate the company's downfall. Insightful direction coupled with fast action is the order of the day. Unlike those in Aristocracy or Stability, the company in Recrimination has no time to spare.

A benevolent dictator, like the founder who ruled the organization during its Infancy stage, needs to take charge, giving the company the same treatment accorded infant organizations: frequent 16-week cash-flow projections, weekly reviews of inventory and accounts receivable, effective follow up of delinquent customer accounts, and detailed accounting that highlights costs that are out of line with budgets. Recrimination calls for treatment that—first and foremost—will arrest cash outflow and the free-fall loss of market share.

After those steps, the company needs to apply the therapeutic

treatments prescribed for companies in Aristocracy. A company trying to escape Recrimination requires a considerably higher rate of intervention—in terms of both length of time and frequency—to get it to
Prime. There are no short cuts, magic pills, or fast liposuctions.

As soon as the situation stabilizes, it will seem as if the company
has moved to Aristocracy. Then the company should use the treatment aimed at an aristocratic company and work to get the structure,
information systems, and reward systems in place. Once it has
achieved those goals, the company will employ the treatment for a stable company.

AGING: SIX ELEMENTS
OF SUCCESSFUL COMEBACKS

Style

The system has taken over, and the administrators have been suffo-
cating the company with controls. Bring back an entrepreneurial,
results-oriented, and—for a company that has been balkanized—
no-nonsense dictator. Return to the Infancy stage where positive direction emanating from the company's leader fostered growth and
expansion. Now is the time to look beyond the company's walls and
refocus on customers' needs, identify new market niches, and find
the capital to fund them.

Structure

If the company had already established accountability with decentralized authority paired with responsibility, it wouldn't be in such
sorry shape now. It faces what is almost certainly its last chance. Remove layers of managers to bring the company closer to its clients,
and consolidate costs into the profit centers that ought to organize
around specific markets or products: strategic business units. Each
unit should end up as autonomous as possible, focused on its spe-

cific market needs without sacrificing the economies of scale of the larger organization.

The human hand provides an excellent analogy for understanding the goals of restructuring. Each finger of the hand is different and serves a different purpose. Together, however, they perform as a unified hand.

Restructuring usually transforms an organization once structured according to functions to one structured around products, and/or markets, and/or geography. I say and/or because the structure cannot follow one principle exclusively. In the end, it is a combination of principles that optimally produce a structure.

Start with market segmentation and see what the first draft of the structure yields. Then look to see what limitation such a structure will impose on product lines. Marketing theory says that market segmentation should be translated into product differentiation. That is not usually practiced by aging companies. They have the same product for multiple markets. Once the structure reflects products and markets, it is time to add the dimension of geography.

While you want to plan and think globally or nationally, you must pay attention to the local action: What are the needs of the local markets, and what do local offices offer? The goal is to provide optimal authority both globally and locally while recognizing authority for markets and product lines.

In the course of its construction, the draft of the structure may emerge as a matrix. That adds to the complexity because the delineation of authorities and responsibilities may get everyone entangled into a web of cross purposes. Finger pointing in such circumstances is inevitable, and the structure must be such to eliminate negative interaction. The next step is to determine which common services (engineering, manufacturing, and so forth) should be shared and which should be specific to individual units.

We next define workable financial and managerial relationships among the different units. My approach, I would like to emphasize, is neither humanistic nor psychological. I spend almost no time on the individual dimension, although I do allot a minimal amount of time to group dynamics. Most of my time, however, I dedicate to traditional Management 101 principles: Who has the authority to decide? How does he or she decide? Who should participate in the decision and how? How should we calculate transfer prices between units?

One helpful approach involves hanging the draft of the chart on the wall and having all the participants review the chart and note all their questions, doubts, and disagreements on three separate lists. I focus on the question lists only, and the group discusses the questions one by one until the participants come up with answers. My role is to offer the benefit of my experience and principles from the field of management, marketing, and production. I do not provide solutions. I provide tools.

As we answer the questions, the chart changes and cloudy issues are clarified. New questions arise that reflect those changes. What used to be the lists of doubts become the new questions. When we have answered the new set of questions—again one at a time—and a new chart has emerged, we collect lists of questions again. The chart is done and ready for implementation only when there are no more questions. By definition, there are no doubts or disagreements either.

Occasionally, there are a few people who aren't completely content with the final chart, but as long as they participated in the process, and we dealt with their questions, they accept the chart. Those people might say that they fail to see where they fit on the new chart because their jobs seem to have disappeared. But because they recognize that the new chart is good for the company, they agree to support it.

Strategy

It is too late for the diversification and growth that might have saved the company in middle age. The best option at this stage is to get rid of high-priced, unproductive bureaucrats and either sell or close irretrievably unprofitable units. Be careful, though: Some good units are unprofitable because they're overburdened with such valueless expenses as corporate retreats, airplanes, and lavish headquarters.

Many an unprofitable unit in an aging company has turned into a gold mine once it was sold to a private entrepreneur. The company needs to identify the worthy components before it starts excising the bad. Don't sell profitable units just because they will bring the highest prices. This was the Massey Ferguson mistake. It sold worthy units to protect the losing units.

Staffing

While it is ridding itself of hidebound bureaucrats, the company should be recruiting energetic outsiders who haven't been poisoned by the moribund culture. Warning: Don't fire the wrong people. Remember the camels in polar bear skins? Those who were misfits during Bureaucracy may be frustrated entrepreneurs who passionately want to build the company's new culture and new businesses. Restaff with high achievers. It is the time to reinstate the ascendancy of entrepreneurship and producer functions.

Rewards

With negative cash flow, it is time to think about commissions and bonuses again. During this near-Death stage, incoming cash should exceed outgoing cash. Rewards, for that reason, ought to reflect short-term performance. Consider introducing a pay-for-performance compensation system. Pay cash bonuses to salespeople who bring in new business, and keep base salaries relatively low. Put as many internal employees as possible on bonus, but take steps to ensure they receive enough salary to keep them going until the bonuses kick in. Defer as much compensation as possible, but do not force excellent performers to leave the company.

Planning and Goals

The company needs to develop achievable plans to help restore cash flow and profitability. The plans need to express the company's new-found creativity within strict budgetary guidelines. All employees need to understand the importance of Cash conservation, cost control, and cost reduction. Reinstate cash flow accounting. As in Infancy, recovering companies need 16-week, forward-rolling, cash-flow projections. The company's salespeople need to understand that their budget projections for sales must be realistic and on target.

————

CHAPTER 10

Bureaucracy: Can the Patient Be Resuscitated?

Bureaucracy: Two Parables

An acquaintance of mine swore to me that the following story is absolutely true.

My friend visited a military camp, and when he attempted to enter a certain building, the guard at the door informed him that no strangers were allowed to enter. There seemed to be no secret archive or activities in that building, so my friend asked around until he discovered the reason for the guard and the prohibition. He found that some time ago, a guard had been assigned to the building's entrance to keep people from entering and marring its newly painted floors. The floor had dried months earlier, but the instruction to guard the place still stood, and in the military, orders are orders.

Another True Story

I treated an aging sales-representation company in Chicago. Every year, the company spent thousands of dollars photographing merchandising efforts. The pictures were filed and seemed to have no use. After some investigation, I found that years earlier, a client had asked to see some pictures of the merchandising effort. Someone else thought it seemed like a good idea to extend the service to all clients. The company issued a camera and allotments of film to every salesperson. Initially, pictures did go to clients. Over time, however, the practice languished due to the clients' apparent lack of response. Still salespeople took the pictures, and the pictures were filed. As the sales force evolved, new salespeople learned protocol from the veterans. They gave the film to company secretaries, who had it developed and filed as documentation. Of what? Thousands of dollars were spent annually with no clear benefit.

BUREAUCRACY

Those two stories exemplify behavior that is typical of but not exclusive to organizations in Bureaucracy. The older the organization and the more rituals it has rooted in forgotten history, the more it wastes on resources and the more it hinders its future growth.

The end can be ugly. If a company's leaders fail to save it from the morass of turf wars, paranoia, and customer neglect, it can go bankrupt. It can turn around, or—in a state of unmitigated Bureaucracy—it can get government protection. A company in Bureaucracy endures only by virtue of artificial life support: either through its monopoly of the market or its access to the government trough.

A company can even start life at birth as a Bureaucracy, a monopoly supported by external, noncustomer entities. In such cases the lifecycle is accelerated from Courtship through Infancy and Go-Go to premature aging. The company skips Prime altogether.

An organization need not be a governmental agency to become a Bureaucracy. If its resources for survival are not driven by its customers, the organization is on a fast track to Bureaucracy. Its people oversee archaic systems that produce self-perpetuating forms, rules, and procedures whose apparent purpose is to immunize the bureaucrats from accusations of violating rules, laws, or principles.

The armies of people who receive, open, stamp, route, copy, and file letters are far more extensive than the few troops who act upon the contents of that mail. Responsibility for action always appears to belong to another department, and there is little communication or cooperation among departments. Corporate bureaucrats view customers as a source of disturbance against whom they install a protective shield. That shield can take many forms. For example, some organizations require all customers who have queries to pass through a single entry point, regardless of the nature of the query, before they can get anywhere near a person who can give them the information they need.

Bureaucracies show all the signs of both internal disintegration and alienation from their external markets. Because their existence does not depend on customers, their executives, naturally, perceive no reason to serve customers, much less strive to please them. I recall with a shudder my efforts to renew my passport at a government office in New York City's Rockefeller Center. I do not exaggerate when I say that the behavior of the administrators in the Passport Office is alarmingly reminiscent of the guards at the Nazi concentration camp that detained me during the Holocaust.

You might expect that its employees would find the somnolence of corporate Bureaucracy a punishment. Quite the contrary: Although they complain, bureaucrats do like their jobs. They hang on to them with all their might. They experience little pressure due to their scant concern for results. Bureaucrats have comfortable jobs that are secure as long as they raise no questions.

People who from childhood or by their culture have been conditioned not to make waves remain charming until someone demands explanations for the arcane rules by which they make decisions. Strange as it may seem, even administrators at the top have no explanations. Many bureaucratic policies are without logical explanation because they were set without any long-term rationale. They are policies that filled a specific need at a specific moment in time. With the passage of time, the policy seems immovable in spite of its archaic reasoning that no one remembers.

A full-blown Bureaucracy is nearly always far too rigid to respond easily to therapy. I myself know of no strategy, structure, or surgery that will definitely and predictably reverse the disease.

I worked with one of the world's largest county departments of social services, which employed 3,500 social workers. Finally, after three years, it was starting to look as if we were making some progress. Sad to say, though, it took a new, political appointee less than three months to erase any signs of our work. I have discovered that after I help governments reorganize themselves, what actually happens in those organizations has little to do with what we all agreed on. The political process, rather than the goal of enhancing organizational effectiveness, drives design and decisions.

I helped design Ghana's health delivery system, which the World Health Organization recognized as the best for developing nations. Nevertheless, it took only one change of government to eliminate all traces of our years of effort. I have grown so frustrated with the public sector that I responded quite cautiously to the possibility of beginning the program of change for Fernando Henrique Cardoso, the president of Brazil. I hesitated even though Clóvis Carvalho, the first minister in Cardoso's cabinet, had been my client in the private sector and had applied my methodologies to mobilize the decision makers to arrest the country's runaway inflation.

Bresser Pereira, Cardoso's minister for reorganization of the civil sector, introduced an exceptional plan for rejuvenating his government's machinery. He recommended reorganizing the government so that agencies—either privatized or semipublic—would be administered by commissions with the profit motive constrained. The employees of those entities would not be considered public servants, and they would not enjoy the law's employment protection should their organizations fail to perform. His plan also recommended reorganization of the public sector so that each different concern—foreign affairs, police, defense, and so forth—had its appropriate rules of employment and expected behavior.

I strongly supported that proposal because it promoted diversity that reflected the various constituencies served. (I recommended to both President George Bush and President Bill Clinton a similar reorganization of the executive branch. My analysis of the White House and the executive branch, which I had conducted with the late Bob Haldeman, had revealed an unmanageable situation.)

Mr. Pereira's proposal, to the best of my knowledge, got bogged down in political decision making, and I have had no response to my recommendations to the White House.

You can easily recognize executives and managers of a company facing imminent Death. They demonstrate the following signs:

- They are not committed to any course of action that introduces change. In the terminal stage of the lifecycle, administrators ignore their customers and competitors, and shun meaningful contact with the world beyond the company's walls. They enfold their company in a protective (and fatal) cocoon.

- The company's executives steadfastly resist any diminution of their functional ranks. The company may be as much as 50 or 60 percent overstaffed. That engorgement is the result of the need to perform and respond to the changing market without having to risk the circumstances of uncertainty that characterize change. Let me offer an analogy by way of explanation of that point.

If you were playing doubles tennis, would you—to avoid all debate and confusion about who should take which balls—take chalk and mark your area and your partner's? No player I know would do that, but that is exactly how bureaucracies try to avoid possible debate or potential misunderstanding. They avoid being out of control—even for a short time. Their organizations have manuals that are hundreds of pages long, written in legalistic language by battalions of lawyers who, naturally, are the people who interpret the directives.

But that is not the entire story. Assume you did put chalk marks on the tennis court, and both you and your partner are in position. What happens when the ball lands somewhere around the line between you? If the ball flies toward you in extremely slow motion, there might be a chance for you and your partner to identify who should deal with it.

Likewise, bureaucracies try to slow the ball to avoid violating rules and policies, and, of course, the customers suffer the consequences of long delays. To speed up the solutions while maintaining a no-risk profile, bureaucrats assign someone to take charge of the gray areas around the line. Now with three people on the court, we have to draw additional lines of demarcation because the new personnel have introduced new areas of uncertainty. The process is endlessly repetitive as the Bureaucracy grows to accommodate the multiplying areas of uncertainty. Eventually, with so many divisions of responsibility, action slows to a standstill. Engaged in turf wars, everyone watches everyone else, guarding individual mandates and areas of authority.

To continue with the tennis analogy, I can assure you that, in the aforementioned scenario, nobody goes for the ball unless it hits him or her between the eyes.

Lines of demarcation are requisite in a Bureaucracy because, first and foremost, people cannot tolerate doubt, lack of clarity, or uncertainty. They defer to a legalistic management approach. Why? Because bureaucrats' accountability is not to customers but to the politicians who grant them funding. And what politician wants to risk being labeled irresponsible?

Another reason why bureaucracies minimize risk and maximize control is that their systems are based on lack of trust. The electorate has no faith that its public servants will not abuse power. The public servants, for their part, do not trust the public to behave responsibly, so they design control systems that themselves need control. The system continues to grow increasingly ponderous.

Often, political infighting leaves bureaucrats so afraid to expose themselves to criticism that they discover it is safest simply to talk, promise, criticize opponents, and do nothing that in any way, shape, manner, or form invites criticism. The overriding goal of politicians is, of course, to stay in power. Politicians, by the way, are different from statesmen. Politicians worry about the next election; statesmen fret about the next generation. Statesmen, however, look so far beyond the horizon that they do not see the current needs of the systems they lead.

Although the organization in Bureaucracy is indeed dying, it may linger for years before it finally expires. In a business Bureaucracy, profits eventually disappear, dropping to zero and moving into the red when creative accounting has exhausted its imagination. Depending on how much capital the company has reserved, it can go on a bit longer, selling off assets to cover expenses, downsizing ever so slowly, and terminating a relatively few people every quarter. For those without work prospects elsewhere, it is an agonizing process.

Shock Treatment

A dying company is staffed with an overabundance of administrators. Growing numbers of consultants busily implement management information systems that choke initiative for change by further institutionalizing the processes that handle uncertainty. Bureaucracies need fewer systems, forms, and procedures. Their people need more discretionary power to make decisions. That is anathema in the public sector: The public does not trust government to use power responsibly, and every effort is made to control this power. As a result, we have an enormously expensive control system that, by definition, can be neither effective nor optimally efficient.

In the private sector, even if the consulting effort improves the process, the new system will, over time, lose its effectiveness because of change. Furthermore, chances are that the new systems, which grow obsolete, will become obstacles themselves. Administrators will request more help, more consulting, more new systems, and more procedures. They impose systems on top of systems, destroying forests to satisfy the need for paperwork.

A business organization at this stage of the lifecycle continues to crank out more manufactured products, but the absolute numbers of units sold diminishes every quarter. The product or service is out-dated. Stricter controls on internal operations will not make the difference. The salespeople are nervous. They have never contemplated a gloomier future. They want new products and services to sell, but they are beginning to realize that nothing new will be coming their way any time soon. Prices are already higher than those offered by competitors.

Consequently, salespeople—the real producers whom the company can't afford to lose—are leaving the company as fast as they can. And where do they go? They go where their understanding of the market will be appreciated: The competition is happy to get them, and they are pleased once again to see a future with promise. Most of those with entrepreneurial spirit are, by this stage, long gone. They left for offers in companies more receptive to their ideas, or they have headed off to start companies of their own.

Entrepreneurs who still remain hate coming to work. There is little for them to do: There is little anyone will allow them to do. The strong get stronger, and the weak grow weaker. That is the Darwinian rule of survival of the fittest organization.

At this frightening stage, the company's executives decide that shock treatment offers the only hope of rehabilitation. Change, even accelerated change, they reason, will no longer suffice. But shock treatment—mass layoffs, managerial realignments, unrealistic demands on survivors—often introduce unanticipated results. Rather than turning the company around by bringing all its people back to their senses, shock treatment often terrorizes employees.

Because they feel cornered, employees leap frantically at any solutions that seem plausible. Given the opportunity, employees accept the first jobs they find—even when they are lower paying—as long as they are more secure. Shock treatment has plunged many failing companies into irreversible comas.

Facing insolvency, many boards of directors elect to fire the whole top management team and install other executives who have garnered reputations as turnover specialists. The board retains a high-priced executive search firm, and within a few weeks or months, depending on the board's urgency, the new hired gun arrives. The board endows the new CEO with wide powers to turn the company around. The new CEO gets a generous compensation package that should reflect expected results.

I am not going to cover in this book how the turnaround strategy should be implemented in a business environment simply because that is not my field, and I have had little experience in it. It is a field in which turnaround consultants with deep understanding of financial instruments and legal expertise thrive. I do, however, offer words of caution, which I base on firsthand observation.

You shouldn't measure a surgeon's capabilities by how fast he cuts. The measures of surgery's success are the patient's recovery and long-term prospects. When the body is weak, vulnerable, and susceptible to disease, postoperative treatment makes or breaks patient health. The same holds true for organizational surgery. I find too many consultants (some among our country's most prestigious) who come in; analyze; recommend realignment, restructuring, and layoffs; and then leave. They are long gone when the real pain and dangers of the implementation emerge. If a surgeon's success rate were measured by the percentage of patients who leave the operating room alive, their records would be virtually perfect. If, however, over time, only half of those patients survive the surgery, their records look somewhat tarnished.

You ought to view corporate turnaround specialists—replacement CEOs and traditional consultants—from a similar perspective. There are some who engage in whirlwinds of activity—creating new organization charts, moving people, imposing systems, and cutting costs—and then quickly take their leave. Their work is neither complete nor acceptable.

Effective turnaround specialists should remain with their companies, nurturing them back to health. They should take responsibility for their actions and stand ready to bolster the many changes they find it necessary to make.

Once they have restructured the organizations to their liking, the real pain of adaptation begins. The newly hired managers and the managers retained from the earlier regimes have tough jobs ahead of them. Some of the changes are wrenching, and only the most stalwart will survive. Most managers suffer their pain silently, hopelessly praying that the new CEO won't schedule additional surgery. He will, of course, because a badly designed restructure or badly implemented change calls for yet more restructuring. That pressure to produce instant results botches reorganizations. Even before the organization has a moment to recover from its initial surgery, somebody wheels it back to the operating room.

Is drastic action ever appropriate? That depends. If the previous management had experimented with seemingly endless cures for the company's problems, any new approach the new CEO attempts may overload the organization and tip the scales against recovery.

One of the least effective cures is the therapy that depends exclusively on training. Because that approach seems so simple to implement, it is extremely popular. But when a company is dying, it needs to restructure and recreate itself, and to design a reward structure that encourages desired behavior organization-wide. When—and only when—an organization has achieved all that it can, should training for the new behavior be introduced.

Starting with training alone is, at best, a waste of money. What is worse, though, is that the false hopes raised by those programs will delay correct treatments. So why is the training approach so popular? It is not painful to implement, and it reflects the organizational culture. A control-oriented company seeks solutions that appeal to its culture: solutions that increase control. Training is the way to further condition people's behavior while eroding tendencies for spontaneity.

I find that it is difficult to lead aging companies through therapeutic sessions. Management insists on agendas detailed to the point that they preclude spontaneity. It is true that some companies spend money on training for creativity, spontaneity, and risk-taking, but the applicability of those skills falls short because nobody wants the trained staff working on real, strategic issues.

Who Should Lead Change?

Companies in the throes of Bureaucracy have an overabundance of systems. They lack the functional orientation of marketing and sales, without which there can be no return to Prime. Administrators have organizational dominance. The company has more systems employees than it needs, and it continues to hire more. Those new hires churn out more and more procedures, which stifle creativity and individual contribution and call for even more control people. Control breeds controls. The more controls, the more violations arise that need to be controlled. It is an endless cycle. For the most part, companies nearing Death need to seek outside help.

The best initial treatment calls for hiring or promoting an entrepreneur to run the organization. The organization's entrenched managers will fight the new entrepreneur. To get the entrepreneurial division to start operating, the organization needs to facilitate participative change, coalescing authority, power, and influence.

The therapist and the chief administrator need to establish a high level of mutual trust and respect. If the chief is a typical political appointee who says one thing and means something entirely different, the therapist will be easily outmaneuvered, lose credibility, and end up paid but ignored.

The chief administrator takes a chance on the therapist, too. Therapists who are not politically careful become liabilities the chief cannot afford. I believe that the older the company, the more critical it is to have good chemistry between the therapist and chief administrator.

Many large and midsize organizations have established internal consulting functions to deal with troubling questions. Specialists whose expertise runs from industrial engineering to organizational development fill those functions. The industrial engineers address the so-called hard subjects: productivity, quality systems, and reengineering. The organizational development experts focus on such soft subjects as establishing trust among departments, team building, and related behavioral concerns.

Companies can benefit from having such in-house expertise during their growing years, in Prime, and even in the very early stages of aging. When, however, an organization finds itself in the aging stages, I find the help of internal consultants and agents of change limited at best.

When a company faces serious trouble and its executives and managers are preoccupied with nothing less than survival, the people who staff the internal consulting function are no less affected by the company's bad news. As insiders, they, too, fear getting the boot.

As their company nears its Death, internal consultants are less useful than what I term insultants. Insultants, by my definition, are consultants with no dependency ties to the languishing organization. As outsiders, immune to the political implications of their actions, they can analyze the company's problems objectively and facilitate whatever action is appropriate for survival. Insultants have one goal only: the company's revival. They are the shock troops that the board calls in as its last line of defense.

Internal consultants are the organization's trained integrators, its development experts. Internal organizational development experts can bring about change when its pace is slow and moderated. In my judgment, they are not effective when fast and resolute action is indicated. They should be swimming upstream politically, but they might not be able to afford that risk and survive. An insultant must be a person who can afford to be fired. Internal consultants usually do not have that luxury, and they end up reinforcing the culture rather than changing it.

STYLE

Management should not tolerate failure. The company has had enough failures to take it to the end of several lifetimes. You can accept nothing less than excellent performance from each employee. Establish your rejuvenated organization with the best performers. Be hard-nosed but empathetic. Support your people in every way you can: They are fighting a fierce battle to save the company. The leader's style should be tough and hands-on while remaining extremely fair and honest. In an aging company there are no romantics; everyone is a cynical veteran of manipulation, lies, and broken promises.

STRUCTURE

In a government agency, the words marketing and process engineering have no meaning. Nor does the word finance. The only departments in the public sector that resemble those in the business world are the ones that tend to human resources and operations. Every organization, however, needs the missing functions. Marketing's function is to analyze the changing needs of clients. Governmental bureaucracies need that too. In those cases where that function exists, people usually call it planning. Be careful. Planning in a Bureaucracy means number crunching. It has little to do with analyzing needs and organizational capabilities to see what clients get and do not get. That's why I avoid words like planning. I recommend creation of a unit dubbed client satisfaction. Because its exclusive role is to audit the department's performance in terms of client satisfaction, that unit must report to the chief administrator so the information comes through loud and clear.

The purpose of process engineering is to improve how we manufacture. Although on the surface a Bureaucracy doesn't seem to be a manufacturer, its mission is "manufacturing services," and someone must continuously improve those services. Again, let me interject a word of caution. Government agencies' units called systems and procedures are easily mistaken for fulfilling the process-engineering role. Usually, those units focus their energies on producing additional forms and procedures when what their organizations need is to reduce the number of procedures, forms, and rules. It is time to think about what tasks can be eliminated.

Instead of systems and procedures, we should talk about streamlining. And as we redirect our focus, instead of finance we should talk about fund-raising: What are the sources of money? Who will be responsible for writing proposals, lobbying, recruiting volunteers, and the like?

One of the causes of bureaucratic paralysis is the remoteness of the authority to approve change. That stems from institutionalized mistrust. Early in the 1970s, I was involved in a revolutionary attempt to professionalize the United States Postal Service. In the course of my investigations, I discovered that postmasters of major post offices who worked with multimillion-dollar budgets were allotted discretionary funds of less than $10,000.

Likewise, the chief of the Los Angeles County Department of Children's Services had neither discretionary funds nor authority to make strategic changes. Getting to those who are authorized to approve change is complicated: Authority is often scattered throughout the organization. The people who ran the computers and information systems reported to a different county organization, and the people who worked directly on children's services had no authority to affect their access to that electronic information. What's more, the court system on which the children's services staff depended for the protection of endangered children operated independently of the children's services staff. There were no mechanisms to facilitate joint planning and cooperation.

The sheriff had his own political agenda and his own unit of volunteers to deal with children. The people appointed by the County's Board of Supervisors to serve on the Commission for Children's Services were well-meaning citizens who, because they didn't trust the bureaucrats, criticized them continuously. As a result, the chief of the department spent a major part of his time preparing explanatory reports for the commissioners.

To design effective structures for bureaucracies, it is essential to build units that interface with and mobilize the sources of authority and power. That enhances flexibility, and it does not impose an additional financial burden on the organization. Because a Bureaucracy always carries people who are underutilized, our restructuring can convert fat to muscle.

Among the challenges we confront as we restructure organizations in Bureaucracy is the relationship of people's ranks and salaries to the number of employees who report to them. Thus downsizing is difficult to effect due to understandable self-interest. What elected politician wants to lay off voters? Our first step, in the case of the Department of Children's Services, was to obtain a ruling that would protect the ranks of the current staff members even after we reduced their staffs. Only their replacements, hired in the future, would have the new rank designations. We also obtained a ruling that allowed, for example, a person of rank 18 to report to a person of rank 13, even though that practice ran counter to all the rules of the Civil Service Commission.

In planning the change, we encouraged the involvement of union leaders: Some of the changes we recommended were not in concert with union positions, so we needed their support to avoid a massive strike. All of our efforts were complicated because several unions were involved, each one responding to direction from outside the children's services department. Furthermore, because those unions had no clear leadership, we never knew whether those not involved in the change process would cooperate. We had to worry about whether they would feel threatened enough to sabotage the leaders who were working with management.

To achieve cooperation, we created a compelling vision centered on a deeply emotional commitment to helping the endangered children. Over several months, we held a workshop for some 30 participants, including the chief administrators of the department, the representatives of the court system, the union leadership, the providers of services from the private sector, and the leadership of the children's commission. Our goal was to build mutual trust among the parties, trust that would allow everyone to work cooperatively to make changes.

Strategy

The board of directors and the management team must focus all their energy and attention on survival. They must start with an analysis to determine which pieces are functionally justifiable. They need to determine the organization's purpose and how its pieces fit together.

We start by identifying the clients. My experience has shown that most organizations are not at all sure who their clients are. In the case of the children's services department, we received revealing responses to the questions "Who are our clients?" and "Whose needs do we satisfy?" Answers included the family court, the local commission for children's services, and the departments of social work at several universities. Endangered children seemed almost lost on the long list of the answers. The confusion between stakeholders and clients prevails in every stage of the lifecycle save one: Prime. In aging organizations that confusion is potentially lethal.

Once the analysis identifies the purpose of the organization's existence, it is time to pose other questions: Are there client needs the organization fails to satisfy? Why does it fail? In aging organizations, it is an enormous undertaking simply to identify the unsatisfied needs. Often those organizations lack strong units devoted to environmental and market scanning. They easily produce such risk-free, generically applicable platitudes as "People want fast, reasonably priced service." Because charges in the government sector are minimal or irrelevant, price may not seem to be a factor. That, however, is a misconception. Price comprises such terms as the distance a person is willing to travel and the length of time people will willingly wait in line for a product or service.

Strategy must focus on what the organization can do to improve the way it satisfies clients within the constraints of its other stakeholders. In the case of the children's department, the question addressed in the structure and driven by this strategy was how to reduce the number of file transfers. The goal was to have each child deal with only one social worker, to avoid losing the endangered child in the constant shuffle of files

The problem was to learn how to control and meet the interests of both the family and the child. There was a big debate that called on the courts to play a major role. We needed the leadership of the court to help the discussion and to design a workable system.

Strategy should focus on who the client really is, how to maximize allocated resources, and how to increase organizational freedom—that is, its flexibility. However, that strategy—to increase flexibility and become client focused—is useless unless the organization's power and authority structure reflects it.

STAFFING

Maintain minimal staff levels in administrative areas. You need to maximize the impact of producers in sales, manufacturing, and client-serving capacities. Of course, for the company to survive or be effective, those employees must be productive. Motivate more. Control less. It is time either to hire or to find within the organization a few key entrepreneurial people with positive visions for the company's affirmative future. Keep those people moving energetically in directions that are most promising.

Often, people believe that their Bureaucracy has no entrepreneurial types in its ranks, and the company will have to import people to fill that entrepreneurial role. I strongly disagree. There are always entrepreneurial types hidden around organizations. If they are intelligent, they have protectively disguised themselves as bureaucrats to survive or progress. After the Berlin Wall fell, I was invited to Russia to consult on privatization. People expect to find apparatchiks and only apparatchiks. I found, instead, throngs of eager capitalists willing to do anything, anytime, anywhere—for a buck. Granted, they did not know how, but they were surely willing to learn.

People's behavior is a reflection of their environment. Change the environment and notice how many of the polar bears are intelligent camels who eagerly drop the polar bear pelts they wore to survive the harsh climate of the North Pole.

REWARDS

In a bureaucratized business organization, salary increases and other compensatory arrangements typical of healthy, growing companies should not even be topics of discussion. During this difficult period, the sales force should earn commissions that motivate selling, selling, and selling. The biggest—in fact, the only—reward at this stage for all other employees is simply to retain their jobs.

It is up to management to assure all employees that if they endure the troubling times, they can anticipate rewards after the crisis passes and the company's future is certain. Don't just utter the words. Unless you remember to compensate them for their loyalty and hard work during trying times, you will lose your newly won future. You should, on the other hand, motivate entrepreneurial enthusiasm with significant stock options.

In the public sector, I find one of the major reasons for bureaucratization is the reward system: salary administration. To get paid more, public employees need to get into management and out of the front line that serves clients. To earn the higher salaries, they need to increase the number of people who report to them. The ratio of doing to administering shifts in favor of administering. You can recognize an aging military: More people want to sit behind desks than want to fight the war.

To rejuvenate the public sector, therefore, we need to change the incentive system: Pay more for results and less for administering. At IBM, for example, where successful salespeople can earn more than their managers, more people want to sell than to manage.

PLANNING AND GOALS

Only after you have grasped the enormity of your predicament can you hope to stop the bleeding. Once the company returns to profitability—or you have, at the very least, stanched the flow—it is time to face the future and plan the company's return to Prime. Establish goals that reflect those plans. Make the goals tough but achievable. Plan to maintain the lean operating style the company perfected during its life crisis.

———

Principles of Organizational Therapy: An Introduction

I have designed a process that comprises 11 steps to promote progress to—or back to—Prime. Just as doctors prescribe specific courses of treatment and medication for their individual patients, the Adizes Program follows a defined sequence of restorative procedures. Their application differs depending on the nature of each corporate patient's problems and its stage in the lifecycle. The wrong treatment or inappropriate application of the right treatment can cause damage, more loss of hope, and further erosion of energy.

Supported by the principle that complementary teams with organizational authority, power, and influence have considerably more firepower than individual contributors, the 11-step therapy is a comprehensive and practical way for companies to handle their own problems through teamwork.

Teamwork mitigates resistance to change: Those busy rowing have no time to rock the boat. An analogy from sailing may help make my point. If, for example, waves rock a sailboat, some people will be nauseated. To overcome their nausea, they should take a turn at the helm and watch the horizon. Likewise, organizational change, especially if it is continuous and unpredictable, can make people sick to their stomachs. To overcome the sickening sense of being a victim of circumstances, people need to get involved in controlling the situation as they fix their eyes on the mission.

Let me repeat some of the principles of organizational therapy:

- Why: The aim is to bring the company to Prime.

- How: The vehicle is participative change.

- What: What you work on depends on your organization's stage on the lifecycle.

Now, we must consider who participates. The therapist needs to form a team of people who together exercise authority, power, and influence on the subject worked on. Working as a team, those people have the authority to say both yes and no to the potential changes the team will be making.

The team members start by collecting the problems—the potential improvement points—they have to address. I use the modifier potential because it is impossible to solve all the problems at once, and we don't want to build unrealistic expectations that could foster a new sense of failure. From the complete list, we select those problems we will work on and those we will put on the back burner.

The therapist keeps vigilant watch over the work of the team: Are the team members discussing a certain change in terms of we or they? The moment it appears that a certain course of action requires the approval of people who are not in the room, we table that discussion until those people join the team. If we can't get them to join us, we change the definition of the problem, scaling it to fit the capabilities and authorities of the people in the room.

Note that the driving force of the process is to increase the organization's sense of potency. We increase faith by picking problems the members of the group can solve. What is crucial for therapy is not what they do but how they do it. As the team solves a problem, everyone gains in self-confidence and mutual trust. With faith in themselves and the organization growing, the group can tackle a broader range of problems.

Like any other therapy, the process is one of building trust. It starts with trust in the therapist, followed by trust in themselves, expanding to trust in other members of the team, and maturing into trust in the organization itself.

I once worked with a Bureaucracy that was paralyzed to its core. The legislature had passed laws the organization could not adhere to, the administration passed requirements the organization had no budget to fulfill, and the unions issued demands and set limits that completely eliminated all maneuverability. What was our first act? We assembled a team to take care of the water fountain in the corridor. It wiggled. My colleagues at UCLA laughed at me. "You are cleaning the faucets of the Titanic," they said with smirks on their faces.

We really had no choice. Considering the health of their organization, that was the most those people could manage autonomously. Once they solved the problem of the wiggling water fountain, they decided they needed to move the water fountain itself and the wall it stood by. Therapy does not start by fixing the problem we most want to change but by fixing the problem we can change.

One aging company welcomed me with a big banner strung across its entrance: "Thanks: For a change we can make a change."

To achieve a sense of self-reliance, we compose autonomous teams of top managers who work together to decide what, where, how, why, and who. They do not just study the problems, they do not just make recommendations, they take action, and they take the credit. It is not enough to hire consultants to make a study and not see them until they present their findings for your approval. You cannot undergo therapy by sending someone else to the therapist. You cannot hire someone to exercise for you several times a week.

Along with those participants who have decision-making authority are those in a position to bring about implementation. They are people whose cooperation is crucial. Those are the people who, I claim, have power. Since many people are in positions of power, we invite those leaders others will follow. The third group we invite are those with know-how who can influence the success of what we are discussing. The entire group could include as many as 30 people.

Sometimes our discussion extends across so many organizational boundaries that we need to include hundreds of people to form a team that truly coalesces authority, power, and influence. Older organizations, which are generally the more disintegrated, need to assemble very large groups to solve a strategic issue.

When I worked with the large bank described previously, I found that for us to establish a strategic new business unit for processing payments, we needed an autonomous team. The team needed to have authority and the cooperation of those who might undermine implementation and the influence of those who knew what needed to be done. The team, therefore, had to include more than 150 people.

We had no choice about the size: The problems we had to deal with crossed the organizational boundaries of retail, wholesale, finance, marketing, and information technology. There were even a few consultants from a leading international consulting group that worked on the subject for more than a year. We assigned certain subgroups to address subcategories of some questions. The heads of those groups then formed an interlocking group that integrated their solutions and presented those solutions to their teams for approval. The process of achieving agreement and cooperation was as difficult as keeping a snowball from melting in hell. Every group had its own agenda and could have, at any time, withdrawn its cooperation.

Nevertheless the methodology is robust, and the team was able to create the new, 15,000-person division out of a number of existing units.

Once the team agrees on a change, implementation is quite swift;

partly because the planning and deciding are so time-consuming, implementation can proceed apace. The old, familiar process, which sidesteps participation, has a faster planning component, but implementation—if it ever happens—is slowed by resistance that our system handles up front. Here are the 11 steps.

THE PROGRAM

STEP

Conduct an organizational diagnosis.

Conduct an organizational diagnosis to pinpoint the problems facing the company and the root causes of those problems. A superficial analysis can lead to a misdiagnosis and subsequently to mistreatment.

The diagnosis involves an analysis of both the company's structure and the processes it uses to identify and accomplish its intended mission. The process, led by the organizational therapist, reveals the potential for organizational improvement. The diagnostic workshop helps the company identify where it is positioned in the corporate lifecycle, then describes specific steps the company will need to take to get back on the road to Prime. An implicit aspect of this phase of the program is engendering desire to make necessary changes, and the company must make it clear that it stands ready to make ironclad commitments to achieve those changes.

STEP

Form teams.

Form teams to address and solve cross-functional problems and exploit opportunities. This step is important because of the often intractable nature of the company's problems. Those are not problems readily corrected by individuals, or they would have been solved by now. In most cases, the problems have been around for a long time. Those intricate problems usually require cooperation among different functions and different individuals, and that doesn't come easily to most organizations.

Problem-solving teams of people from opposing camps are not easily managed. Managers and other employees, who have functioned well individually, need to learn both effective teamwork skills and powerful problem-solving methodologies. During this intense phase, the teams perform and receive instruction on how to solve the problems assigned to them in a way that accomplishes four activities simultaneously: problem solving, team building, style enrichment, and cognitive management training.

STEP

Train integrators.

Train integrators who will get the company to meld its disparate organizational functions and produce change effectively. The goal is to coalesce authority, power, and influence to enhance organizational effectiveness.

In this phase, we build organizational structure that parallels the staff meetings and allows change and openness.

Those first three phases help employees feel they can climb mountains to get their jobs done. The teams learn to chase down problems, identify their root causes, and either eliminate those problems or reduce their impact on company operations. All this is accomplished without the witch-hunts that typify failing companies.

STEP

Define you organization's mission.

Working together in the environment of trust and respect created in the first three phases, this fourth phase brings employees together to take a collective peek into the future. Their collective diversity helps shape a plan of action for the future. The definition of the mission will include the markets and customers the company should serve; analysis of the company's strengths and weaknesses in marketing, manufacturing, and distribution in comparison with its competition; and a projection of the future environment (internal and external) and its likely effect on the company.

STEP

Create structure that follows mission.

The teams design the organizational structure they think is best suited to carry out the company's mission.

This phase, among the most complicated of the entire program, should defeat corporate colonialism or dysfunctional parental control that could destroy nascent efforts or hamper their ability to grow.

STEP

Test the new structure; establish and verify accountabilities.

In this phase the teams define and clarify responsibilities among different functions of the company. To be sure the teams can implement their recommendations, it's crucial to associate appropriate levels of authority with newly defined responsibilities. Information systems that track performance, operational and financials, throughout the organization establish clear accountabilities.

The right information systems encourage trust and cooperation. Information that fails to pinpoint accountability encourages political infighting.

STEP

Enlist organization-wide involvement.

At this point, it is time for information to extend beyond the upper echelons and permeate the company. Unless there is an honest attempt to integrate the total organization, a chasm will open between top management and the rest of the company.

STEP

Set goals and budgets.

Set goals and budgets in a way that encourages risk-taking, committing to goals that are not easily achieved and establishing goals and budgets based on mutual trust and respect. During this phase, the company prepares its annual operating budgets. Setting goals is an art, whether for an individual or a group. With teams, the challenge is magnified. If you try to touch the ceiling, simply throwing up your hand will extend your reach only so far, but if you first stretch your arm, then your side, then the upper part of your leg, the calf, and finally your feet and toes, you will come closer to the ceiling. The same principle applies to organizations. The entire team must stretch as far as it can—together.

STEP *9*

Develop a long-term strategic plan.

Develop a long-term strategic plan for increasing market share, identifying new market opportunities and increasing profitability. The organization's plan for regaining Prime will be a communal vision with the full support and commitment of the managers responsible for results. The managers are ready to prepare the company's capital budget.

STEP *10*

Infuse every organizational function with the Adizes methodology.

During this stage, the organizational therapist prepares company managers to take over the reins. The company's top managers devise a plan to integrate all company units into the company's vision, mission, and strategy.

The original diagnosis guides the units' handling of organizational functions and their individual problems. The units establish timetables and assign each problem either to teams or to individuals.

STEP *11*

Design reward systems.

This last step demands that all other steps already be in place. Employees' rewards are tied directly to their performance, and their performance is tied directly to the company's performance. Top management joins with the teams to devise incentive systems that reflect how well teams have achieved their goals and how those goals have affected company performance.

If all the previous 10 stages have been implemented successfully, team performance should be high and consistent with the company's vision and mission. Information systems will reflect actual versus budgeted or planned performance, and there will be systematic accountability for all of the company's teams and individual performers.

With direction, resources, structure, and rewards to get the job done, the organization will reach the payoff point, and all stakeholders benefit. Clients get satisfaction at a price they are willing to pay, investors enjoy higher stock prices, and employees earn higher compensation and recognition.

But it is important to remember that as soon as the company successfully completes the 11-step program, it is time to start over. Why? In the course of the year-long program, the organization uncovers new problems and new opportunities, and all of those will require new teams, new missions, and new structures. The greater goal of the process is to institutionalize itself. Just as taking your car to the garage for regular tune-ups keeps it running smoothly, preventive maintenance keeps organizations running at peak performance.

The focus of the Adizes methodology is continual rejuvenation. It helps the company recognize problems before they grow into ugly, expensive crises. When the information system needs to be revised and updated to reflect changing conditions, the company's managers know what to do and when to do it. When market share in certain regions shows signs of decline, the company's attention is drawn to the trouble spots, and teams take corrective actions. When the established organizational structure shows signs of wear, the company revitalizes it before it becomes unresponsive.

The process is never ending. It is a journey, not a destination.

THE PROCESS

I work as a facilitator and coach rather than as a traditional consultant. My job is neither to find answers to all the questions nor to preach to troubled companies: "Here is the solution. Work with it."

I reverse the flow of energy. I ask the questions, and the company provides the answers. When a patient consults a psychotherapist, the doctor does not give answers. The doctor asks the questions, and the patient searches for answers. A good therapist knows the right questions to ask at the right time. I, too, ask questions to provoke answers that will help organizations discover for themselves how to resolve their problems. With the tools I give them, they can diagnose their position in the lifecycle to determine which of their problems are normal and which abnormal.

After I teach and put organizations in the position to solve some of the normal problems, we proceed to the mission phase: What business are we in? We work to understand what questions to ask—when and how—and, more important, which questions not to ask.

That task presents significant challenges. As a matter of interest, you should know that the Adizes Graduate School for Organizational Transformation awards master's and doctoral degrees in the discipline of organizational therapy. That is a field of study that involves a program of no less than three years and includes supervised internship and clinical work.

FUNCTIONAL IGNORANCE

Clients often ask me to visit their offices and factories to get a real understanding of their problems. "Let us tell you about our company," they say. "Let us educate you." I refuse, and I have a reason for refusing. I don't want the clients to educate me and make me responsible for solving their problems. My clients should never think that once I have learned their problems, I should be the one who comes up with the solutions. By not knowing, I can honestly claim ignorance and continually remind them that the responsibility is theirs. I provide the tools and the teaching, and they provide the content. If they do not possess content expertise, we hire a content consultant.

In the course of a diagnosis, I total the lengths of company service of each of the session participants. Let's say the sum comes to 189 years. I point out to them that among themselves they have 189 years of experience with their company. My experience with their company totals two hours—max. Who knows better, I ask, what is causing their problems and which solutions are potentially workable? Now, I continue, none of you, alone, has 189 years, and my job here is to use my 30 years of experience to lead you to make decisions based on your cumulative wisdom.

My role is not to solve the problems, it is to create the right environment and provide the tools for them to solve their problems themselves. Like a homeopathic medical practitioner who maintains that a body has all it needs to identify and cure its own ills, I insist that my job is to enable the organizational body to treat itself. I will help you find the path, but you must make the journey.

There are consultants who interview practically every employee of their client companies, and their reports regurgitate the problems and their resolution. What they are doing is telling the company what it already knows. My job is to help managers coalesce their authority, power, and influence to implement the solutions they already suspect will make a positive difference.

Here is an example: One of the largest banks in the world asked for my assistance. It was losing market share rapidly, and that was the problem I was asked to address. The organization was in Aristocracy and rapidly approaching the Recrimination stage.

"Everyone is complacent; how do we mobilize the change?" the bank's CEO asked me. He and I assembled the executive nucleus of the company. We began with fundamentals: What, I asked them, is a bank and what does a bank do? That, may I interject, was a courageous question. The executives believed that consultants worth their salt should know more than they did.

After prolonged discussion, the executives arrived at the conclusion that the banking industry (remember, this was back in the beginning of the 1980s) had not changed conceptually since the Middle Ages. Banks attracted depositors and paid them "x" percent interest. Then they sold loans to businesses and consumers, charging them "y" percent. The bank earned a margin as long as what it paid was lower than what it charged.

It became clear that traditional banking is an endangered species. For some banks, it may not be at all profitable. The multibillion-dollar losses of the savings and loan associations proves the point. Both businesses and consumers know they can get a higher rate of, return by investing in financial instruments ranging from Treasury notes to common stocks. What's more, businesses have other sources of financing outside the banking system. Banks faced growing competition on both the demand and supply sides while the law restrained them from effectively competing in those arenas. "Making money on the margins is passé. We must make money on providing services for fees," the executives concluded.

Now, I asked, what is the bank's fundamental strength? Well, aside from accepting deposits and selling loans, the executives responded, "We know how to move money around, and we have the largest network in the world." As a matter of fact, the bank had so many branches that it looked as if it was in the real estate business. With the advance of electronic banking, which at that time was still in the beta-testing stage, this real estate was becoming more of a burden than an asset. All in all, there was a good chance that this largest bank would become the largest white elephant of its industry.

Some time before those meetings, the bank had engaged a major consulting firm in a multimillion-dollar investigation of the problem. After more than a year of study, the consultants concluded that there was a tremendous need for payment systems between individuals, between organizations, and between individuals and organizations. The results of that analysis were at the bank, in nice red covers, typed clearly, and presented very professionally. No one, however, had acted on it because there was no coalescence of authority, power and influence and there was no conscious recognition of the need for change. It was a typical consulting report: paid for, filed, and forgotten.

So we started with a diagnosis of one of the divisions. We accumulated all the division's problems and classified them into two groups: those they had authority to solve and those they did not believe they had the authority to solve.

It turned out that most of the critical problems fell into the second category. We took those problems to the CEO and showed them to him. He was quite annoyed. "This is exactly the problem," he said. "They are responsible for finding solutions to these problems, but their complacency is blocking us. How do you change that?"

We reviewed each problem, one by one, asking him whether the unit had authority to act. It became quite apparent that while the executives had the responsibility, they did not have the authority. They were paralyzed. It was not an attitudinal problem. It was not a problem of complacency. It was an organizational problem. Authority was separated from responsibility.

When we tried to discover who did have the authority, the problem grew increasingly complicated. Even units with authority to decide could not exercise their decisions. They needed the cooperation of any number of other departments with their own agendas. Even the CEO could not make a decision by verdict.

Aha! The light bulb went on. A structural problem had been misunderstood as an attitudinal problem. We started barking up the right tree, or, should I say, we stopped peeing on the wrong tree? That is a typical—and very human—mistake. Because it is difficult to analyze systems, whenever we fail to understand something, we look for someone to blame. If there is no logical culprit, we accuse God, who is always available to take the blame.

Once, when my two sons were little, perhaps six and seven years old, I asked them to collect avocados that had grown on the tree in our yard. I told them to put the avocados in a bag and to put the bag in the garage. They filled the bag and tried unsuccessfully to lift it. The older one shouted, "Sho (the nickname of the younger one) does not want to lift." I looked, and poor Sho was red in the face from the effort of trying to lift the bag. The bag, of course, was far too heavy. Clearly, both of them were trying. How many times has this picture come back to haunt me? We always look for somebody to accuse rather than contend with the complexity of the task or situation that stymies us.

After our success with the bank's small problems had given people confidence, we tackled the big one: Banking is dead. Long live financial institutions. At that point, somebody rediscovered the consultants' report on payment systems. The teacher can teach only when the student is ready: We started working on the payment systems, structure and strategy. There we encountered a new problem. The bank had been making money on the float, the money that was in the channels. Providing efficient systems of payments meant giving up that source of income. This is the next human problem: A bird in the hand is, as we all say, worth two in the bush.

Nevertheless, there was a market need. The cost of having money resting in channels of transfer was extremely high to those needing liquidity. Considering the advances in electronic banking, it was only a matter of time before some bank would offer that service. After deep discussion, the group concluded that a better way to make money was to add value by focusing on clients' needs and solving them. They reached that revolution in thinking—putting clients' needs first—only after gradually building faith in each other and in the organization.

The executive group continued its discussion of how moving assets around makes money. Those are fee-based services as opposed to traditional banking services, which make money on the margin. Are there other services beyond moving money around for which we can charge fees? Yes: insurance, brokerage-house services, investment advisory services, and other financial services we don't even know about today. We must get organized to identify them early and act on them earlier than others.

A mission and structure were starting to emerge. The bank needed to convert from the traditional business of making most of its money from the differential between the amount it pays and the amount it charges for money, to a financial services institution that makes most of its money from fee-based services.

The Incompatibility of Effectiveness and Efficiency

How did the bank find itself in such a condition that it needed help? The process is similar to human aging. By the time a man reaches his middle age, he has accumulated extra fat due to a naturally falling rate of metabolism. When he was younger, his metabolism was higher, and whenever that man gained a few pounds during his youth, he could easily shed them. But that was long ago.

In their growing stages and coming-of-age stages, companies can stumble, make mistakes, and return to fighting shape with reasonable ease. Younger, more vital organizations are leaner and more flexible. They resolve problems and exploit opportunities with alacrity.

But as they enter the aging stages, they lose the resilience of those earlier years. They become more set in their ways. Flexibility gives way to control. Companies grow less responsive to change. Managers, who once worked together for the common good of the company, no longer communicate. They define their responsibilities individually— rather than in a collective or integrated sense.

Remember those doubles tennis players we talked about in the last chapter? They split the court, and each played on one side of the line, never crossing to the other's side. Who played the middle? What happened when smart opponents repeatedly lobbed the ball to the center of the court?

The tennis players did a bad job of defining their responsibilities. They would have been better off to watch the ball and each other. Perhaps both of them should move for the ball. The first one to reach the ball can take the swing. But, you think, that's not efficient, is it? No, it is not efficient, but it is effective.

The way to become more effective is to become less efficient. That is the approach aging companies need to take. For growing companies, the approach is just the reverse. To become more effective in the long run, you need to become more efficient, which means that in the short run you might have to sacrifice your short-term effectiveness. Effectiveness and efficiency are incompatible. Efficient systems, by definition, are ineffective in the long run. An aging company, to be efficient, needs to be controlled, and controls reduce flexibility, which is required for long-term effectiveness.

Each task that falls in between individual tasks is better defined as ours. Not yours, not mine. Ours. An efficient manager can perform his own tasks beautifully, but he stands alone, exposed and vulnerable, until he connects with other managers in the organization. When every manager stands alone, the organization is fragmented, not integrated. Individual efforts will come to naught. It is the collective power of all the managers, integrated to provide a common direction, that makes the organization a powerful entity. The role of the organizational therapist is to provide integration, a sense of interdependence, and a uniting consciousness.

My approach to changing a client's location on the lifecycle calls for helping its people to grow more attuned to the needs of their customers and to one another. As together we slaughter sacred cows, our clients overcome their fear of change. We accomplish all this not through the bloodletting of downsizing but by building faith; by taking a realistic problem-solving approach; by integration, not disintegration; by long-term therapy, not short-term surgery; by building strength from the inside, not the outside; and for long-term effects, not for short-term cosmetic improvements.

———

CHAPTER 12

Management Myths Revisited

——— *Management Myths: A Parable* ———

The board of directors of Plug&Play Software, Inc., a relatively young, fast-growing company, brought in Jack Sampson as the company's new CEO after deciding that the company's hard-charging founder, Sharon Glass, needed support. That was the public reason. Privately, they said that Sharon was too "uncontrollable." She retained her position as a member of the board and as the chief engineer in charge of product development.

There wasn't much she could do about the management change. She had long ago lost control of the company. She used generous stock options to lure talented engineers to the company, and she sold large chunks of stock when she needed capital for expansion. Although she was bitter, she accepted the decision in the hope that it would help the company.

Several years before that momentous meeting of the board of directors, Glass had started Plug&Play. She recognized that literally millions of people wanted to take part in the information revolution, and many of them, who possessed neither technical training nor inclination, felt constrained by fear of the unknown. So she and a few of her close associates—all technical people— developed a trendy line of software that gave novices instant access to their computers' power.

The software hit the market at just the right time. And even though it was pricey, millions of frustrated computer users embraced it. Sales zoomed off the charts for awhile, but new programs were needed as competition entered the market. Tom Wixom, Plug&Play's chief financial officer, was worried about the company's ability to cover its skyrocketing costs. Glass insisted on developing new software to respond to market demand. "What we did with computer education," she insisted, "we can do with 'edutainment' software, software that is educational and entertaining."

The education part fit well with Plug&Play's product line, all right, but the company's people knew little about entertainment. As a result, the new software was, according to the critics, neither entertaining nor educationally effective. The product bombed. In response, Glass redoubled her efforts and went after the market for pure entertainment. "We know how to educate; we missed on the entertainment. So we must develop our capabilities there. That is where the future lies," Glass asserted.

Each development was a major financial undertaking. Because the major investment was in systems architecture, there was little to dedicate to the product's promotion. Its packaging was mediocre, the marketing budget was virtually nonexistent, and the sales effort was ineffective because the company had little leverage with the sales channels. Because the big, established software companies demanded that retailers stock the complete line of their products, Plug&Play was bumped off the retail shelves. And shelf space was at a premium. New and competing products were arriving like an avalanche.

Glass found herself fighting with everyone. "All we need is a winner. One winner! The difference between a losing software company and a winner is one, I repeat, only one, good software package." She was actually yelling. "That is where we must concentrate our efforts. If we produce a winner, the sales channels will have to stock it."

Her strategy to develop a winner meant that the company had to develop many products. After all, who could predict which development would be the winner? So Glass initiated a dozen developments that devoured money the company did not have. "Don't worry," she recommended, "when we get our next winner, it will pay for everything handsomely. Money is available. We just need to make ourselves available. Investors will back us. We have the track record. I can get new investors next week. We could go public."

At first, investors shared Glass' excitement, but she was losing credibility rapidly. Her vice presidents started to doubt that her approach was a strategy.

"How can it be?" lamented the CFO. "Every new idea is a great idea, and so many great new ideas have miraculously become projects-in-the-making without any discussion. And, we have no money."

Glass used to love to hold company pep rallies, where she would proclaim: "Microsoft, watch out! Here comes Plug&Play!"

As Glass was losing the trust of her vice presidents, the members of the board also started to worry. The vice president of sales cultivated a friendship with a member of the board. He described—in disturbing detail—the haphazard process that governed development decisions. He also explained why he could not sell the products the company did develop. The vice president of marketing was sending a flurry of memos that asserted that without different packaging, the products would never sell.

The CFO submitted his resignation on a weekly basis: The company had no money in the bank, and the pressure at work was just too much.

Glass, however, was relentless. The vice president of sales, Glass accused, "has no imagination, but he still wants to decide what software gets developed. He has no clue what to do." She presented examples from the past to prove that the same sales vice president had been opposed to products that had been extremely successful.

As for the vice president of marketing, Glass dismissed her with a sniff: "She's just a Harvard MBA. All she does is quote pages from the textbooks. We hired her because the board believed that professionally trained management is what we need. But from the day she arrived, she has been an obstacle to my capability to create. And," she continued, "the CFO is simply incompetent. He has no idea whether we are making money or losing it. His cash projections are constantly off. If the board would let me, I would fire the three of them and bring in some real talent."

The board was worried. Incoming cash was trailing cash outflows. The company's line of credit was exhausted, and several times in the recent past Glass had gone to the board for additional equity contributions because there was inadequate cash to cover even payroll.

The board finally decided the company needed a professional manager to impose controls.

Jack Sampson was a veteran of IBM where he had enjoyed steady, if not spectacular, advances in the company. His background was mostly in marketing and sales. The board thought that he would help Plug&Play do a better job of choosing software development projects. Sampson had earned a reputation for being the kind of guy who could work with teams. He would be able to get factions to reach agreement. He was empathetic, considerate, and thoughtful.

Sampson attacked his new duties at Plug&Play with relish. His first move was to assemble the staff so that he could let them know how much he respected teamwork. He explained that he expected everyone who reported directly to him to work as a team. Each of them, he added, should serve as an example for the rest of the company. The board had charged him with uniting the company in this time of crisis, and he had every intention of doing so.

In his first meeting with his staff, Sampson asked all of the participants to feel free to express opinions. Did they ever. The accusations and interruptions were such that one of the participants actually started to hyperventilate and get dizzy. Glass threatened to leave the company, and the dissenting vice presidents encouraged her to go. Weathering that maelstrom, Sampson remained calm. Although people continually interrupted his presentation, he never got upset.

No decisions were made. Sampson announced his intention to appoint a team to study the problems and present recommendations within two weeks. Glass wanted the results sooner. She needed to know which products would be developed and which would not. The CFO wanted to know where money was going to come from: He needed to know Monday morning at the latest. The marketing vice president insisted that she needed a decision on the packaging for Christmas sales "last Monday, not next Monday."

Sampson realized he needed help. He retained an organizational-development facilitator for team building and effective communication training. He explained to his senior managers, "We need to work together as a team. We need to pull together, to realize our interdependencies, to communicate and be open and honest."

The consultant brought the managers together and got everyone to agree on rules of engagement. People had to be absolutely honest and open.

So they all told Glass, honestly and openly, how much they did not trust her, and she, in turn, told them that they were incompetent and ought to be fired. Sampson tried to calm everyone, reiterating the need for trust, respect, constructive conflict, open systems, harmony, and understanding. By the end of the meeting everyone was completely miserable.

"No pain, no gain," the trainer intoned.

Paralyzed, no one knew what was coming, who would stay, or who would get fired. Sampson developed a bleeding ulcer and had to go to the hospital. Glass could feel her blood pressure rising. The vice president of sales refused to come to any more meetings, and the vice president for marketing let everyone know that she was willing to leave—if they would vest her—effective immediately.

Meanwhile, the company's sales were going from bad to worse. A sudden decline in earnings reflected the drop in sales, and the company, which had been consistently but marginally profitable, plunged into the red. CFO Tom Wixom reported the alarming news to Sampson and the board of directors.

The board, which included major investors who had a lot to lose, asked CFO Wixom to launch an immediate investigation and make recommendations. Wixom, who had initially hoped to replace Sharon Glass as CEO, was no friend of Sampson. He told the board that Sampson had failed to take control of the company's affairs and its galloping costs. What's more, he was trying to run the company by consensus. Wixom told no lies, but he made no attempt to support Sampson either.

When a board member pulled Sampson aside and confronted him with what Wixom had said, Sampson responded that he had used the same approach at IBM, and he had no doubt that his management style would be just as effective at Plug&Play. He said, however, that his health was so bad that if the board would honor his golden parachute, he would resign.

The board accepted his resignation and appointed Wixom as the new CEO. He had a plan that the board found appealing: cut costs rapidly to match the company's resources, fire 60 percent of the development engineers, focus and get development under control, and recruit a world-class cost accountant as soon as possible. Wixom spoke with the assurance of one who knows exactly what to do, and he presented the numbers that proved his plan would save the company.

Glass was the only board member to vote against the plan and the appointment. Because she had lost so much credibility, when she spoke, people were so embarrassed they focused their eyes anywhere but on her face.

Soon after Wixom's appointment, Glass resigned and opened another software company practically across the street. She financed it out of her savings. The most talented development engineers from Plug&Play respected her creativity. They promptly followed her to the new venture. Wixom was having his way with the engineering department anyway. He kept only those who were willing to work within the parameters he set: "Forget the fireworks; forget the exotics. Watch what is successful in the marketplace and copy it. Do not try to be the first kid on the block. It's too dangerous. Follow success and be cost-effective."

The first product of Wixom's regime did not make it on to most retailers' shelves. It sunk into oblivion. The vice presidents of both sales and marketing resigned, and, Wixom, trying to save further costs, undertook those roles himself.

The word was out: Plug&Play was in trouble. Even those employees who did not have their resumes out in the street were hearing from headhunters. The fast-growing software industry always needs talent. Investors who had been attracted by Glass's vision were reviewing their position. Many of them sold their stock at a fraction of their investment. With no source of new funds, the company was incapable of meeting the interest payments on its debt, and Plug&Play found itself facing bankruptcy proceedings.

Management Myths

That story leads me directly to the subject of this chapter: The myths of guaranteed business salvation promise that if companies simply embrace team building or delegation of power or autocratic management or cost efficiency or a more-is-better approach to product planning or who knows what, then prosperity will surely be theirs. Plug&Play's board of directors; its founder, Sharon Glass; its second CEO, Jack Sampson; and its last CEO, Tom Wixom, all believed in the infallibility of one or another of those myths.

The myths all originate from one fundamental mistake that many management books make. They ignore the it-all-depends aspect of situations. They describe what businesses should do as if they were in Prime. I believe that even Tom Peters, for whom I have great respect, made that mistake in his book In Search of Excellence. Peters described companies' optimal behavior as if they were in Prime. But what is a desirable behavior for a company in Prime does not necessarily bring companies to Prime.

That approach is as hopeless as describing an emotionally mature adult to a child and telling him, "Now, be like that." For that matter, it isn't much more useful to tell a feeble, old person that "the way to rejuvenate yourself is to be like that young, athletic neighbor of yours."

What is right at one stage of the lifecycle can easily be the wrong thing to do at another stage. You should not treat your babies as if they are adults, nor should you treat your adult children as if they are still babies. To raise emotionally healthy children, you must do the right things at the right time.

Absolute principles create myths: delegate; use teamwork; be open and honest; decentralize; manage with, by, and for chaos; downsize; reengineer; manage by results, not by process; manage by process for results; hierarchy is good; hierarchy is bad; love; fight; act; wait. The list goes on and on.

For me, there are no absolute solutions. It all depends. What is right and what is wrong depend on what needs to be done and how. Understand that I am not talking about values: Values are absolutes, and I do not compromise on values. I am talking about tools, and their correct use depends on the task at hand.

MANAGEMENT MYTH

Companies don't thrive under autocrats.

That is not always true. Companies in their Infancy, or in deep trouble as we have seen, require a strong arm to keep them on course. A participative management approach at this early stage may be inappropriate. Teamwork, by definition, calls for delegation of tasks. Delegation requires capability and sufficient experience to articulate what to do and what not to do. In Infancy it is too early for the founder to achieve this level of articulation.

The founders during the Infancy stage usually don't yet know whether they will see the realization of their dreams or their nightmares. In the early stages, founders learn from their experience. For that reason, when someone challenges them, founders raise their voices and even get upset. They may well retort, "Just do what I tell you."

Those people who too frequently pose challenges to their authority become irritations, and many founders try to get rid of such pests. Delegation without control is abdication, but you cannot control until you can systematize what you want and what you do not want.

It is too early to delegate in Infancy. But be aware: If you don't delegate in Go-Go, you may face disaster. Autocratic, centralized decision making gets Go-Go companies into trouble. Remember Sharon Glass and Plug&Play?

Autocratic leadership is again desirable should a company find itself in Recrimination. That's when it needs leadership that imparts a sense of certainty and security, galvanizes the company, and unites efforts to eliminate waste. In the Plug&Play parable, Sampson was too weak to decide, act, and eliminate dissension.

Infant companies cannot progress swiftly without directed leadership. What all infant companies need is more, more, more: more sales, more production, more new markets, more products, more services. Everyone in an infant company must be action oriented, with an unquenchable thirst for results. But results don't come easily.

Leaders—the founders who are struggling to transform their visions into realities—need to control their experiments or they will lose interest and abandon their creations to die from neglect. They have to be the people who hire, train, motivate, and coach their sales teams, which they usually lead since founders know their products, markets, and customers better than anybody else. They must visit customers frequently and let their people know what they have to do to keep those customers happy.

They cannot delegate because they do not yet know how, and if they did know how, they would need better people than themselves. At this stage of their companies' development they can't afford people who are better than they are. They must make every major decision until the company stabilizes with repeat sales, positive cash flow, and predictable demand. That's when they can articulate and systematize their companies' experience. And, then, they should start delegating: first the producing functions, followed by administrative functions, and eventually the entrepreneurial functions.

When they delegate the entrepreneurial role, they are no longer delegating. They are decentralizing, and that should occur only when companies reach Prime.

Autocratic management does not mean being obnoxious and disrespectful. It means being strong, decisive, and fair.

Leaders of infant organizations have to learn how to persuade, order, explain, cajole, or command employees to get the job done. During Infancy, founders are like the wagon masters who led the pioneers across dangerous, uncharted territories to reach the West.

Committees, teams, and groups can take the place of founders only if they are so committed to one another that they are one, and they act like one. Like the suffering children of parents who bicker, companies languish when their leadership disintegrates. Team decisions and consensus building are better left to companies in the more advanced stages of the corporate lifecycle.

MANAGEMENT MYTH

Every meeting should have a strict agenda.

Some should not. If every meeting adhered to a strict agenda, how could participants explore the future of their companies, dream about new markets and products, and build common values?

At their best, meetings bring together employees from disparate functions to discuss common goals and share the information participants need to do their jobs well.

In their Go-Go stage, companies hold meetings that follow no set format. They can address any topic that strikes their founders' interest. For the most part, these meetings are impromptu, taking place almost anywhere: in corporate corridors, at water fountains, on production floors, in the company lunchrooms over vending-machine coffee and doughnuts. Meeting subjects range across the entire spectrum of company affairs. Usually there is no single subject under discussion, and every participant has the authority to introduce new topics as long as the CEO finds it interesting.

As companies grow older, they have a tendency to formalize the structure of their meetings. In Prime, meetings take on lives of their own. They become the working ground of middle managers: They provide the arena for resolving major issues through liaisons with peers and others who can help them.

Formal agendas, for more mature organizations, are de rigueur. Those agendas spell out not only what will be discussed, who will participate in the discussions, and how much time will be allotted to each topic, but also the anticipated results. Attendees conform to established dress codes. They take their places in accordance with the recognized pecking order.

Such oppressive atmospheres asphyxiate initiative. The meeting protocol (who says what, how he or she says it, and to whom it is addressed) snuffs out the possibility of give and take. Managers, too scared to depart from established procedure, toe the line. For them the above principle is a myth that needs debunking.

Meetings like those accomplish very little except the sharing of information, and they are usually boring. Even before the meetings convene, managers know what to expect. The cleverest managers carefully shape outcomes by conducting informal discussions beforehand with other managers. Anyone who dares depart from the agenda risks being tagged a troublemaker, a corporate pariah whom other managers studiously avoid. Form crushes function.

What, then, is the answer? Should organizations shun or require strict meeting agendas? It all depends. In Infancy there are usually no formal meetings. People see decisions being implemented before they even hear that there has been a decision. In Go-Go–stage companies, the decision-making process, dominated by the CEO, is extremely fluid and unpredictable, and there is scant accountability. Go-Go companies must have formal meetings with agendas just to counterbalance the ad hoc attitude that permeates the company.

Meetings in companies that have left Prime grow increasingly structured and impotent. Those companies should set time aside for meetings with a general topic, no strict agenda, and no prepared overheads. Such meetings should supplement, not supplant, the formal meetings.

A Prime company has both types of scheduled meetings: blue-sky and formal meetings, in the right balance.

MANAGEMENT MYTH

The companies that win are those with the most flexibility.

This is a good one because it is a fad of the 1990s. In the attempt to rejuvenate bureaucracies, many management-fad gurus recommend doing away with structure and hierarchy. "It will increase the flexibility of companies," they assure us. For aging companies, they may be right, but such a path will destroy a growing company.

Flexibility is characteristic of companies in their growing stages, and control, its counterbalance, is characteristic of companies in their aging stages. Absolute flexibility means a complete lack of control, and absolute control means a complete lack of flexibility. Those absolutes determine the limits of the flexibility-control continuum. Companies in Prime are at the center of the continuum, engaged in a continuous struggle to maintain the delicate balance between flexibility and control.

I deliberately use the word "delicate" because it takes so little to push a company in either direction. When administrators gain the upper hand, the company's balance swings in the direction of excessive control, and the company sacrifices flexibility. If entrepreneurs gain the upper hand, the company grows more flexible and loses control. The top management of a company in Prime needs to be always alert to that teetering balance.

A company with excessive flexibility is unable to accomplish much in a predictable manner because people are flying off in too many different directions. While that complete flexibility is acceptable in a growing company in its Infancy, it will prove disastrous for a company in Go-Go.

On the other hand, a company in its Aristocracy stage has already been weakened by excessive control. Reducing controlling structure and process and introducing a culture that encourages risk-taking and embraces flexibility will interject forces of rejuvenation that will retard the company's decline.

Companies in Adolescence are at the right stage to establish a measure of control. As they grow and progress through Courtship, Infancy, and Go-Go, companies have to remain loose and flexible, ready to change direction and grasp emerging opportunities at a moment's notice. Adolescence calls for companies to prepare themselves for the next stage, Prime. To achieve Prime, companies must first gain control over both finances and operations. That, by definition, calls for controls. I do not mean controls that smother initiative. I do mean controls that maintain consistent and predictable operations. Flexibility, at least too much during Adolescence, can prevent a company from attaining Prime and may cause it to bypass Prime altogether and head directly into the Founder's Trap.

MANAGEMENT MYTH

The sooner a company attracts investment bankers, the sooner and the faster it will grow.

On the surface that statement may seem to be an axiom of business. After all, doesn't every company need capital to grow and finance operations? In their early years most companies are cash starved. Their CEOs and other senior managers devote a lot of time and energy to attracting investors. And the faster companies grow, the more they need large cash infusions to sustain that growth. Under certain circumstances—when payables outpace receivables, for example—it can be difficult for companies to generate expansion capital from operations. Working capital to finance the increasing sales might not be available and, as the company's sales grow, will go dry. That is when astute investors show up.

Founders, be cautioned. Certain investors are interested only in the short ride. They are looking for a fast return. If they do not share your dream, they will become the vultures your mother warned you about. I strongly recommend that no founder lose control of voting stock until the company reaches Prime.

This principle might not always work since some founders, drunk with success during their Go-Go phase, start making decisions that are dangerous to their companies' health. They become overly adventurous. They believe in their own infallibility, and they take their companies over the cliff. Those founders need a strong board of directors with a stake in the company to control the elusive founder. But they must be careful: Those founders may still be indispensable to the company's survival.

MANAGEMENT MYTH

Marketing and sales should work hand in hand.

Well, yes, but the question is how. Marketing's job is to create opportunities: to explore the possibilities of new products and services. Marketing defines niches competitors have not yet discovered or that have not yet been truly satisfied. By identifying distribution channels, advertising, and promotional opportunities, marketing expands customer receptivity and interest. Marketing uses brand management to enhance product-line profits.

The job of sales is to respond to opportunities. Its managers take marketing's niche information and sell. Marketing plans; sales executes. Marketing, you might say, is the thinking part of the selling process, deciding what to sell at what price and through which distribution channels. Sales is producing. Sales carries out marketing's plans and contributes information that indicates the effectiveness of those marketing plans. That feedback contributes to a continuously self-adjusting marketing strategy. Sales is a source of marketing information and the execution arm of marketing.

It is clear, then, that the two functions need to cooperate. But since marketing's function is to locomote change, and sales' function is to deliver that change, marketing and sales often clash. Their styles are incompatible.

The conflict is not evident at the beginning. Infant organizations have neither a sales nor a marketing orientation. These companies, simply struggling to survive, are in the order-taking business. Sales happen when orders arrive. Marketing is what the founders dreamed about when they started their companies. The conflict is not evident because, for all practical purposes, people ignore both functions in Infancy. They are busy making the product work and finding "who is on first."

In Go-Go, the strong sales orientation is frequently called marketing, but the founder or CEO actually fulfills the marketing function. The company in Go-Go is opportunity driven: It chases every opportunity that looks promising whether or not it fits the so-called marketing strategy. Opportunities without a strategy are distractions, and companies in the Go-Go stage are riddled with distractions. Again, the conflict is not evident because the organization does what the CEO wants it to do, and the CEO monopolizes the marketing function.

In Adolescence, companies need to institutionalize and depersonalize the marketing function by moving it from the creative founder to a marketing department. That, of course, is easier said than done, particularly for those companies that enjoyed Go-Go success because of their founders' marketing talents. The source of earlier successes becomes the cause of future failures.

The founders refuse to release their holds. They refuse to give up their discretionary powers. They refuse to give up making decisions as they please. They want their babies always to continue admiring them and emulating them. They do not want to lose the pleasure of having a dependent entity responsive to their dreams. They clutch their babies even though those babies are now 40 years old. They are like overly possessive mothers who keep their adult sons from dating women who might marry them and change their habits. Several of my clients come to mind. The struggle to transfer marketing authority from the founder to another person can take a lifetime, and I mean a lifetime: Everyone says, "It won't happen until the old man (or the old lady) dies."

If the transition occurs and the entrepreneurial roles (marketing, process or production engineering, finance, design or developmental engineering) are institutionalized, the company has moved to position itself in Prime. But will it stay there? Marketing and sales may bicker and fight. Marketing will campaign for a change, but sales will resist, saying, "You guys without the responsibility to execute speak with great authority. You don't understand the repercussions of your recommendations."

CEOs, especially if they come from the ranks of the bean counters, do not want to get in the middle of those arguments. Their response is to unite the two functions under one vice president with the title vice president, sales and marketing. Notice that the position is not called marketing and sales. This is no accident. As a consequence of uniting those two roles, it is usually the marketing function that is suppressed. The company stops making waves and the short-term pressures of sales dominate.

More than 30 years ago, the American economist Herbert Simon postulated that when confronted with the choice of doing a long-term or short-term task, people almost invariably postpone the long-term task. As a matter of fact, a continuous stream of short-term pressures can postpone the long-term assignment indefinitely. When marketing and sales report to the same vice president, I find that marketing degenerates. It becomes sales support. No longer making waves, marketing is reduced to helping sales ride the waves. That is when the company starts its departure from Prime.

Conclusion: After Adolescence make sure to have independent—but cooperative and communicative—sales and marketing vice presidents.

MANAGEMENT MYTH

If a company consistently beats its sales and costs projections,
that is a sign that the company is managed well.

Wrong. When actual sales levels are consistently higher than budget, and actual costs are always below budget, the message is that the budgeted numbers are much too easy. The company has grown lazy. Its goals are far too accessible. Its employees are not challenged. It is a company headed for trouble. When the company's employees get lazy, the next crisis—and there is always a next crisis—may find them totally unprepared and too complacent to discover the problem's root causes and make changes. They just lower expectations.

Worse, the company's managers may ignore the crisis, refusing even to recognize it. After all, they might reason, "Haven't we consistently surpassed our projections? This problem is simply an anomaly. We're doing fine."

The problem is aggravated by a reward system based on how well people beat their budgets. To be sure that they surpass their goals, they fight to set their goals as low as possible. To avoid that problem, the latest fad recommends you benchmark your company's performance against the stars of your industry.

Does it motivate your son or daughter if you post the grades of the best in their class all over the house? Can you reasonably expect them to meet or surpass those grades? Some of us parents have tried that, but what does it do to our children's self-esteem? Why not sit down with them to evaluate their performance and set goals that reflect the best they can do? I would rather my children get a low grade while trying their best than cheat their way to a high grade. In many companies, people do cheat or pass the buck to meet their goals.

Establish budgets through planning. As Dwight D. Eisenhower said, "Plans are useless; planning is priceless." What is really important is not the budget itself but the process of making the budgets. That process makes us ask how we can do our best and how we should go about doing it. When the results we achieve either fall short or far exceed our expectations, we ought to view those deviations from the budget not as opportunities to dress down or applaud but as opportunities to analyze our assessment of our capabilities.

How does a company slip into a state where it regularly surpasses its goals? It is easy. The older a company grows, especially a company that has been consistently profitable, the more its managers get rewarded for being predictable. How you do counts more than what you do. If someone surpasses the goal, the threshold rises. So executives build reserves into their projected budgets that only they know about. Compounded reserves reduce the agility of the company. They establish intra-organizational deception, and they sow the seeds of mistrust throughout the system.

How does everyone grow so attached to budgets? Companies in Infancy rarely have budgets. If they do have budgets, the actual is distinctly different from the projected. It starts during the Go-Go phase when budgets are usually late, and the difference between actual and projected budget is always high. The company is clearly not under control. Go-Go companies often spend large sums of money on projects that were never even budgeted. The lack of budgetary discipline continues until the company gets in trouble. That happens in Adolescence so predictably it seems as if it is scheduled on someone's calendar. The organization slams the brakes to the metal, bringing the runaway vehicle to a screeching halt. Now the company rigidly enforces budgetary restraints. It punishes violators and establishes rewards to encourage predictability. Entrepreneurial types complain, fight, resign, or moan. Flexibility suffers.

A company that is enjoying a healthy Adolescence has controls that don't stop the vehicle but simply prevent it from tumbling down. When controls are pathologically tight, the company stalls like Plug&Play in this chapter's introductory case.

When budgets stimulate improvements as much as controls—the company is in Prime.

MANAGEMENT MYTH

Having lots of cash in the treasury is a sign of a well-managed organization.

The truth is nearly the opposite. Huge cash reserves indicate an aging company with failing vitality. The company has neither the vision nor the drive to seek out new and promising opportunities to spur growth and profits. It is a company well into the aging process.

A company that is either growing and pursuing Prime or returning to Prime never has enough money set aside to finance growth. Employees bombard top management with so many promising ideas that the company's executives need to rank the ideas before they can even consider them. With so many rich ideas, the company might have a cash squeeze. Nevertheless, such a company is a moving company. It is better to be approximately right than precisely wrong.

The employees of a company with bulging coffers either aren't advancing ideas or are advancing ideas that top management rejects, approving only those projects with low risk.

It is difficult to imagine a company full of employees with no ideas. That is rarely the problem. Most employees are at least creative enough to find better ways and means to do their jobs. Discovery of opportunities is the rule rather than the exception, unless management has imposed an environment hostile to new ideas. Remember there are no bad soldiers, only bad generals.

I become alert when a CEO tells me that he would love to invest his company's cash in promising new companies. Why does he not have projects indigenously grown? While such aspirations might be appropriate for a Prime company, they could be a sign of a company in Aristocracy. Companies in Aristocracy are much more interested in acquiring technology or products and services than in developing them themselves. Why? Because they cannot develop them, that's why.

Being cash rich has another distinct disadvantage: The company is a ripe takeover target. Other, more aggressive companies—usually companies in Go-Go—need that cash to finance their expansion. The company with too much cash is a sitting duck.

MANAGEMENT MYTH

A healthy company exhibits a consistent management style.

This is as misleading as saying that parents' relationship with their children should not evolve over the years, or both parents should use exactly the same approaches with their children.

A company in Prime embraces a diversity of management styles. It is a company that is comfortable with strategists and tacticians, people who love detail work and those who hate it. It is a company of entrepreneurs, administrators, producers, and integrators—all of whom have their own distinct management styles. And everyone has learned to work well with everyone else.

New companies that make sure everyone has the same style cannot survive much beyond the Infancy stage—certainly not beyond the Go-Go stage. No company should grow exponentially up because it has only one direction to take when problems intervene: down.

People should build companies by following the principles of tunnel digging in the gold-mining business. If you simply keep digging deeper, you can be sure the tunnel will collapse on you. You must dig and dig and then stop to install infrastructure. Why do companies so often fail to build the infrastructure? That requires a different style of leadership. Those who dig hate to spend time on supports, and those who build the supporting system resent the diggers. They argue that "what is gold for you is a lot of dirt for us to clean."

In young companies, the entrepreneurial types dominate, and the administrators are in the penalty box. In aging companies, the power shifts. Administrative people dominate and the entrepreneurial people are relegated to the penalty box. In both cases, they are doing the wrong thing. A company needs them both: The offensive and the defensive teams must be involved if we want to win the game in the long run. In Prime, everyone plays together.

Companies, like children, need both the feminine and masculine energies, the yin and the yang, to grow successfully. The energies are in balance only in Prime, and even in Prime, the relationship between the two forces is not static. One leads while the other supports.

For healthy growth, entrepreneurial types should lead, supported by the administrative types. In Adolescence, the driving force should switch. And in Prime the integrators should take the lead, supported by the administrative and entrepreneurial roles in tandem.

Children need feminine energy to begin with, and then they need masculine energy to continue their growth. After a while, their parents need to free them, and the parent who is the better integrator generally takes the leadership position.

Companies in Aristocracy, Recrimination, or Bureaucracy stages tend to collect managers with the same management style. In a dying company, nobody wants to make waves. Managers who do not want to be ostracized or fired seek the protective cover of conformity.

The same principle applies to company structures and strategies. Excessive uniformity indicates decay. Clashes between marketing and sales are normal and expected. The trick is to insure their arguments don't become destructive.

Diversity of styles and the changing of styles as organizations progress from one stage of the lifecycle to another are necessary factors for successful development. It is essential that a company have, develop, and nurture that diversity.

When a company is having problems tracking its financial and operating information, it probably needs a new, more powerful computer.

More often than not, the problem is not the company's computer technology or information system. A new computer will not solve the problems caused by inadequate structure.

The difference between data and information is that information is data designed for decision making. It is apparently no mistake that in their early days, computers were in the electronic data processing (EDP) departments. But for EDP to provide information, the company needs to establish which people have authority over what and what data those people need to make decisions. The next questions they must answer are: Who should know about those decisions? Who should know whether those decisions are working out or not? To achieve those goals, the company must articulate its structure and identify authority and responsibilities.

I have encountered numerous inefficient companies that decided they needed to reengineer and redesign their business processes. One company, in particular, hired highly qualified and experienced consultants, assigning them the project of business-process redesign with the following limitation: Do not change the company's structure. "It is a very treacherous field," the company's management assured the consultants, "politically loaded."

You can, I am sure, recognize that the company was an organization in an advanced stage of aging. It was on the verge of Recrimination. The consultants accepted the task. More than a million dollars and one year later, the company had a computer system few could use. It further petrified the company and reduced its flexibility more than ever. When the company wanted to refocus responsibilities on its markets and restructure, it could not: The computerized budgetary system was too difficult and too expensive to change.

The same problem arises in Go-Go–stage companies. With no structure, those companies are often highly centralized. They have no controls and little, if any, discipline. They erroneously believe that the right computer system will bring order and impose discipline. Instead they end up with new confusion, pain, less control, and even more centralized decision making: Now the CEO really can reach everyone and everywhere.

Before computerizing, a company needs structure and discipline.

MANAGEMENT MYTH

Strategy precedes structure.

It is one of the cornerstones of management theory that strategy precedes structure. It makes sense, doesn't it? How can you structure an organization without knowing what it intends to do—what its strategy is? Architects and design engineers will all agree that form follows function.

My experience has led me to a different conclusion: Strategy should precede structure, but in reality it does not. In reality, structure precedes strategy. Tell me the structure of your company, and I will describe its strategy. I have done it many times for my clients. I analyze the organizational structure of the competition and predict its behavior, that is, the competition's strategy.

For example, financier Mike Milken told an audience that AT&T invented the cellular phone and estimated that demand would not exceed 750,000 by the year 2000. What's more, AT&T predicted that nobody would spend more than $1,000 a year on it. Consequently, AT&T decided the market was too small to merit its attention, and it sold the business only to buy it back just a few years later, in September 1994, for $11 billion from McCaw Cellular.

Now, how could AT&T make such a blunder? And how did IBM nearly miss the PC market. For that matter, why did the British textile industry miss the mechanical loom?

The reason is that strategy is neither decided nor implemented by an individual. It is set by a group of people who interact, decide, and implement their decision. What they decide and implement is a result of their interests as they perceive them. Their interests are brought about by the power and responsibilities that the organization chart offers them. If there is a vice president for sales and marketing, and a CFO to whom finance, the controller, accounting, internal audit, human resources, legal services, information technology, and facilities maintenance all report (bureaucrats of the world, unite!), chances are the company has a very short-term, conservative outlook on the market.

The CEO might be an entrepreneurial, risk-taking individual, but in a structure as described above, he or she will encounter plenty of resistance from the vice president of sales and marketing and the CFO. I would not be surprised to find the CFO subtly undermining the CEO's position with the board. The CFO's comments appear, on the surface, to be innocent, but they hamper the CEO's ability to maneuver and lead change.

If one product line is successful, and the unit that produces it has enjoyed generous rewards for that success, chances are slim that the unit's leaders will lend wholehearted support to a new product, technology, or market expansion that threatens their product line. It was IBM's enormous success with the mainframe that produced a structure dominated by mainframe-dedicated people who could not create a supportive or nurturing environment for PCs.

To understand and know the enemy's intentions, a military commander looks at the positioning of the enemy's forces. If the tanks are in front of the infantry, they intend to attack; if they are behind the infantry lines, they intend to defend.

The power structure, which is partially reflected in the organization chart, determines the future strategy and subsequent behavior of an organization. That is why I maintain that if you want to change behavior and strategy, you must change the structure first.

When I purchased a new fish for my saltwater aquarium, the salesperson told me, "If you put a new fish into the aquarium, the current 'residents' might attack and destroy it. However, if you rearrange the coral before you introduce the new fish, you will create a new environment in which all residents, new and old, are equal. Territorialism will no longer be the driving force."

And that is what I do when I help companies rejuvenate. To introduce new strategies, I first change the structure to make the organization more flexible. With the support of a newly flexible structure, we work together to design a new strategy, returning to further refine the structure in light of that developing strategy. The back-and-forth process can take a year or longer. I have been working with a television broadcasting company for more than two years, continuously refining the structure. Just as a surgeon cannot complete a burn victim's skin graft in a single operation, this process takes time.

Set a strategy and then design a structure that reflects it. That is how it should be done. I, too, do it that way, but only after I have created an environment where the new strategy will be supported and accepted. We need to remove the stumbling blocks: self-interests that work to sustain powerful positions and the existing reward structure.

The issue of strategy and structure is one that emerges during Adolescence with the installation of a decision-making apparatus and the administrative support needed to progress to Prime.

Putting structure into a Go-Go–stage company involves a cultural conversion. People resist, fight, and avoid it. Up to this time, their success derived from breaking, ignoring, and violating boundaries. Now the organization requires discipline and boundaries. Structure, discipline, and rules are both threatening and alien to the people in Go-Go companies. "We are losing the asset that made us what we are today," a client, a founder of a leading cosmetics company, warned me. "You are bureaucratizing the company."

Those leaders need to learn that without structure, supplies do not arrive on time, inventory control is a riddle, field support is haphazard, and delegation of decisions is impossible. And when the leader is busy all over the globe, the inability to make decisions on a timely basis imposes hopeless hurdles for the rest of the company.

Most Go-Go organizations fiercely embrace the proposition that strategy should precede structure, and they spend both time and money on strategy formulation. That fits their culture: In Go-Go everyone loves to discuss new directions the company can investigate.

People in an aging company resist discussing structure, too. But they have different reasons. Structural change is a threat to the powerful positions and rewards they have spent years working for. Strategic planning is far less painful: They know that they can simply go through the motions, and unless a strategy fits into the current power and rewards structure, nothing will come of it anyway. A high percentage of strategic plans never see the light of day.

Although the value of that palatable medicine is questionable, strategic planning is a growing consulting industry.

MANAGEMENT MYTH

There is no optimal organizational structure.

Here my critics have a field day. "How can you say it all depends and then claim that there is a one and only optimal structure? You are speaking from both sides of your mouth."

And I can't say that they are wrong. Just as there is no optimal house design that applies to everyone, there is no optimal business structure. Still, there are design rules that should not be violated: No one would be pleased to have the sewers back up to the kitchens. Everyone expects the wastes to flow to the sewer. You would not want the kitchen in the middle of your bedroom, would you?

By the same token, marketing and sales should not report to the same vice president. You should also avoid the rage of the '90s: the CFO role. Furthermore, you should not have human resources development reporting to human resources administration, which is what used to be— and still is in spite of the new appellation—the personnel department. You should not mix short-term-goal roles with long-term-goal roles. You should not mix roles that you know have conflicting interests. You should not have an Infancy stage organization reporting to a Go-Go: That parent will neglect the baby. Do not expect a company in Bureaucracy, Recrimination, or Aristocracy to conceive new companies easily. They will talk and spend millions on strategic planning, but they won't act.

- Do not decentralize in Go-Go: You will lose control.

- Do not decentralize in Aristocracy: Nobody can handle it.

- Decentralize when you get to Prime.

Those are a few rules you should apply when you design your organization chart.

Let me warn all readers, however: I have designed structures for very large companies-some of the largest companies in the world. I have designed structures for governments. In one organization, our changes moved more than 100,000 people. I can do it, and I do not lose sleep over it. But there is one organization that does cause me to lose sleep. That organization is my own institute.

As I mentioned very early in this book, surgeons cannot perform surgery on their own children. No lawyer, no matter how good, represents himself or herself in court on a matter of significance. It is unreasonable, therefore, to expect CEOs to restructure their own companies without the collaborative help of a professional outsider.

MANAGEMENT MYTH

There is an optimal reward system.

You have, no doubt, read plenty of articles in magazines about how to motivate and reward your employees. They all tell you that what is right depends on the role the person performs. I would like to add that the right reward system depends also on the organization's stage on the lifecycle.

- In Infancy, the desirable norm should be low, fixed salaries with high commissions for measurable, verifiable results. Try to avoid giving equity.

- In Go-Go, raise the fixed pay, reduce the commission rate, and establish commission thresholds that reflect company profitability. Be careful not to set limitations too tight. After all, only the founder or CEO is in a position to affect profitability.

- In Adolescence, add profit sharing, cut fixed pay and individual bonuses a bit. Add stock options for a select few.

- In Prime, fixed salaries should be the smallest component of the entire compensation package. The next largest component should be bonuses for individual achievement, followed by profit sharing based on corporate achievement. Stock options, distributed to all full-time employees, should play a major role. Those options would vest over time.

As companies move into the aging stages, stock options are insulting rather than rewarding. People feel less and less powerful, and the declining stock price serves only to remind everyone that the company is decaying. The more aged the company, the more its reward system should resemble that of a growing company: low, fixed salaries with high bonuses for individual achievement of measurable, verifiable results.

MANAGEMENT MYTH

A strong planning division is a sign of health.

Don't kid yourself. The truth is just the opposite. The role of a planning unit is not to plan. It is to see to it that people throughout the organization are planning. Go-Go–stage companies centralize planning in the founder or CEO, and aging companies centralize planning in a single unit. In either situation, the rest of the organization is left with no incentive for creativity or responsiveness to change. At best, everyone else simply responds to pronouncements from the center.

Back in the 1970s, the postmaster of a post office in Hawaii told me about a response he received to a memo he had submitted to the Washington, D.C., headquarters of the United States Postal Service. He had written asking for budgetary approval for equipment to load mail at the dock. It would, he explained, increase the efficiency of his operations many times over. Headquarters, however, denied his request because "the equipment cannot survive the snow on the docks." Now, for those of you who may have missed the point, it never snows in Hawaii, and it does snow in Washington, D.C.

It is easy for a central planning unit to get entangled in its projections, tables, charts, and number crunching. It ends up devoting more time and energy on devising convincing communications of its findings than it spends on actual implementation.

Planners should be working in teams of at least two people. One facilitates the process of planning in the units; the other serves as a resource, providing data, teaching, and contributing content. That approach allows those responsible for the results of their plans to actually plan, with the aid of professionals.

MANAGEMENT MYTH

Always use teamwork.

This is as good as saying, "Always be happy." Who doesn't want to be happy? Who is against motherhood, apple pie, and the flag? Nevertheless, people did burn the flag because to them it symbolized a problem they wanted to see changed. You might see that teamwork carries a similar burden. It has been abused rather than used by managers who didn't want to act. They wanted to avoid leadership in times of crisis: Those are the times that call for action and commitment to a direction despite opposition and ambiguity.

Managers invoke teamwork when they have feared taking stands in times of discord. "People are not ready yet," they explain.

For me, teamwork is fine—when you can afford the time it takes to achieve consensus. If there is no time, don't even consider it. Everyone knows how frustrating it is to have a leader start a meeting by saying, "We have a very important decision to make, but there is significant pressure to reach a conclusion quickly, say, within two hours. I expect you to reach agreement and make a decision that you will all support. I want teamwork and full consensus." It will not happen. It cannot happen.

People need time to air differences of opinion, fears, and hopes. Under pressure they will act as if they agree, and they will support a decision out of fear. Because nobody opposed the decision, it will only appear as if there had been teamwork. I have been to meetings where people sit, bite their tongues, nod in agreement, and, after the meeting, in the corridors, tell their trusted colleagues that a terrible decision has just been made.

MANAGEMENT MYTH

There are people who are born leaders, and there are those who are born followers.

This kind of talk gets to me. I call it managerial racism. It is a kind of Aryan theory of who is the best and who just had the bad luck to be born with the wrong kind of brain.

The things that make leaders are not simply personality traits, upbringing, or past experience. In my opinion, every person is a born leader, or, to paraphrase Andy Warhol: Everyone will have his or her 15 minutes of leadership. What makes people leaders are the personality attributes that respond to the needs of the moment.

The traits that make people perfect leaders of organizations in Infancy will make them disasters later on if they do not change their style. A loving, protective embrace of a mother is just what a baby needs, but it suffocates a teenager. A participative, integrating leadership style will be just right for a company once it reaches Prime, but it is highly dysfunctional for a company in Infancy.

There is a time to lead and a time to follow, and those with experience know the difference.

MANAGEMENT MYTH

Downsizing improves efficiency.

That is as good as saying that losing weight is good for your heart. Sure it is! But the real question is not what and why we do what we do. The question is how we do it. Downsizing can be outright dangerous to long-term organizational health if it is done in a way that destroys mutual trust and respect. That can leave organizational scars that increase the costs of internal marketing.

Cutting costs is exhilarating if you are the one who is cutting them. If you cut the workforce by 30 percent, you will see results almost overnight. The impact on the bottom line is pleasingly predictable. But that is only one side of the equation. What about the effect on revenues? The depleted workforce will certainly have trouble increasing that top line.

How about downsizing if the company is going under? Yes, that makes sense, and it is indispensable. It is an acceptable option when there are no other choices: Management, after obviously ignoring the decline (when it is almost too late), has to take action. But the situation reminds me of a person who has a heart attack and needs a bypass after years of eating badly and maintaining other unhealthy habits. Heart surgery is not the recommended solution to a lifetime of bad habits. Downsizing in a race against time to avoid bankruptcy is a sign that management was not doing its job. How did the company get to that sorry stage in the first place? Surgeons bury their mistakes. Managers downsize.

Downsizing when there is still time means that management does not want to spend the time and money to retrain and turn fat into muscle. The liposuction and other quick weight-loss solutions, which we are inflicting on our corporations, leave us looking attractive for a while, but we are destroying our self-image, and, unless we change our eating habits, we will get fat again.

MANAGEMENT MYTH

The CFO should have all administrative and financial functions reporting to him or her.

As I have emphasized already, that structure can work only for companies in Go-Go because they need to strengthen the administrative roles to counterbalance the strong entrepreneurial role of the CEO.

After Prime, a politically strong CFO spells disaster. That structure will send a company sailing toward Bureaucracy. Strong CFOs dominate the budgeting process and centralize power to the point where they sap the authority of those with responsibility. But the CFOs—with all the authority to decide—do not have the responsibility to produce.

In Adolescence such a powerful CFO will balance the founder's authority and—if the two work well together—will be a desirable phenomenon. Companies in the growing stages need to unite the administrative roles and divide the entrepreneurial roles. After Prime, divide the administrative roles and unite the entrepreneurial roles.

MANAGEMENT MYTH

Long-term leadership is desirable.

People are impressed with stability: the same person leading a company for, say, 30 years. At the end of that tenure, should the company celebrate in recognition of the extended contribution or should there be a celebration of the belated emancipation and the release from a lengthy oppression?

Again, it depends. What was that leader's style in the beginning? If it has remained unchanged, celebrate liberation. If it has evolved over time, celebrate personal growth. It probably mirrors the company's growth.

As parents, we change our style as our kids grow. The same is true for the people who lead companies to Prime from either direction.

MANAGEMENT MYTH

Business is business, and private life is different.

I have found that what applies to business applies to family life, personal life, the bees, and the butterflies. There is a lifecycle to everything, and the rules that govern everything govern business too. We all either grow, or we die. We change for the better or for the worse. Life does not stay in one place. There is neither heaven nor hell all the time. Our lives are either going to heaven or going to hell, and that is up to us—depending on how well we integrate.

MANAGEMENT MYTH

Management books know what they are talking about.

Not even this one. Not long ago, an interviewer on Israeli radio asked me, "Now that you have achieved some fame in your field, what is your hope for your future?" I responded that I hope that next year, I will renounce everything I now say with passion and conviction. I hope that I will have grown and changed.

Every time I finish a book, I realize that in the process of writing it, I have learned a great deal more, and it is already time to rewrite: There is so much more I need to tell my readers. Each book brings me a step closer to a higher level of truth. As Professor Eli Ginsberg of Columbia University, himself a prolific author, explained to me, every creation is nothing more than a progress report. This is mine.

———

For Futher Reading

BOOKS BY THE SAME AUTHOR

Industrial Democracy Yugoslav Style. New York: Free Press, 1971. Soft Cover Edition, Los Angeles, California: Adizes Institute, 1977.

Ichak Adizes and Elizabeth Mann-Borgese (Eds.), *Self-Management: New Dimensions to Democracy.* First publication, Santa Barbara, California: ABC/CLIO, 1975. Reprint, Los Angeles, California: Adizes Institute, 1978.

How to Solve the Mismanagement Crisis. 1st printing, Homewood, Illinois; Dow Jones/Irwin, 1979. 5th printing, Santa Monica, California: Adizes Institute, 1985.

Corporate Lifecycles: How and Why Corporations Grow and Die and What to Do About It. New York, New York: Prentice Hall, 1988.

Mastering Change: The Power of Mutual Trust and Respect in Personal Life, Business, and Society. Los Angeles, California: Adizes Institute, 1992.

The Pursuit of Prime. Santa Monica, California: Knowledge Exchange, 1996.

TRAINING MATERIALS

The Adizes Institute Publishing Department distributes the books of Dr. Adizes as well as videotapes and audiotapes by Dr. Adizes.

Audio Programs

Analysis of Management (6 cassettes) 1988
Corporate Lifecycles (6 cassettes) 1989

Video Programs

Program A: Overview of the Adizes Process of Management (set of 3 videotapes)

- The Adizes Process of Management

- The Adizes Program. Questions and Answers #1

- The Adizes Program. Questions and Answers #2

Program B: The Management Process (set of 4 videotapes)

- The Roles of Management

- The Structural Causes of Deadwood

- What Is a Good Manager

Program C: Organizational Lifecycles (set of 4 videotapes)

- The Growth Phases of Organizational Lifecycles

- The Aging Phases of Organizational Lifecycles

- Treating the Growing and Aging Problems of Organizations

Program D: Decision Making and Implementation (set of 2 video-tapes)

- CAPI: Predicting Managerial Effectiveness

- The Adizes Process of Decision Making

Other video programs are periodically made available to the public including:

- From Entrepreneurship to Professional Management (Speech to the Council of Growing Companies)

- The Young Company's Lifecycle: Are You Ready for the Future? (Keynote address to the *Inc.* 500 Awards)

OTHER TRAINING AND EVALUATION MATERIALS

The Adizes Institute has available special questionnaires for management roles and lifecycles and special training materials such as the PAEI card inventory and analysis.

Adizes Institute

Adizes Institute, Bel Air (Los Angeles), California. An innovator in the field of organizational transformation, the Adizes Institute is dedicated to the research, clinical practice, publishing, and training in the field of organizational transformation. Through its division of the Adizes Associates, it has been coaching and facilitating corporate change since 1975, directing the transformation of over 500 organizations worldwide, from governments and Fortune 500s to young entrepreneurial companies, non-profits, and social organizations.

The Institute has offices and representatives in eight countries, offering a full range of long- and short-term programs for organizational transformation, The Adizes Program includes major organizational restructuring, training of in-house facilitators of change, diagnostic workshops, executive development programs, and bootcamps for young companies. The Institute also offers a number of speaking programs, from three-hour lectures to three-day conferences.

The Adizes Graduate School was approved in 1995 by the State of California to award Master and Doctorate degrees in the emerging field of Organizational Transformation. The Institute also administers the Association of Certified Adizes Professionals, a network of professionals of 100 certified Adizes practitioners in 30 countries. An annual convention is held each year.

The Publishing Department distributes the books as well as videotapes and audiotapes by Dr. Adizes. The Publication Department makes available working papers by Adizes Associates and students. It also publishes an annual report, communications, and ACAPI newsletter.

The Adizes Web page includes information and articles by Dr. Adizes, which can be downloaded, along with application materials. The Adizes Web page may be found at the following location:

HTTP://WWW.ADIZES.COM/ADIZES

Adizes Institute
International headquarters

820 Moraga Drive, Los Angeles, CA 90049
Tel: (310) 471-9677
Fax: (310) 471-1227
E-mail: adizes@adizes.com
Web page: http://www.adizes.com/adizes

THE ADIZES GRADUATE SCHOOL
FOR ORGANIZATIONAL TRANSFORMATION

The Adizes Graduate School for Organizational Transformation is approved by the State of California Council on Private Postsecondary and Vocational Education to award Doctorates, Master degrees, and certification in the emerging field of Organizational Transformation.

The AGS trains CEOs, senior manager, consultants, and HR managers in the coaching and facilitation skills needed by leaders of organizational change. Student enrollment is international. Courses are taught by certified Adizes associates, practicing professionals who have ongoing experiences in coaching and facilitating organizational change.

The program involves training in the school and supervised internships at the client's facilities. Companies who desire the services of the Institute at discount rates engage practicing associates to work with them under the supervision of instructors. For information, contact:

The Dean of Students, Adizes Graduate School
820 Moraga Drive, Los Angeles, CA 90049
Tel: (310) 471-9677 Fax: (310) 471-1227
E-mail: adizes@adizes.com

Visit the Adizes Web page for more information on the AGS.
HTTP://WWW.ADIZES.COM/ADIZES

Acknowledgments

I am indebted to Wordworks, Inc. of Boston, and particularly to Donna Sammons Carpenter, Elyse Friedman, and their team, which included Bill Birchard, Christina Braun, Maurice Coyle, Erik Hansen, Martha Lawler, Martin Smith, Mel H. Pine, Robert Shnayerson, Sebastian Stewart, and G. Patton Wright for helping me with the clarity of presentation, for the professionalism, patience, dedication, and support without which this book would not have been what it is. I want to add to this list and acknowledge: my literary agent, Helen Rees, whose wit and enduring faith and encouragement made the "writing trip" an exciting one, and the head of Adizes Institute Publications, Dr. Patrick Griffin, who continuously supported me with all the details that accompany book writing and from whose advice I benefited greatly.

Index

Knowledge is Power

This maxim best describes why Knowledge Exchange (KEX) is dedicated to helping business professionals achieve excellence through the development of programs and products specifically designed to give them a competitive edge.

KEX's divisions include strategic consulting services; executive education, conferences and seminars; and multimedia, book, and online publishing.

The company's publishing division produces books that demystify the Internet, general business, management, and finance as well as audiobooks, videos, and CD-ROMs. KEX books and audiobooks are distributed throughout North America by Warner Books, Inc.

KEX was founded in 1989 by President and CEO Lorraine Spurge. Formerly a senior vice president at Drexel Burnham Lambert (1983-1989), she raised more than $200 billion for companies including MCI Communications, Turner Broadcasting, Viacom, Barnes & Noble, Mattel, and Tele-Communications, Inc.

KEX Chairman of the Board, Kenin M. Spivak, is also Cofounder, President, and Co–CEO of Archon Communications, Inc. He has served as President of the Island World Group; Executive Vice President and COO of MGM/UA Communications Co.; and Vice President of Merrill Lynch Investment Banking. He is also an attorney and a film producer.

For more information about the company or its products, visit the KEX Web site at http://www.kex.com or write to: Knowledge Exchange LLC, Publicity Dept., 1299 Ocean Ave. Suite 250, Santa Monica, CA 90401.

The Accelerated Transition®

Fast Forward Through
Corporate Change

**MARK L. FELDMAN, Ph.D., and
MICHAEL F. SPRATT, Ph.D.**

An in-depth analysis of companies that have gone
through corporate change, with a concise outline of
proven steps to insure a fast, efficient and successful
transition.

Hardcover/$22.95 (Can. $28.95)
ISBN 1-888232-28-5

Coming to bookstores in 1997

Customer Intimacy

Pick Your Partners, Shape Your
Culture, Win Together

FRED WIERSEMA

Taking business far beyond the concept of good
customer relations, bestselling author Fred Wiersema
presents a new way of defining customer relations,
which has produced exceptional sales, profits and
customer satisfaction.

Hardcover/$22.95 (Can. $27.95)
ISBN 1-888232-00-5
Audiobook/$14.00 (Can. $17.00)
ISBN 1-888232-01-3
Read by the author

Available in bookstores now

Changing Health Care

Creating Tomorrow's Winning
Health Enterprise Today

**KEN JENNINGS, Ph.D., KURT MILLER
and SHARYN MATERNA
of ANDERSEN CONSULTING**

An inside look at the health-care industry by a
team from the world's largest consulting firm,
laying out the essential strategies that companies
must follow to survive and thrive in the turbulent
health-care market of tomorrow.

Hardcover/$24.95 (Can. $29.95)
ISBN 1-888232-18-8

Coming to bookstores in 1997

Fad-Free Management

The Six Principles That Drive
Successful Companies and
Their Leaders

RICHARD HAMERMESH

A step-by-step program to implement the six
bedrock management principles that have a
proven track record in helping companies
achieve their goals.

Hardcover/$24.95 (Can. $29.95)
ISBN 1-888232-20-X

Available in bookstores now

Failure Is Not An Option

A Profile of MCI

LORRAINE SPURGE

A case history that reads like a novel, this is the story of the tension, suspense, personalities and brilliant thinking that catapulted MCI from a start-up to a telecommunications powerhouse, forever altering the American business landscape.

Hardcover/$22.95 (Can. $27.95)
ISBN 1-888232-08-0

Coming to bookstores in 1997

Prescription for the Future

How the Technology Revolution Is Changing the Pulse of Global Health Care

GWENDOLYN B. MOORE, DAVID A. REY and JOHN D. ROLLINS of ANDERSEN CONSULTING

In a time of tremendous flux in the health-care industry, this book shows how those who can understand and harness changing technologies will be able to create the successful health-care organizations of the future.

Hardcover/$24.95 (Can. $29.95)
ISBN 1-888232-10-2
Audiobook/$12.00 (Can. $15.00)
ISBN 1-888232-11-0
Read by the authors

Available in bookstores now

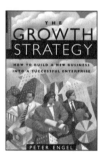

The Growth Strategy

How to Build a New Business into a Successful Enterprise

PETER ENGEL

A book that entrepreneurs have been waiting for, it shows businesses how to get beyond the start-up phase to become professionally managed businesses that will create true wealth for their owners.

Hardcover/$22.95 (Can. $28.95)
ISBN 1-888232-30-7

Coming to bookstores in 1997

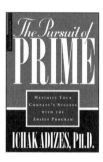

The Pursuit of Prime

Maximize Your Company's Success with the Adizes Program

ICHAK ADIZES, Ph.D.

The renowned author shows companies how to successfully navigate the various growth stages of a business and reach prime—the stage at which they are most healthy and profitable.

Hardcover/$24.95 (Can. $29.95)
ISBN 1-888232-22-6

Available in bookstores now

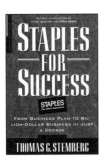

Staples for Success

From Business Plan to Billion-Dollar Business in Just a Decade

THOMAS G. STEMBERG

Written by the man who made Staples a reality, this is the gripping story of how a simple idea was turned into a new, multibillion dollar industry (with key lessons for those who want to do the same).

Hardcover/$22.95 (Can. $27.95)
ISBN 1-888232-24-2
Audiobook/$12.00 (Can. $15.00)
ISBN 1-888232-25-0
Read by actor Campbell Scott

Available in bookstores now

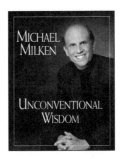

Unconventional Wisdom

MICHAEL MILKEN

The man the *Wall Street Journal* called "the most important financial thinker of the century" shares his global vision, insight and ideas for the next millennium, providing a guidepost for the next wave of successful businesses.

Hardcover/$25.00 (Can. $30.00)
ISBN 1-888232-12-9

Coming to bookstores in 1997

The Tao of Coaching

Motivate Your Employees to Become All-Star Managers

MAX LANDSBERG

A must-read for anyone who wants to get the most out of their *human capital*, this book presents a new way of approaching people management that will allow your managers to use their time better while motivating, developing and creating loyalty among employees.

Hardcover/$22.95 (Can. $28.95)
ISBN 1-888232-34-X

Coming to bookstores in 1997

The World On Time

The 11 Management Principles That Made FedEx an Overnight Sensation

JAMES C. WETHERBE

Learn how Federal Express became a phenomenal success and discover the eleven innovative management strategies they employed, which have set the standard for the way businesses manage time and information, handle logistics and serve customers.

Hardcover/$22.95 (Can. $27.95)
ISBN 1-888232-06-4
Audiobook/$12.00 (Can. $15.00)
ISBN 1-888232-07-2
Read by the author

Available in bookstores now

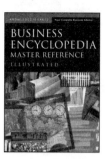

Business Encyclopedia: Master Reference

**KNOWLEDGE EXCHANGE
EDITORIAL BOARD**

The ultimate business tool and the ultimate business gift, this illustrated reference book provides a wealth of information and advice on eight critical disciplines: accounting, economics, finance, marketing, management, operations, strategy and technology.

Hardcover/$45.00 (Can. $54.00)
ISBN 1-888232-05-6

Available in bookstores now

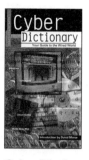

CyberDictionary

Your Guide to the Wired World

**EDITED AND INTRODUCED BY
DAVID MORSE**

In clear, concise language, CyberDictionary makes sense of the wide-open frontier of cyberspace with information useful to the novice and the cyber-pro alike.

Trade Paperback/$17.95 (Can. $21.95)
ISBN 1-888232-04-8

Available in bookstores now

Business Encyclopedia: Management

**KNOWLEDGE EXCHANGE
EDITORIAL BOARD**

Volume two of the Business Encyclopedia series, this book is an essential management tool providing in-depth information on hundreds of key management terms, techniques and practices—and practical advice on how to apply them to your business.

Hardcover/$28.00 (Can. $34.95)
ISBN 1-888232-32-3

Coming to bookstores in 1997

60-Second Net Finder

**AFFINITY COMMUNICATIONS
AND KNOWLEDGE EXCHANGE
EDITORIAL BOARD**

For people who want information from the Internet and want it now, this book shows where to find anything you want, in sixty seconds or less.

Trade Paperback/$24.95 (Can. $29.95)
ISBN 1-888232-26-9

Coming to bookstores in 1997